D0463341

One

TOSS OF THE DICE

One
TOSS OF

The Incredible Story of How a

Translation of
"UN COUP DE DÉS JAMAIS N'ABOLIRA LE HASARD"
by J. D. McClatchy

THE DICE

Poem Made Us Modern

R. Howard Bloch

LIVERIGHT PUBLISHING CORPORATION
A DIVISION OF W. W. NORTON & COMPANY
Independent Publishers Since 1923
NEW YORK · LONDON

For information about permission to reproduce selections from this book, write to

Permissions, Liveright Publishing Corporation, a division of W. W. Norton & Company, Inc.,

500 Fifth Avenue, New York, NY 10110

For information about special discounts for bulk purchases, please contact

W. W. Norton Special Sales at specialsales@wwnorton.com or 800-233-4830

Manufacturing by Quad Graphics, Fairfield

Book design by JAM Design

Production manager: Louise Mattarelliano

ISBN 978-0-87140-663-7

Liveright Publishing Corporation

500 Fifth Avenue, New York, N.Y. 10110

www.wwnorton.com

W. W. Norton & Company Ltd.

15 Carlisle Street, London W1D 3BS

1 2 3 4 5 6 7 8 9 0

To Caroline, Clara, and Louisa

All the Great masters, ancient and modern,
plagiarized Homer, and Homer plagiarized God.

—STÉPHANE MALLARMÉ

CONTENTS

INTRODUCTION

The poet Stéphane Mallarmé slept badly in the summer of 1896. He suffered periodically from insomnia, and took analgesics to put him to sleep. Once he joked with a journalist, who asked him about his dreams, that he had not closed his eyes in twelve years. But the bout of insomnia that began that May was especially severe, though in the beginning it was nothing more than worries about house cleaning and home renovation that kept him awake at night.

For twenty-three summers, Mallarmé and his wife, Marie, and daughter Geneviève had rented the first floor of an old boatman's house on the banks of the Seine. From the entrance facing the river, one could see the Pont de Valvins, with its steel crisscross girders on stone, a monument to the new technology favored after the Franco-Prussian War of 1870–71. The bridge would be destroyed by explosives on the morning of August 23, 1944, as General George Patton's Third Army, on its way to liberate Paris, engaged German troops stationed on Mallarmé's side of the river. An Allied shell penetrated the poet's study. On the far bank lay the eastern edge of the thick Forest of Fontainebleau. The castle had once been a favorite of the Emperor Napoleon III, who was baptized in its rococo chapel. In 1814, his uncle Napoleon I bid farewell to the Old Guard of his army in the courtyard of the castle, after a coalition from Austria, Russia, and Prussia forced him into exile on the island of Elba.

Napoleon III had been gone for twenty-five years, and summers along this particular stretch of the Seine now brought a harvest of artists and intellectuals. A fourth member of the Mallarmé family, eight-year old Anatole, rested in the nearby cemetery of Samoreau.

Each year, the poet preceded *les dames* to Valvins to prepare the house for their arrival. This summer was different, however. Mallarmé had retired from his day job as a high school teacher of English to devote himself to art. The thought of spending more time in the country house, which would now be more of a second home than a summer retreat, meant that repairs could no longer wait. So, having hosted his last of the season's Tuesday evening gatherings for a circle of select writers and artists, the poet traveled on the morning of May 6, 1896, seventy kilometers by train from Paris to Fontainebleau, where he was met by one of the local residents, Charles Guérin, who took him by carriage to Valvins. There were plasterers, painters, and masons to be hired and kept on task over the long Ascension weekend, minor damage from the winter to be repaired, all combined with a fear that the owners would object to the changes he had made. "I haven't closed my eyes, with all the worry and bother," he wrote to Marie and Geneviève after the first week.[1]

Mallarmé was no stranger to domestic tasks. He was deeply fascinated by the workings of this house while attuned to the new consumer goods that were making daily life in Belle Époque France easier and more aesthetically pleasing. For a brief period in the mid-1870s, he had edited a ladies' fashion magazine, giving advice about the latest dress, home decoration and remedies, vacation destinations, and menus for special occasions. At home in Paris and Valvins, the poet surrounded himself with beautiful objects—paintings and drawings, which were gifts from fellow artists: Édouard Manet's portrait of the poet smoking a cigar, a seascape by Berthe Morisot, a pastel of flowers by Odilon Redon, the plaster cast of a faun by Auguste Rodin, and James McNeill Whistler's sketch of Geneviève. Stéphane and Marie Mallarmé treasured a few pieces of well-chosen furniture and accessories that had accompanied them on their moves through southern and eastern France before they settled in Paris: an oriental lacquered chest, an elaborate Venetian mirror, and a Saxony porcelain clock that they had purchased in 1863, before their marriage.

Alongside these inanimate objects were animate ones as well, exquisite pets. "He needed these small living presences, with all their naiveté," wrote Geneviève: greyhounds named Yseult and Saladin; an owl, Clare-de-Lune; a bluebird, a waxbill, and small green parrots whom the poet referred to as "little academicians"; a white angora cat called Snow and her son, Fog; and the black cat Lilith, who was the granddaughter of poet Théodore de Banville's cat Éponine, for whom Charles Baudelaire wrote his famous poem "Les Chats." In an interview about his pets, Mallarmé declared cats to be as worthy of respect as human beings. We may chase them outside because of their intemperance, but they come back inside, "like household gods, the idols of the apartment." He traveled back and forth between Paris and Valvins with Lilith in a basket.

On neither his meager salary as a teacher nor his pension of 5,000 francs per year could Mallarmé afford the costly furniture and refined knickknacks of France's Belle Époque. So, he indulged in *bricolage*, do-it-yourself tinkering about the house. "I tried to imitate English furniture with your dressing stand, you will see," he wrote to his wife. "Tomorrow, I will set about painting in off-white the winged chair, a delicate task in view of the trimmings." When it was done, the poet was as fastidious about the finish as he was about his verse: "My winged chair, too white and shiny, looks new; I am going to apply a coat of matte." While attempting to clean house amid all the disorder, he realized that the key to a silver clock was lost, and the one he borrowed broke the mainspring. Juliette Hubert, the woman who prepared the poet's meals and did his laundry when he was alone in the country, promised to have it fixed in nearby Fontainebleau. "I slept badly because of this," he confessed.[2]

In the course of his first stay in the country, the mailman brought news of various kinds: a copy of Émile Zola's latest novel, *Rome*; word of the death of Trixie Whistler, the wife of his friend, the painter James McNeill Whistler; and a copy of *Argus* magazine, which informed its readers in one of its "gossips" that Stéphane Mallarmé received visitors with a bottle of wine, salad, and a round of Camembert cheese. Who was the informant? he wondered. Could it be the Irish novelist George Moore, whom he had invited to lunch the previous summer?

Local visitors were not shy about dropping by the Mallarmé cottage in Valvins. Thadée Natanson, editor of the high cultural *La Revue blanche*, and his ravishingly beautiful wife, the pianist Misia Godebski, rode their bicycles over to invite the poet to dine with them at the nearby summer home of Misia's father, the sculptor Cyprian Godebski. This was before Natanson made a deal with Misia's lover, Alfred Edwards, the wealthy editor of the daily newspaper *Le Matin*. Edwards agreed to pay for publishing *La Revue blanche* as well as for the costs of Natanson's political activities, in a divorce settlement that was most unusual even for such heady times, when private life was often the stuff of public spectacle. Edwards, in turn, soon replaced Misia with the actress Geneviève "Ginette" Lantelme. Misia was so furious that she sent her rival all of the Edwards family jewels. When Lantelme mysteriously fell off Edwards's yacht and drowned in 1911, her tomb was desecrated by robbers seeking the jewels with which it was rumored she was buried in Paris's Père-Lachaise Cemetery. Misia later married the Spanish painter José Maria Sert. Henri de Toulouse-Lautrec, Auguste Renoir, Édouard Vuillard, and Pierre Bonnard all painted portraits of Misia Sert, who was one of the deadliest femmes fatales of fin-de-siècle France.

Mallarmé may have suffered from insomnia, but he saw to it that in just three weeks the kitchen of the little house in Valvins was enlarged and made lighter. Cracked walls were patched and tiles replaced. Four rooms, the circular staircase leading to the second floor, and both indoor and outdoor furniture were painted. The baking oven was rebuilt, the floors waxed, the garden replanted, and the trees trimmed. "In spite of the workers' inexperience, it will be pretty; and the faults of execution will disappear in the harmony of the ensemble," he wrote to Marie and Geneviève on the eve of his departure to fetch them. "Nonetheless," he mused with typical humor and the understated irony known to anyone who has undertaken home renovation, "these have been strange weeks. . . . One day, I will look back on it perhaps with curiosity. To have something built, only to move back in!"[3]

In these final years of the nineteenth century, the poet, despite his modest means, was at the height of his poetic reputation and powers. He was still healthy. On the forms required by the French government for retirement, he testified: "My daily food regimen is mixed; I believe you asked me to indicate my height: 1 meter, 63 centimeters; width of shoulders: 41 centimeters; weight: 150 pounds; age: 53. Exercise, moderate. No medications."[4] He planned in retirement to spend more time sailing and fishing in the ten-kilometer stretch of river between the lock of Héricy and the village of Thomery. Once the house in Valvins was restored, the poet would finish a number of difficult writing projects that had haunted him all his life.

The poetry review *La Plume* had elected Mallarmé to succeed Paul Verlaine as France's "Prince of Poets" after Verlaine's death in

January 1896. Two months later, the editors published a special issue devoted to their new prince, with several of his major poems and a portrait by the celebrity photographer Félix Nadar. Just a few days before his departure for the country, the popular newspaper *Le Figaro* included in its "Concerts and Spectacles" column the review of a public lecture dedicated to France's most esteemed poet, delivered at the Théâtre Mondain: an "enormous, exquisite, elite audience interrupted the eloquent lecturer often with applause." Mallarmé had begun to be known abroad, not only in England, where he had lectured at Oxford and Cambridge, but even across the Atlantic in the United States. The week of his arrival in Valvins, his article on the poet Arthur Rimbaud appeared in *The Chap Book*, edited in Chicago. "Tuesdays" *chez* Mallarmé, these renowned after-dinner gatherings in the French tradition of literary salons, attracted an international array of poets, novelists, painters, and composers, who, once a week in winter, climbed four flights of stairs on the rue de Rome to the "little house of Socrates."

Upon his return to Paris in the middle of May, Mallarmé sent get-well wishes to the writer Léon Daudet and a letter of condolence to the journalist and art critic Théodore Duret, whose brother had been killed in Africa. He then changed the address of some of his magazine subscriptions, forwarding them to the country. He agreed to head the committee to erect a monument in honor of Verlaine. The poet dined at home the night of his arrival in the capital, and, the next night, at the home of his lifelong confidante and muse, Méry Laurent.

In the days between his initial trip to Valvins and his return to Paris, Mallarmé heard rumors about a Jewish army officer who had been arrested two years before. Alfred Dreyfus, a graduate of the French military academy Saint Cyr and the son of a wealthy textile manufacturer from Alsace, was tried for espionage and exiled for life to the penal colony on Devil's Island, off the coast of French

Guiana. In May 1896, however, the case against Dreyfus began slowly to unravel. Mallarmé's disciple, the journalist and polemicist Bernard Lazare, had been contacted by Alfred's brother Mathieu and was one of the first to cast doubt upon Dreyfus's conviction for selling French military secrets to the Germans. On May 14, Émile Zola, journalist, playwright, and France's leading naturalist novelist, published an article in *Le Figaro* decrying the dangers of anti-Semitism: "I am stupefied that such a return of fanaticism, such a fomenting of religious war, could happen in our era, in our great Paris, among our good people." Zola was promptly attacked by Édouard Drumont, founder of the Anti-Semitic League of France and author of the incendiary *La France juive*, which had been hugely successful in stirring up anti-Jewish feelings after it appeared in 1886. Drumont predictably accused Zola of being a lawyer for the Jews and even to be like the Jews themselves because of the "filthy, blasphemous, basely smutty character of his books." These initial seeds of doubt about Dreyfus's guilt, planted by Lazare and Zola, would quicken over the next two years into the Dreyfus affair.

Such unpleasantries did not weigh heavily on the poet's mind when he brought wife and daughter back to their pastoral home in Valvins. The first task upon his second trip to the country was painting the little sailboat, which brought him solace amid the storms of life. Mallarmé had always been fascinated by water, which he associated with poetry itself. "I no longer write a poem without an aquatic reverie running through it," he had written some thirty years earlier to Frédéric Mistral, the poet and leader of the Félibrige, or indigenous Provençal literary association.[5] Two decades later, in 1885, Mallarmé described himself to Verlaine, who had requested biographical information, as a "simple wanderer in mahogany skiffs, but a furious sailor proud of his flotilla."[6] Boating and writing were deeply entwined in the poet's mind, poetry, in his own phrase, like an "oar stroke," and the sail, like a "white page" on which verse is written.[7]

The return to Valvins was filled with distractions. Members of the Verlaine memorial committee arrived with the Swiss sculptor Auguste de Niederhäusen, a prominent student of Rodin, to discuss a list of patrons willing to pay for the commission. The painters Pierre Bonnard and Édouard Vuillard also came to visit late one afternoon. Since their earlier visit, the Natansons had bought their own place, La Grangette, so close to the Mallarmés that the sounds of Misia's piano could be heard in the evenings. The circle of writers and painters around *La Revue blanche* gathered there nightly, the loudest among them, apparently, Toulouse-Lautrec, who loved to tend bar, his specialties being a multicolored layering of liqueurs known as the "Pousse-Café," designed to push afterdinner coffee out of the way, and a mixture of absinthe and cognac known as the "Earthquake." Because of his underdeveloped legs, the painter walked with a cane, which he had hollowed out and filled with alcohol so he would never be without liquid refreshment. One afternoon, Toulouse-Lautrec dropped by the Mallarmés to borrow the poet's little boat, and, when the "Master" consented, had the effrontery to ask if he might borrow a swimsuit as well. Mallarmé was not very tall, but Lautrec was of such a size that the poet's bathing trunks drooped about the painter's knees.

Julie Manet, whom Mallarmé and Auguste Renoir had cared for after the death of her parents, the painters Eugène Manet and Berthe Morisot, was staying nearby with her cousins Paule and Jeannie Gobillard. There were boating parties for everyone, expeditions to paint along the Seine, long walks in the forest, and home concerts with Julie playing the violin, accompanied by Geneviève or Jeannie on piano.[8] If ever life imitated art, it was in and around Valvins in the summer of 1896. Boating on the Seine was a favorite subject of the Impressionists. Vuillard painted several views of the Mallarmé cottage during his stay with the Natansons that year. Julie Manet and Jeannie Gobillard had posed for Renoir's painting *Young Girls at the Piano* in 1892.

Valvins, summer 1896. Seated left to right: Mme Gabriel Séailles,
Geneviève Mallarmé, Mme Marie Mallarmé, Mme Henri Normant;
standing left to right: Julie Manet, Jeannie Gobillard, Stéphane Mallarmé,
Gabriel Séailles, Paule Gobillard.
Bibliothèque littéraire Jacques Doucet, Paris, MNR ms. 1851.

When the time came to put pen to paper in the newly renovated
rooms at Valvins, Mallarmé picked up a long dramatic poem, *Hérodiade*, which he had begun at the age of twenty-two. Here, the poet
sought to capture via the story of Salomé and Saint John the Baptist
a vision of what he referred to through his life as the "Ideal" or
"ideal Beauty." Of the three sections of this exotic treatment of violated virginity and sacrifice, only one was published during the
poet's lifetime. A second writing project, conceived around the same
time as *Hérodiade* and related to it, remained shrouded in mystery.
Mallarmé referred to it simply as *The Book*, a work whose ambition,
the poetic equivalent of Richard Wagner's *The Ring*, was nothing less
than "an orphic explanation of the earth" that would "change the
nature of the human community."[9]

A third writing project, which may have been part of *The Book*, took shape around the theme of water and sailing—"ONE TOSS OF THE DICE NEVER WILL ABOLISH CHANCE" ("UN COUP DE DÉS JAMAIS N'ABOLIRA LE HASARD").

Some of the notes that Mallarmé left for *The Book* indicate that he conceived of writing a work which would hark back to the origins of Western literature and would supplant Homer, in what would be a new source for poetry in the epic mode. So, in a mythic move that reached all the way back to the beginnings of voyage literature and Homer's *Odyssey*, Mallarmé, an avid sailor, took to the sea in this masterwork. "One Toss of the Dice" is, in fact, a seafarer's tale of a shipwreck, filled with images of water, of a captain, master and helmsman, of waves, surges, and of the shell, sails, tilting deck, plunging prow, toppled mast of a ship, listing to this side or that. In the distance, the horizon frames the sinking boat, while winds howl. Closer in, the general litter of driftwood crowns the depiction of disaster.

Published first in 1897, "One Toss of the Dice" broke with the expectations of two thousand years of metric verse. Nothing like it had ever been seen. Even Lewis Carroll's *The Hunting of the Snark, An Agony in Eight Fits* (1876), another seagoing poem full of enigmas that border on nonsense, had none of the visual boldness of "Un Coup de dés." Mallarmé's manuscript looks in places like sheet music, and the poet saw the layout of his poem as a musical score whose ups and downs indicate the rising or falling intonation of the voice. The typography, with different letters ranging from 3 to 22 points in size, of varying weight and typeface (bold, normal, italics), and blank spaces, resembles the poster art of Belle Époque Paris, with its varied type sizes, forms, and irregular spatial design.[10] "One Toss of the Dice" brings to mind the original punch cards that Joseph-Marie Jacquard invented at the end of the eighteenth century for the programming of textile looms, that the English polymath Charles Babbage adapted for his calculating "Analytic Engine" (1864), that Herman Hollerith used for the tabulation of census data in the 1880s, or that Mallarmé encountered in the barrel organ, organette, and player piano rolls, that were popular in fin-de-siècle France, even after Edison's invention of the phonograph in 1877. The poet originally envisaged a disposition of print that involved reading not down, but across an open double page. He insisted on great patches of blank space between verses of wildly different lengths. Some lines were to contain a single word, others to stretch fully across two pages. Some folios of "One Toss of the Dice" hold only a single word, while others are densely packed, in what, in the phrase of fellow poet Paul Claudel, is a "great typographic and cosmogonic poem."[11]

The balky syntax of "One Toss of the Dice" is unsettling, its logical leaps a form of grammatical dissonance that assails the reader, as the music of Stravinsky and Schoenberg, or the paintings of Picasso and Kandinsky, would jar listeners and viewers only a decade later. Print gives pattern to space, and scatters, becomes mobile, aggressive even. Intelligibility is constantly under threat. The task of the reader is to disentangle main from subordinate material in order to make the lines of a sentence, to make meaning, to distinguish subjects from predicates, order from chaos, arguments, explanations, chronologies, causes and effects, narrative structures.

Reading "One Toss of the Dice" is an active process. As we begin, we are made insecure. In the place of a founding story, guiding directives, or description, which might orient and comfort us, we sense randomness and danger. Through careful reading, however, we begin to recognize certain patterns; and, by the end, on the last folio, the constellation of words on the page aligns fully with the constellation of the stars to which the words point, like the needle of a compass after a geomagnetic storm.

Part of the challenge of "One Toss of the Dice" stems from the newness of its ideas, and from a change in the look of the poetry to which we are accustomed. Mallarmé recognized at the end of the preface originally printed with the poem that new forms are appropriate for dealing with "subjects of pure and complex imagination or intellect." Yet the poem's rigor also derives from a performance of meaning that coincides with meaning—language that appears somewhat arbitrary and haphazard used to describe a chaotic universe, a dice throw about a throw of the dice. The poem dramatizes the difficulty of making sense of a world in which truth, meaning, and order are no longer given, and are constantly changing. The spatial layout—without the margins that contain the body of text in a conventionally printed book, without fixed line lengths or a set number of lines on a given page—renders a work beyond borders, without limits, out of bounds. Seven of the ten double pages of "One Toss of the Dice" contain lines that cross from the verso, the left-hand page, to the recto, the right-hand page, requiring us to read across the open fold, or gutter.

"One Toss of the Dice" is a disaster poem, and the experience of reading it is akin to being tossed overboard in a shipwreck. We grasp at bits of linguistic debris or meaning as if words and phrases were the flotsam and jetsam of the scattered pieces of a foundering ship. The lines on the page sink to threaten us, or remain aligned to keep us afloat. Mallarmé's masterwork is full of counterintuitive reversals having to do with space. "The first words of the Poem, so that those that follow, arranged as they are, lead to the last, the whole of it without novelty except the spacing of the text," the poet states in the preface.

Space in "One Toss of the Dice" has the function of punctuation, a have-stop function. It distracts and destabilizes, disrupts the normal expectation that the order of appearance of syntactical units will correspond to the logical sequence of meaning, and that meaning will coincide with the world. The empty spaces leave hanging elements of language that cannot stand alone, e.g., "than playing" (*que de jouer*), "no matter where" (*n'importe où*), "or the event" (*ou se fût l'évènement*), "not so much" (*pas tant*). Space dissolves what the printed elements of the poem unite. The spaces encourage us to pause, to seek another method of reading, other paths to follow, such great unexpected reversals, surprises, ellipses, and setbacks all being part of verbal modernism, and of the hypertext of the information age in which we now live.

Mallarmé described himself as a "sacred spider," the inventor of a "marvelous lacework." The appearance of "One Toss of the Dice" thus colluded, in its lacy lack of transitions, with the Lumière brothers's *cinématographe*, which had burst upon the world in late December 1895 and was barely up and running before Mallarmé began his optical oeuvre. Bravely conceived and fiercely written against the long tradition of verbal poetry, "One Toss of the Dice" marked a great shift in the direction of the visuality of our own era, with its still and moving projections, hand-held personal data devices, monitors, and screens.

Is "One Toss of the Dice" a verse or prose poem? Or both? A lyric, dramatic, concrete, or metaphysical poem? Is it a picture poem? Something akin to a Chinese ideogram? Or not a poem at all, but a visual work of art, which was known in the nineteenth century as a *livre de peintre*, the painter's or artist's book?[12] Whatever its origins or type, "One Toss of the Dice" makes meaning not in the traditional way, by the sound and rhythm of its verses, but by the visual layout of the letters on its double pages and the spaces between them.

Mallarmé's masterwork, presented here in a new translation by J. D. McClatchy, cut a wide swath across twentieth-century literature and the arts, and deserves more recognition in the English-speaking world. "One Toss of the Dice" was the birth certificate of modern poetry in the same way that Picasso's *Demoiselles d'Avignon* was the inaugural work of modern painting, and Stravinsky's *Rite of Spring*, of modern music. Mallarmé's poem became an icon of modernism, in a line that associates difficulty and modernity, from "One Toss of the Dice" to "Zone" (1912), Guillaume Apollinaire's epic of urban dislocation, to *The Waste Land* (1924), T. S. Eliot's jarring poem of disintegration and regret. In fact, the logical leaps of "One Toss of the Dice" were the first signs of what would become the free-associative modernist novel—Marcel Proust's flashbacks of involuntary memory, Franz Kafka's wild mixings of fantasy and everyday life, James Joyce's and Virginia Woolf's streams of consciousness, and Gertrude Stein's "continual present." Joyce kept a copy of "One Toss of the Dice" close at hand while writing *Finnegans Wake*.

Mallarmé's epic poem laid the groundwork for the temporal and spatial dislocations of cubist painting and poetry. It anticipated, among other things, Italian futurism, and French and Swiss Dadaist visual displays. Elements of "One Toss of the Dice" surfaced in the concrete sheet music and the syncopated beats of Erik Satie. Cy Twombly's word pictures and John Cage's chance-controlled music looked for inspiration to "One Toss of the Dice," as did the *musique aléatoire* of Pierre Boulez. In his longest composition, "Pli selon pli" ("Fold by Fold"), Boulez set five of Mallarmé's poems to music, "so, fold by fold," the composer states, "as the five movements develop, a portrait of Mallarmé is revealed."

"One Toss of the Dice" is an atomic poem, conceived a full four decades before the discovery of nuclear fission in 1938. Words are broken into particles. Negatives are supplanted by further negatives. Prepositions lose their weight. Parentheses gain in substance. Each phrase is potentially a nucleus around which others may be construed, a large semantic periphery beyond which wide spaces separate similar clusters of scattered print. The poem, in a happy coincidence, appeared just five days after the publication of the British physicist J. J. Thomson's article announcing the discovery of the electron as the fundamental unit of matter. Mallarmé, despite his anglophilia, could not have known Thomson. Yet the preface to "One Toss of the Dice," which defines the originality of the poem as a scattering of words upon the page, resonates uncannily with Thomson's radical spacing of the basic elements of the material universe.

The vision of a word genius like Mallarmé—no less than scientific geniuses like Thomson and Einstein for physics, Watson and Crick for molecular biology, and Freud for psychology—shaped the perceptual world out of which scientific breakthroughs emerged. Art this great is the fellow traveler, if not the lubricant, of science and technology. The effects of simultaneity that "One Toss of the Dice" produce in the reader contributed to the coming into being, beginning in the 1880s, of universal time and fixed longitudinal zones among the nations of the world. Einstein went to work on clock coordination for the Bern patent office just five years after Mallarmé strove to produce the sensation of time simultaneity in his masterwork. The first theory of relativity, which can be understood in terms that resonate with those of "One Toss of the Dice," would emerge out of the scientist's experience with the mechanics of time just four years after that.

"One Toss of the Dice" marked an enormous break with the conceptual world in place since the Renaissance. Its verbal and visual dislocations make it more like an interactive poem of the digital age than like any kind of traditional verse. A great existential crossword puzzle, Mallarmé's masterwork invites the reader to fill in the stretches between words, the gaps in his or her understanding, to organize a wide array of scattered bits of meaning. Many works of literature, both poetry and prose, elicit multiple interpretations, yet none before it maintains so fully a lack of hierarchy in its word order or its sense. None offers the kind of multiple paths through disparate interconnected images and ideas of "One Toss of the Dice."

At the furthest reach of its effective horizon, Mallarmé's poem is an early avatar of the hypertext of our era, with its modular possibilities of reading up and down, backward, forward, and obliquely, with great leaps. In its juddering jumps from one place of meaning to another, "One Toss of the Dice" is the zero point of a change of mental universe that culminated in the World Wide Web.

What will taking the chance of reading "One Toss of the Dice" do for you? Why should you, in such a fissionable age as our own, read it?

I am convinced that part of the benefit of reading "One Toss of the Dice" has to do with the sheer pleasure of cracking something hard. A great poetic Rorschach test, the poem is an exercise in mastering words as a way of mastering the world. Mallarmé tells you what his great work means in its title, the capitalized, centripetal sentence that runs like a verbal skewer through the poem: "ONE TOSS OF THE DICE NEVER WILL ABOLISH CHANCE." Yet, the dispersed constellation of words begs for order, and the way we understand the poem's title tells us more about ourselves than the words on the page, which are, after all, mute until they are read and infused with sense.

A masterpiece about the enduring question of beating, cheating, or gaming the odds attached to every life worth living, "One Toss of the Dice" is about risk management and tolerance for the unknown. Engaging with it is risky in the way that committing ourselves to any consuming passion, work, hobby, sport, spiritual quest, journey of self-discovery, creative or intellectual project threatens a loss of the self. It is dangerous in the way that falling in love threatens to take the lover to unfamiliar places, the danger, of course, being part of the thrill. That risk taken, arranging and dispersing the poem's shards of meaning around its central phrase puts us up against the question of whether we think of our world as ordered from the start and from without, or chaotic and wild, without design or purpose—or somewhere in between.

Rightly understood, "One Toss of the Dice" sheds new light upon the condition of modernity, which is sometimes associated with a loss of moral direction, with skepticism, anxiety, self-criticism, paralysis, doubt, and despair. Mallarmé, against the grain of discontent of the period of great upheaval between 1870 and World War I, unites us with a tradition reaching all the way back to the Greeks and with questions so deep and enduring as to clarify what it means to be fully human. This "desperately modest man" with a "sweeping cosmic manner," the poet who could fuss about the paint on his easy chair while contemplating the metaphysical nature of human language, has much to teach us about how to live, both spiritually and in a myriad of small ways.[13] "One Toss of the Dice" contains a great lesson in how to negotiate, after Nietzsche's declaration of the death of God, the treacheries of a rootless secular world.

One

A POET IS BORN

Stéphane Mallarmé's last poem, an epic drama of shipwreck and survival, reached so far into the poet's past, so deep into the psychic recesses of what it meant to suffer, recover, and write, that it can be said to have been growing in him his whole life.

Étienne, as he was known as a child, was born in March 1842 to a comfortable, even affluent, middle-class family of lawyers and soldiers, alongside bureaucrats, notaries, and clerks who had worked for the government both before and after the Revolution of 1789. A measure of the solidity of Mallarmé's origins can be seen in the two witnesses who signed his birth certificate in Paris's second arrondissement. His maternal grandfather, André Marie Léger Desmolins, head of the Service of Registration and Domains in the Ministry of Finance, and his uncle, Jules Charles Adélaïde Mallarmé, lieutenant in the Garde Municipal, both had been awarded the Legion of Honor, France's highest prize for national service. At the time of Étienne's birth, his parents, Numa and Élizabeth Mallarmé, lived with the Desmolins in Paris. The infant was put out to nurse. The birth of a second child, Maria, two years later, encouraged Numa to buy a house on the rue de l'Hameau de Boulainvilliers, in what is now Paris's chic sixteenth arrondissement.

Louis-Philippe, king at the time of Étienne Mallarmé's birth, was the third royal to govern during the restoration of the monarchy, after the second exile of Napoleon I in 1815. More liberal than his Bourbon predecessors, the Orleanist "Citizen King" had ruled, after the July Revolution of 1830, as "King of the French," and not as "King of France," by national sovereignty limited by a constitution, and not by divine right. Louis-Philippe presided over the industrial revolution in France, the building of roads and railroads, the development of factories and mines, and a consolidation of the power of the wealthy bourgeoisie—landowners, merchants, those who exercised liberal professions, and civil servants—at the expense of the working poor. The nation as a whole expanded its territorial reach and its sense of national pride by the conquest of Algeria between 1830 and 1847, as a result of intense colonial competition among the European powers over the continent of Africa.

As a midlevel government employee, Numa Mallarmé profited little from the economic takeoff of the July Monarchy. This may have had to do with a genuine lack of ambition. But it may also have had to do with a desire not to draw attention to the role played by one of his ancestors during the Reign of Terror, the ten-month period between September 1793 and July 1794, when tens of thousands of "enemies of the Revolution" were executed by guillotine. François René Auguste Mallarmé had presided over a meeting of the National Convention that voted for the execution of King Louis XVI, "without appeal and without delay." With the return of monarchy after the departure of Napoleon I in 1815, the members of the Convention were banished from France. François Mallarmé, Numa's great-uncle, who had served under Napoleon I during the Empire as well as during the Hundred Days of his return between March and

July 1815, went into exile in Belgium, where he died in a mental hospital in 1831. He was one of the relatively lucky ones. According to a reckoning compiled in 1829, only 86 of the 338 members of the Convention died of natural causes; 33 were guillotined; 14 committed suicide; 7 were assassinated; 5 perished in French Guiana, having been deported; 2 drowned; and 5 died, as François Mallarmé soon would, as a result of madness.

The legacy of a regicide in the family was still alive long after the event. One of Stéphane's high school teachers, Emmanuel des Essarts, mentioned it in a memoir about his famous student. Paul Verlaine, in preparing a book on contemporary poets, wrote to Mallarmé in 1885, to ask him about this ancestor. Verlaine was especially interested in how François died, a question that his fellow poet, despite the lifting of any moral sanction with the disappearance of monarchy altogether after 1848, simply neglected to answer. Numa Mallarmé, however, had every reason to maintain a low profile as a civil servant in the government of Louis-Philippe, whose own father, along with the revolutionary Mallarmé, had voted to execute his cousin Louis XVI and had himself been put to death during the Reign of Terror.

The Desmolins had other reasons for not participating as fully as they might have in the economic and national expansion of the July Monarchy. They were preoccupied by the health of their only daughter, Élizabeth, who suffered from rheumatoid arthritis and heart trouble. André Desmolins's wife, Fanny, an extraordinarily pious woman and the driving force of both households, spent much time in prayer, trusting in the will of God as much as in the skill of doctors. Élizabeth followed in her mother's footsteps. When her health worsened in the summer of 1847, the Mallarmés left Stéphane and Maria with their grandparents and undertook a pilgrimage to Rome in search of a cure. The hoped-for miracle did not materialize, however. That August, Élizabeth Desmolins Mallarmé died, probably still clutching the cross that had been blessed by the Pope in the Vatican.

A family council was convened. While Numa would remain the legal guardian of the Mallarmé children, grandfather Desmolins was appointed their deputy guardian (*subrogé tuteur*), representing the interests of their dead mother in the absence of their natural father, or even against him, if need be. Such an arrangement protected the inheritance that would come to them from their mother when they attained majority. It also attested to a certain confusion in the parental status of the two generations. From then on, the children would live either with their father on the rue de l'Hameau de Boulainvilliers or with their grandparents in Passy, which was then a nearby suburb.

Étienne was only five years old when his mother died. His childhood comprised a series of devastating blows. A second shock came a little over a year after Élizabeth's death, when Numa married Anna Mathieu, the nineteen-year-old daughter of a military officer. Fanny Desmolins described the children's reaction to their father's remarriage in a letter to her cousin and confidante Mélanie Laurent as "a ruinous piece of work." A half sister, Jeanne Mallarmé, was born a year later, which caused Fanny to complain to Mélanie that it fell to her to "encourage affection for this new arrival, who does not yet elicit the sympathy" of her stepsiblings. In rapid succession, the birth of two other children solidified the marriage of Numa and Anna Mallarmé.

In the overwhelming loss of wife and daughter and the quick rebuilding of a new family, the Mallarmés and the Desmolins took little note of the tumultuous events of February 1848, which saw the abdication of Louis-Philippe, rioting in the streets of Paris, and the installation of a provisional government led by the poet Alphonse de Lamartine. Louis Napoleon Bonaparte returned to France after almost a decade of exile in London, and was elected president of the

Second Republic in December 1848. In the space of only four years, the government passed from monarchic, to republican, to imperial rule, when Louis Napoleon, after the coup d'état of December 1851 and the referendum of November 1852, declared himself Emperor Napoleon III.

While France as a country was changing all around him, Étienne Mallarmé, whose first name changed about that time to Stéphane, had sufficient upset all his own. Upon the advice of Numa's half sister, Herminie du Saussaye, a woman with aristocratic pretensions, eight-year-old Stéphane was placed in a boarding school in the nearby suburb of Auteuil. The institution was filled with the sons of high nobility, who made such fun of Stéphane Mallarmé's modest origins that he invented for himself yet a third name: the Marquis of Boulainvilliers, a reference to the street on which Numa's house was located. In fact, Numa lived there for only two more years. In 1853, he was promoted in the Registry Office to serve as "keeper of mortgages" in the town of Sens, a distance of some seventy miles southeast of Paris. Stéphane stayed behind, to be looked after by his maternal grandparents.

In the absence of Numa, with whom relations had always been strained, and in keeping with her own piety, which had only been strengthened by her daughter's death, Fanny Desmolins enrolled Stéphane as a boarder in the Jesuit College of the Christian Brothers—in Passy. Reports from the school showed a lackluster performance: "Religious study: passing; work: marginally satisfactory; conduct: leaves much to be desired, religious observance: not satisfactory; neatness: not careful about his belongings; appearance at recess, at the dining table: lack of cleanliness."[1] At the age of thirteen, Stéphane Mallarmé was expelled for insufficient scholastic assiduity and an "insubordinate attitude." After a year away from any formal learning environment, he enrolled as a boarder in the Lycée Impérial of Sens, though his father and stepmother lived nearby. Maria, still supervised by the Desmolins, remained at boarding school in Paris.

Tragedy struck again in August 1857, when Maria, who had last visited Stéphane and her father in Sens the previous September, and whom Stéphane was preparing to visit in Passy, died suddenly of the same rheumatic disorder that had carried off their mother exactly ten years earlier. The pathos of a letter sent five years later to his most intimate friend, the poet and doctor Henri Cazalis, reveals the depth of the shock. Mallarmé described Maria as "this young phantom, who was thirteen years my sister, and the only person whom I adored."[2]

For Stéphane Mallarmé, the first decade and a half of life must have felt like a shipwreck during which he had been tossed overboard. One of his earliest recorded memories, recounted in the journal of poet Henri de Régnier as Mallarmé related it to him many years later, harked back to the bewilderment he experienced a few days after his mother's death. "He was called into the drawing-room where his grandmother was entertaining a friend. As the latter referred to the unfortunate event, the child, who felt embarrassed by his lack of grief which prevented him from acting as he was expected, decided to throw himself on the tiger-skin rug lying on the floor and tear at his long hair which kept getting into his eyes."[3] The passage has been taken by critics and biographers as an indication that Mallarmé felt little grief at the loss of his mother. Yet, such helpless pitching on the floor, conscious of the inappropriateness of his external display of emotion, was akin to flailing in water over his head. It is the primal scene of the powerless castaway that will find expression in his earliest poetry and that will surface fifty years later in the shipwreck of "One Toss of the Dice."

The young Mallarmé had been thrust back and forth between so many parental, grandparental, stepparental, child-care, guardian, and scholastic figures that it must have been unclear to him just where he belonged. In the first edition of a prose poem, "The Orphan" (1867), subsequently published in several different versions, Stéphane saw himself as being without parents altogether: "Orphan, already, child with the sadness anticipating the Poet, I wandered dressed in black, eyes turned away from the sky and seeking my family on earth."[4]

"The sadness anticipating the Poet" captures what must have been a deep desire to grasp something by which the hapless child might anchor himself in the ever-changing and unpredictable world of infancy and early boyhood. As things turned out, he did not have to wait very long.

Anna Mallarmé had a friend on the rue de l'Hameau de Boullainvilliers, Madame Dubois-Davesne, whose daughter Fanny Dubois-Davesne introduced Stéphane to the art of making verse when he was seven years old. He thanked her with a poem in her honor: "My dear Fanny / My good friend / I promise to be wise / All my life / And always to love you / Stéphane Mallarmé." (*Ma chère Fanny / Ma bonne amie / Je te promets d'être sage / A tout âge / Et de toujours t'aimer / Stéphane Mallarmé.*) This is, of course, not much of a poem, but it does rhyme, and it shows traits of character that will be obvious throughout the poet's life: gratitude for the gift of poetry in the epithet "my good friend"; forbearance in the face of difficulty in the "promise to be wise"; and constancy in love in the promise "always to love you" and the rhyme *aimer / Mallarmé*.

Either on the same occasion or in another visit to the Dubois-Davesnes's, Stéphane Mallarmé encountered Pierre-Jean de Béranger, the poet and the most popular songwriter of nineteenth-century France. Béranger was almost seventy at the time, and the meeting clearly meant more to the boy than to the old man. As Mallarmé later wrote to Paul Verlaine, the contact with Béranger marked him deeply, and set the artistic course of the rest of his life: "I lost as a child, at seven [sic], my mother, adored by a grandmother, who raised me at first; then I passed through various boarding schools and lycées, with a Lamartinian [i.e., romantic] soul and a secret desire to replace, one day, Béranger, since I had met him in the house of a friend."[5] The trajectory could not be clearer: from devastating loss, to disorientation in a world of constantly shifting people, places, and things, to poetry as the one activity that might, as he would later phrase it, "fix his place in the universe."

The deaths of Stéphane Mallarmé's mother and sister haunted his earliest verse, as poetry became the way out of grief and provided consolation. "The Guardian Angel" (*L'Ange gardien*), a biographical prose poem written when the poet was twelve, evoked a distant past where safety and stability, and not death and a passing "through various boarding schools and lycées," might sustain him at every stage of existence. The poet appealed to the tutelary gods of Antiquity, which protect each family, each person, through childhood, maturity, and until death. "And when he is launched out into the world, you alone watch over him, only you never leave him, you replace a mother whom he perhaps has lost."[6]

The guardian angel, a mother substitute, reappeared in a poem written after the death of his sister, as, again, poetry made up for irretrievable loss. "Yesterday. Today. Tomorrow" ("Hier. Aujourd'hui. Demain"), dated March 1859 and dedicated "to the one who sleeps," is situated physically "in coming back from the cemetery of Passy" where Maria was buried. In this lamenting lyric—"Oh Maria! Maria! The coffin / Is it cold?"—the dead sister appears as "A beautiful angel [which] under the feather of its wing made me a nest."[7]

"Yesterday. Today. Tomorrow" reinforced the continuity of life among the dead as among the survivors, but it introduced a significant new element: the feathered wing. In the scribal culture of the mid-nineteenth century, the feather was the writing instrument par excellence. The nest under the feathers of the angel's wing points to the shelter provided by writing verse. The tone and context of the two poems connected to the deaths of his mother and sister are explicitly religious. Faced with disorienting loss, the young Mallarmé, who was a devout child, converted the orthodox Catholic religion all around him into the religion of art.

While at boarding school among the Christian Brothers and later at the public lycée of Sens, Mallarmé either could not afford or was denied access to the books of verse he wanted to read. So, beginning at the age of twelve, he copied by hand, like a medieval scribe, more than eight thousand lines of traditional French poetry which he obtained from either edited books or another such notebook that he had borrowed. Here we see just how inextricably religion and writing were entwined. The first line of this notebook, "June 18, 1854: First communion," yokes the act of writing poetry, even if it was copying, with the sacrament of communion.

Three poems written in late adolescence affirm the connection between loss, suffering, and writing, between the feathered wings of a guardian angel and the consolation of putting pen—from the Latin *penna*, plural for "wing feathers"—to paper. The poet wrote a "Cantata for the First Communion" ("Cantate pour la première communion"), dated July 1858, as part of the state-required religious education at the Lycée Impérial in Sens. The following July, he read another poem, "A Mother's Prayer" ("La Prière d'une mère"), at a public ceremony, presided over by the archbishop of Sens. A mother, alone, in tears, on her knees before the cross, emits "bitter pains." Her prayer is received by God as a "joyful song". "Oh! On this day, O Lord, / A song of joy rises to you on the wings of an angel, weak echo of my heart!"[8]

In "The Cloud" ("Le Nuage"), composed around the same time, Mallarmé appealed to another guardian angel. Formations of clouds in the sky are transformed into the shapes of foam in the sea, and the pattern of clouds summons an angel's wing.

> Cloud, are you the foam
> Of the celestial ocean on a limpid and pure wave?
> Are you the white wing
> Detached by the breeze, in crossing the blue sky,
> From the wing of one of our angels?

Eventually, the shifting clouds, sea foam, white feather, and angel's wing assume the shape of a shroud enveloping the body of a dead child:

> "I am the messenger of the Lord.
> I carry on my breast a blond child, of the age
> When one doesn't know about death.
> I took it: it was sleeping on its mother's breast:
> The wing of an angel is its shroud!"[9]

The grieving voice asks the cloud, which reminds him of the censer of the Catholic mass, if "it is" also, "when our praises / fly with incense to the feet of God / the perfume which the child, ravished before the cross, swings in the urn on fire?" "The Cloud" affirmed the power of the imagination to prevail over the reality of a cruel world. Such a parallel universe may exist only in the mind, yet it becomes no less real when the feather of the protective angel's wing is put to paper in the making of elegiac verse.

From the age of twelve, and perhaps even well before, Mallarmé found salvation through the writing of poetry. Those responsible for his upbringing, however, had very different ideas. He complained, in the autobiographical letter to Verlaine, that the notebook in which he kept his verses, the intimacy of which can be seen in its title, "Between Four Walls," was repeatedly confiscated. Somehow, too, the young Mallarmé had acquired a copy of Charles

Baudelaire's *The Flowers of Evil* (1857), which was his first contact with contemporary verse. Grandpa and Grandma Desmolins, in their long effort to direct his moral and professional upbringing, managed to remove this volume as well. The fifteen-year-old aspiring poet immediately procured another copy of the writings of France's premier *poète maudit*.

The Desmolins had every reason to be concerned. Baudelaire's masterpiece, whose original title was *The Lesbians*, was filled with images of death, corruption, and the artificial paradises of alcohol, drugs, and sex. The reviewer for the daily newspaper *Le Figaro* wrote, "Everything in it which is not hideous is incomprehensible, everything one understands is putrid." Under the heavy hand of Napoleon III's censors, the French courts successfully prosecuted the author, the publisher, and the printer of *The Flowers of Evil*. Six of the poems in the collection were suppressed until a Belgian edition appeared in 1866. Baudelaire was outraged at the way his book had been treated. He protested to his mother that he had known that his poems would upset the reading public, and had thus removed fully a third of the most offensive ones from the collection. At other times, however, he tried to appear worse than he was. "Exasperated that people always believed what I said," he wrote to a friend in 1865, "I let it be known that I had killed my father and eaten him, . . . *and they believed me*! I have taken to disgrace like a duck to water."[10]

Baudelaire's reputation for indolence and dissolution must have offended to the core the Desmolins's sense of bourgeois decorum. In the bohemian mode of the late Romantics, and in anticipation of the end-of-the-century decadents, Baudelaire practiced satanic cultism under the influence of laudanum in the Hôtel de Lauzun, his elegant Parisian residence on the Île Saint-Louis and the headquarters of the Club des Hashischins. He had inherited a little fortune from his deceased father when he turned twenty-one, and he began to spend it generously on paintings, furniture, alcohol, clothes, prostitutes, and on his Creole mistress, Jeanne Duval, who for twenty years was his muse. The Desmolins, knowing that Stéphane would inherit money from his mother when he turned twenty-one, must have trembled at the thought that he would follow the example of the profligate author of *The Flowers of Evil.*

During Stéphane's last year at the lycée in Sens, Numa Mallarmé wrote a letter to Grandpa Desmolins expressing concern over "our poor child, who dreams about poetry, and only admires Victor Hugo, who is far from being a classic."[11] Victor Hugo, a Romantic and the most prolific poet of nineteenth-century France, was a liberal opponent of Louis Napoleon. He left France, when, in his own phrase, the "Little Napoleon" became Emperor Napoleon III, and was still in exile on the island of Guernsey when Mallarmé's father sounded the alarm about Stéphane's future. Hugo's political tracts had been banned in France. It just would not do for the son and grandson of two registry officers working for the government of the Second Empire to be reading the poetry of such an outspoken enemy of the regime.

In the same letter expressing alarm at the adolescent Mallarmé's reading habits, Numa confided that "his future preoccupies me greatly, and, all things considered, I would favor our administration, which at least puts bread on the table and might build a nest egg for the future. . . . Try to reinforce this idea, I beg of you." The troubled father had written on the eve of Stéphane's departure to visit his grandparents in Passy. During this stay near Paris, the aspiring poet visited Pierre-Jean de Béranger's tomb in Père-Lachaise Cemetery. Béranger had died in 1857, some eight years after the encounter "at the home of a friendly neighbor," which set Mallarmé on course for a career in the arts.

Numa Mallarmé and André Desmoulins had reason for further concern. Stéphane was supposed to graduate from the lycée the following year, and the family, while moderately well off, did not have sufficient property or revenues to support an impecunious poet. If Stéphane must write, father and grandfather must have reasoned, why not use the pen in the manner of his ancestors. After all, it is his birthright.

Stéphane Mallarmé failed the *baccalauréat* exam, needed to graduate from a lycée, in the summer of 1860, but he did pass a make-up test that fall. To the great satisfaction of his father and grandfather, the title of *bachelier* qualified him for government service, and the following month, Stéphane took a job as a probationer, the equivalent of a student intern, in the Registry Office of Sens.

There was nothing inherently shameful about late-nineteenth-century French writers maintaining day jobs as bureaucrats: the novelist and short story writer Guy de Maupassant, as a clerk in the Department of the Navy and later the Ministry of Public Instruction; the anarchist and art critic Félix Fénéon in the War Office; the decadent novelist Joris-Karl Huysmans in the Ministry of the Interior. Yet the life of a copyist in the Registry Office meant entering into the public record tax assessments, payments, and other official documents, a routine of transcription that the aspiring young poet found crushing. Mallarmé must have felt like Bartleby, the anti-heroic hero of Herman Melville's 1853 short story "Bartleby the Scrivener," a copyist who repeatedly refuses to write or to read proof with the phrase, "I would prefer not to." Stéphane had tried to, but "preferred not to." Copying the words of others instead of inventing new combinations of words of his own provoked a mood of quiet desperation, a hopelessness compounded by the place itself. The town of Sens was so gloomy, he noted, that "everything that passes through it turns gray!"

In 1861–62, the year that he worked as a supernumerary in the Registry Office of Sens, Stéphane lived in the household of Numa and Anna Mallarmé, which only added to the gloom. His father began to show signs of senility: slowness in walking, in finding

words and ideas, and memory loss, followed by a stroke and paralysis. For a long time, the only bright spot in the period following
graduation from the lycée was continued contact with Emmanuel
des Essarts, his teacher and a poet. Though only three years older
than Mallarmé, des Essarts had already published a book of verse.
He must have been privy to Stéphane's difficult situation at home,
and he no doubt recognized his former student's precocious poetic
gifts. Des Essarts expressed a resolve to put young Mallarmé in contact with the poets whom he had met when he lived in Paris. First
among these was his classmate at the Collège Henri IV and another
budding poet, Henri Cazalis. Cazalis and Mallarmé hit it off immediately, and with an intensity that led to an exchange that lasted
almost forty years.

In a long letter to Cazalis in June 1862, Mallarmé complained of
his father's disorientation and of his stepmother's stinginess. "The
cash box is in the desk of my stepmother, who has never understood
what it is to be a young man, and who only has one horrible word on
her lips: thrift."[12] Family life, especially dinnertime, had become
insufferable: "I feel at each silent meal such a discomfort that I am
repulsed." The late adolescent Mallarmé felt a need to step out and
breathe freely, but his stepmother reminded him that "the garden
has paths, and the air one breathes is the best there is in Sens." He
felt constantly under surveillance, "looked at by all as if I had three
mistresses, I who don't have a penny in my pocket, and don't even
sleep with the maid." In the same letter, Mallarmé confided that the
"small-minded and stifling atmosphere" of home life in Sens had
planted in him the idea of escaping to London.

As Numa's health declined, so did his authority over his son,
who again found himself under the strong tutelage of his maternal
grandfather, behind whom stood the powerful Fanny Desmolins.
Stéphane confided to André Desmolins that work in the records
office, despite all his goodwill and effort, had turned out to be abso-

lutely hateful, "to absorb not only my time, but my person as well." With the destination of London still in mind, he announced his desire to become an English teacher, which would not only permit him to grow intellectually over time but carry the further advantage of social distinction. Grandfather Desmolins must have taken umbrage at the suggestion that his career path, as well as that of Numa, lacked distinction. He increased pressure on his grandson and ward to pursue the family bureaucratic calling. He drew attention to Stéphane's delicate health. His grandson had suffered several bouts of what may have been rheumatic fever over the course of the previous two winters. The grandpaternal figure warned of the physical exertion involved in teaching and reminded Stéphane that his writing style was not up to that required of a language instructor, the very charge of obscurity for which Mallarmé would later become famous among critics and journalists trying to decipher his complex verse.[13]

While André Desmolins pressured Stéphane directly about his career, his wife, Fanny, prayed for her grandson to follow the family calling. Deeply devout, she was convinced of the efficacy of prayer in family matters that could not be resolved by argument or reason. At one point, she had believed that her own husband was not sufficiently pious, so she formed a club at whose weekly meetings wives would pray for their spiritually wayward mates. On May 1, 1855, Fanny wrote to her cousin Mélanie Laurent, who had similar concerns about her own father: "I must speak to you about another idea. . . . That is, to form a pious family league, a completely Christian league . . . , for the salvation of the husbands so dear to us, by setting aside each week a day of communion which would be specially dedicated to them."[14] It seems that the Thursday prayers by proxy worked, since, some five years later, which was right around the time of Stéphane's crisis in the Registry Office, Grandma Desmolins reported to her cousin that André had returned to the fold: "With the help of God's grace, all has turned out for the best, and I have had the happiness, for which I longed for forty-three years, of finally seeing my good husband on his knees next to me at the holy table, April 8, the very day one consecrates the Annunciation of the Holy Virgin."[15]

Having saved her husband by Thursday meetings to pray for the intervention of the Blessed Virgin, Grandma Desmolins turned her attention to Stéphane. In the same letter, she suggested, "If you do not want to forget our old family good work on Thursdays, we can replace grandfather with Stéphane." There really was not much need to insist. By the time he was twenty, young Mallarmé had replaced Catholic orthodoxy with faith in the salvific power of verse; and in 1875, he would convert Thursdays in Passy *chez* Grandma Desmolins into Tuesdays *chez* Mallarmé on the rue de Rome.

Youth prevailed in the future poet's struggle with his father and grandfather about the choice of a career. Supported by des Essarts, as well as by his stepmother, who was, finally, less repressive than he had portrayed her to his friends, Stéphane, it was decided, would take private English lessons five times a week beginning that spring.

Two completely unpredictable events in the spring of 1862 prepared Mallarmé's escape from the onerous parental household as well as from the Registry Office. On May 11, 1862, he attended a picnic in an open area of the Forest of Fontainebleau known as the Carrefour des Demoiselles (Girls' Crossroad). Des Essarts and Mallarmé met guests coming from out of town at the train station in Fontainebleau. From there, they proceeded by carriage down the pathways, named by one of Napoleon's Old Guard soldiers, the Road of False Steps, the Road of Beauty, and the Road of Tenderness, which set a tone for the outing. Young artists and poets had come from Paris, such as Mallarmé's new friend Cazalis and the painter Henri Regnault. And there were girls, chaperoned by their mothers: Nina Gaillard, an accomplished pianist, and three young Englishwomen, Miss Mary Green, and Ettie and Isabelle Yapp, accompanied by Mme Yapp, the wife of the Paris correspondent of London's *Daily Telegraph*.

The event itself remained vivid throughout the lifetime of the poet and his friends. Conceived as a performance, the picnic at the Carrefour des Demoiselles became the subject of art. The picnickers ate pâté and strawberries, washed down by white and red wine. As lunch ended, they indulged in songs, charades, and pantomime skits. Des Essarts and Mallarmé recited poems, in what might have

Gustave Le Gray, *Tree, Forest of Fontainebleau*, ca. 1856.
Source: https://commons.wikimedia.org/wiki/File:Gustave_LeGray_-_Tree,_
Forest_of_Fontainebleau_-_Google_Art_Project.jpg.

been the younger poet's first public reading since the recitation of
"A Mother's Prayer" at the lycée of Sens. Henri Regnault did a pencil
sketch of Ettie Yapp, and des Essarts wrote verse in her honor—"À
Miss Ettie Y——" Mallarmé and des Essarts composed a mock
heroic epic, which they labeled a "saw" (*scie*), depicting in rhyme
each of the assembled picnickers. We know from the "saw" what the
poet wore that day, and how his dress was admired by the ladies, or
at least by their mothers. "Amiable mothers of families / Who
delighted to behold / Their daughters' eyes all sunny / And men of
Sens in black from head to toe." (*D'aimables mères de familles / Qui se
réjouissaient de voir / Du soleil aux yeux de leurs filles / Et des messieurs Sens
habit noir.*)[16] Wearing black intentionally displayed the smart bohemian garb of the intelligentsia of the mid-nineteenth century. For
Mallarmé, however, black was not simply the color of his rebellious
youth. In the last Tuesday meeting of his inner circle before leaving
for Valvins in the late spring of 1896, he predicted, at the end of a
lecture on the almost universal style of men in black in fin-de-siècle
France, "that it is so indispensable, so much a part of us, that at the
Last Judgement, we will all rise in a black suit."[17]

Mallarmé portrayed himself in the "saw" as a revolutionary and
an outlaw: "Considered suspect by the gendarmerie / The Garibal-
dian Mallarmé / Still having more arts than arms / Seemed like a
Jud who is very alarmed." (*Fort mal noté par les gendarmes / Le garibal-
dien Mallarmé / Ayant encore plus d'arts que d'armes / Semblait un Jud très-
alarmé.*) The association with Giuseppe Garibaldi, the general who
fought in South America and then helped to unite Italy, and with
Charles Jud, an elusive serial killer in French railway cars during the
early 1860s, reveals the extent to which Stéphane, who was among
the youngest and the least worldly of the entire group, sought to
appear as a daring adventurer.

The two poets specified that their "saw" was to be sung to the
tune of a popular song, "There Once Was a Little Boat That Never

on the Sea Had Sailed." For Mallarmé, the title was significant. The picnic at the Carrefour des Demoiselles was his maiden voyage. The song, moreover, tells the story of a shipwrecked sailor about to be eaten by his shipmates. When he hears them discussing how to cook him, right down to what sauce to choose, he prays to the Virgin Mary and is saved by a miracle. Absent the cannibalism, the narrative arc of "There Once Was a Little Boat" would resurface in the shipwreck of "One Toss of the Dice" and in the miraculous alignment of the stars in the shape of a constellation on the final folio of Mallarmé's epic poem.

The picnic at the Carrefour des Demoiselles affected all who attended. Cazalis fell madly in love with Ettie Yapp. The friendship between Mallarmé and Henri Cazalis had been affirmed such that five years later, the poet would write, "And then, my old pal, we go back to the party at Fontainebleau! It all started there."[18] For the poet, Fontainebleau became "this magic name." His settling at Valvins, with the Forest of Fontainebleau in plain view, no doubt had something to do with that day in May 1862 when it all began. He had been initiated into a world of artistic conviviality. Mallarmé, the orphan in the poem by that name, "with the sadness anticipating the Poet, [wandering] dressed in black . . . , seeking [his] family on earth," found it amid the intellectual youth of his era. The meeting with the Yapps consolidated his plan to visit London, where Ettie would serve as a guide the following year. The poet experienced a sublimated eroticism among "young girls in flower" that was a true sexual awakening, as can be seen in a letter written to Cazalis a little over a week after the event: "You tell me that I pleased the ladies, and I am charmed by that."[19]

Around the time of the picnic at the Carrefour des Demoiselles, Mallarmé spied a woman sitting on a park bench in front of the lycée in Sens. She seemed to be waiting for someone. He, too, was waiting—for des Essarts. At first, he thought she might be English, which would have suited his plans to learn English and to visit London. When they spoke, however, she turned out to be German, born in Camberg to a family of schoolteachers. Keenly attracted, Mallarmé began to lie in wait for her at the end of each school day, to follow her into the Île de l'Yonne where she would walk, and to sit near her in Saint-Étienne Cathedral on Sundays. He discovered that her name was Maria, the same as his sister, and that she worked as a governess in one of the local families of notables. Soon, he obtained her address, and wrote a letter that was somewhat of a toss of the dice: "It's three months now that I love you violently, and several days now that I adore you even more hopelessly. Will you receive this love?"[20]

Tall, thin, blond, and blue-eyed, modestly dressed, not particularly cheerful in her demeanor, melancholic even, seven years his elder, Maria Gerhard must have been plain by the standards of Belle Époque beauty. The poet confided to Cazalis that he was relieved that the woman he loved was not an ideal beauty, for, if she were, he would no doubt someday have been disillusioned. For the budding poet, no woman could match the kind of beauty that belongs rightfully only to the realm of art. Despite his initial bold letter, Mallarmé was not a romantic. He noted in the letter to Cazalis that Maria seemed bored and sad, and that he, too, was bored and sad. "Together," Mallarmé the lover reasoned, "our two melancholies might make for happiness."[21] To Cazalis's warning that she was neither sufficiently exciting nor cultured for his sophisticated friend, the poet replied, "Don't you worry! I will make an artist out of her."

At the end of September, Stéphane and Marie, as he began to call her, took a long walk in the Forest of Fontainebleau, the poet hoping that the magic of the picnic at the Carrefour des Demoiselles might rub off on them. Their meetings were clandestine, hidden both from the Desmoulins and from Marie's host family, the Libera des Presles, one of the richest families in town. In early November, they departed together for London, where Mallarmé was to learn English for teaching in French secondary schools. He had left behind the deadly atmosphere of home, the Registry Office, and Sens. He was at last free to try his hand at becoming a poet. In the autobiographical letter to Verlaine, Stéphane described the scribal genealogy from which he had descended. Yet, he confessed, he was overjoyed "to have escaped the career to which I was destined since I was in diapers. I am happy to be holding a pen for something other than recording administrative acts."[22]

Charles Baudelaire had asked apropos of Victor Hugo, "As a result of what historical circumstances, philosophical fatalities, astronomical conjunction was this man born among us?" The question had to do with how genius might arise amid the mediocrity of everyday life in mid-nineteenth-century France. Mallarmé, who must have felt reborn at the age of twenty, sought to answer this question in his poem "Sonnet," written in the year of his liberation from the gloom of the paternal nest.

"Sonnet" begins with a series of seemingly random events in the life of a bourgeois household, not unlike the one he just left. The dinner meat is not fully cooked, the newspaper contains the story of a rape, the maid forgot to button her collar, the bourgeois glimpses on the bedroom clock an "old and crazy couple," or he is not sleepy, and, without modesty, his leg under the covers brushed fleetingly against another leg. Then, "A fool climbs on top of his cold and dry wife, / Rubs his nightcap against this white bonnet, / And works blowing inexorably. / And since on this night without rage or storm, / These two beings couple in sleeping, / O Shakespeare and you, Dante, a poet can be born!"[23]

Two

THE FOUNDATION OF A
MAGNIFICENT WORK

On his way to London in the fall of 1862, Mallarmé stopped in Versailles, where the Desmolins now lived, to pick up an advance of four thousand francs on the inheritance that would come to him from his mother when he turned twenty-one. His cautious grandparents, resigned to his pursuing a career as a teacher of English, tried to elicit a promise that Stéphane would live while in London in a Catholic residence, where his morals and his daily comings and goings would be properly supervised. He was, after all, still their legal ward, and they must have felt emboldened to exercise their guardianship, given the decline of his father, Numa. Stéphane, who was now in correspondence with poets his own age or slightly older and had a mistress, would have none of it. The lovers had already consummated their relationship sometime in September, though the tie still remained hidden from parents and grandparents. In the small town of Sens, as well as in the conservative monarchist stronghold of Versailles, the scandal of the sudden departure of the governess in a respectable family with a would-be poet, seven years her junior, would have been unbearable. Both the Mallarmés and the Desmolins would have opposed Stéphane's cohabitation with any woman to whom he was not married, much less to an au pair of lower social standing. Mallarmé, however, maintained that one of the things that attracted him to Marie was the "melancholy charm" of governesses, who were always a little *déclassée*.[1]

The arrival in London was not easy. Only a week after Stéphane and Marie had rented a small apartment on Panton Square, the young poet was robbed and ended up in court. "English justice sided with the thief under the pretext that he entrapped but did not rob me. Swindling is permitted here, and the court sent me away saying that I was an imbecile to let myself be taken like that."[2] Such a difficult welcome could not, however, dampen the couple's initial excitement at being on their own.

The young lovers, as tourists still do today, visited Westminster, Piccadilly, Hyde Park, the British Museum, and the National Gallery, where they admired the Turners. They were charmed by the chocolate-colored omnibuses and the tree-lined squares, and by the street life right outside their window—organ grinders, guitar strummers, trained monkeys in red hats, and commedia dell'arte players. And they were delighted by domestic life, right down to the ordinary objects, the teapot and beer mugs, next to a big double bed. "We have put together a true English household," Mallarmé wrote to Cazalis in mid-November, "so much so that I feel the need to write to my notary."[3] The letter to his notary would presumably have been to ask him to send money, which he had begun to spend for more than food and rent. Stéphane and Marie acquired a black cat, the first of their pets, and a German clock, purchased in a London antique shop for three shillings. "A superb façade in porcelain! With two painted roses. . . . It has a friendly tick-tock which seems to say: 'Listen well, you who embrace each other, to how laboriously I work all alone in my little corner.'"[4]

Saxony clock.
Photograph by author.

It was not clear that Mallarmé was in any rush to enroll in English lessons, and, without the encumbrance of family or school, he was free to devote himself to writing, "all alone and in his little corner." "I read, I write, she embroiders and knits," he confided to Cazalis. The usual French complaint about English bad weather did not detract from the poet's experience of the city. He saw poetry everywhere. "I love this perpetually gray sky. You don't need to think. The bright blue sky and the stars are really frightening things. You can feel at home here, and God cannot see you. His spy, the sun, does not dare crawl out of the shadows."[5]

While the joys of domestic life might have excited the young lovers at first, they pleased Stéphane more than Marie. With her reputation now in tatters, she began to doubt the poet's intentions. She suffered from insomnia and loneliness and was often in tears, which elicited guilt. "It's me who is killing her," he confided to Cazalis. Stéphane and Marie moved from the apartment on Panton Square to Albert Terrace, Knightsbridge. After a sad Christmas Eve spent with the Yapps, Marie threatened to leave.[6] Two weeks later, she booked passage back to the Continent. Mallarmé was so dispirited that he would not let her depart from the quay in London, but insisted on accompanying her as far as Calais.

The boat trip from Dover to Calais on the night of January 9, 1863, was no ordinary crossing of the English Channel. It was so tumultuous as to suggest that the portrayal of a shipwreck in "One Toss of the Dice" may stem from the poet's actual experience of a violent storm at sea. The fog that protected the poet in the city surrounded the boat at the mouth of the Thames, and the wind battered it about until the passengers thought they might drown, the result being a thirteen-hour delay. "The night before the boat had been five days to sea. The wind destroyed five hundred boats on the coast of England. Marie was sick, and as for me, I am only exhausted."[7] Once on the French side, Mallarmé could not resolve to return to England. "It is impossible to leave tonight; I feel in this moment a sort of loathing that I cannot overcome for any travel by sea." The ferocity of the elements while at sea was inseparable from the turmoil of the couple's emotional distress—"Oh! A voyage. If I write to you from here nonetheless," he scribbled to Cazalis from Boulogne-sur-Mer, "it is to say that, since this morning, we feel a mortal upset." Occasionally, despite the equanimity of poet's external demeanor, the psychic storm manifested to offer a glimpse at how this mild-mannered man might come to write such turbulent verse.

Marie proceeded to Paris, where she met her sister and Cazalis, whom Mallarmé, who often served as an intermediary between his friend and Ettie Yapp, had enlisted in the effort to try to get Marie to change her mind. His confidant, who had never favored the union, was unsuccessful and wrote to remind the budding poet, "You cannot marry Marie. . . . Marie is your sister: she has returned to her calm duty, as the other has returned to heaven."[8]

Mallarmé did not return to England but, unannounced, arrived in Paris, where he saw Cazalis, but not Marie, who had taken lodging in the house of a woman whose job it was to place governesses in respectable households. He then returned to London, where a letter from Marie awaited him, announcing, "All is finished for me."[9] At his mistress's words, the young poet was again filled with guilt, in his delicate phrase, for "having deflowered her." "It would be dishonest, criminal even," he reasoned, not to marry her. Such self-rebukes summoned the reproaches of the dead: "My mother, my sister, who see things from above." Like the honor-bound hero of a neoclassical drama, he resolved, "I must do it, and I will do it, and I will be proud of it, because it is a beautiful and rare deed."[10] In what was an act of desperation, Mallarmé wrote Cazalis, who was still in contact with Marie, that she had a choice between staying in Paris definitively, coming to London, where they might understand each other better in person than by an exchange of letters, coming back without any commitment on his part, or, finally, coming back to get married. "It's up to her to decide. . . . But she should hurry, because I am going crazy here, yes, crazy." After some hesitation, Marie boarded a train for Boulogne, crossed the Channel, and arrived in London the next day. "I am in ecstasy to see her," Mallarmé wrote to Cazalis.[11] The respite was temporary, however, as a disappointed Marie left London for Brussels at the beginning of March.

Mallarmé gained some small measure of financial and moral independence as the result of the small inheritance that came to him from his mother when he turned twenty-one, on March 18, 1863. On his way back to Sens to complete the paperwork for the transfer of funds, he stopped to see Marie in Brussels and the Desmolins in Versailles. Once in Sens, he discovered that Anna Mallarmé had known all along about his relationship with Marie, and he confessed to having misjudged her. Anna agreed to prepare the Desmolins for the possibility of an impending marriage. On Stéphane's way back to London, he went to visit the Yapps in their sumptuous Parisian apartment on the avenue de Wagram, and it was there that he learned that Numa had suffered another stroke and had lost consciousness. He returned to Sens barely in time to see his father before he died.

A true orphan, at last, with a modest sum of money at his disposal, Mallarmé proceeded to Brussels and reconciled with Marie. The couple returned to London and a new apartment on Brompton Square. Six months of emotional turmoil had ended, with the prospect of calm seas ahead. "The life of a high school teacher is simple, modest, calm. We will be at ease that way. It's what I'm aiming for," the poet wrote Cazalis on June 3, 1863.[12] After a respectable period of mourning, the young exiles were married in the Catholic church of Kensington that August, returning to Paris in time for the September state-administered teachers' exam. From then on, M. and

Mme Stéphane Mallarmé led a quiet, bourgeois existence, what the French call "a little life in the kitchen."

Mallarmé, the poet who would seek in his poetry to raise language to the abstract level of an Idea, to "purify the words of the tribe," was no less taken by the relationship between art and everyday life. There would be no point at which he did not live under constrained circumstances, and he was always anxious about having sufficient money to provide for his family. Yet, he took comfort in his modest immediate surroundings. There, he found physical refuge in a "little corner" next to the German clock where he might withdraw to write. He once described his daily routine to the English poet John Payne as that of a "silent termite, burrowing and working in our little chest of drawers, the apartment."[13]

Despite the turbulent London sojourn, the prolonged absences, and the lack of formal studies, Mallarmé passed the examination certifying his competence to teach the English language at the high school level, although it was without distinction. He was the ninth out of ten candidates. The passages that he was required to analyze as part of the *explication de texte* portion of the exam were particularly appropriate: Shakespeare's *Romeo and Juliet* and Sheridan's *The School for Scandal*. He must have thought to himself at the time that he had managed not to die for love and, given his grandparents' surveillance and their severe morality, he had caused only a minimum of scandal.

After a brief stay in Paris, and a reunion with des Essarts and Cazalis, the novice teacher was dispatched to the Lycée Impérial of Tournon, a town at least as gloomy as Sens and five times as far from the capital. Upon arrival, he wrote to Albert Collignon, a jurist and the editor of *La Revue nouvelle*, whom he had just met in Paris, that the inhabitants of this dismal village live in great intimacy with their pigs. "The pig encapsulates the spirit of the household just as the cat does elsewhere. I have not managed to find accommodations that do not remind me of a stable."[14] When the young couple did find an apartment on the rue de Bourbon, they suffered under difficult living conditions. Charles Seignobos, one of the poet's students at the lycée, who later became a professor at the Sorbonne, reported that his father, a deputy from the Ardèche, socialized with the newlyweds. He described a house exposed to sun, very hot, and so full of bugs that the Mallarmés put the feet of their bed in saucers full of water to prevent the cockroaches from climbing up. Eventually, they moved to live by the Rhône in a house exposed to the northern winds and freezing in winter.

At the beginning of this period of exile, Mallarmé wrote a number of poems—"The Azure" ("L'Azure"), "The Clown Chastised" ("Le Pître châtié"), "Weary of Bitter Rest" ("Las de l'Amer Repos")—while Cazalis and des Essarts, acting informally as his agents in Paris, submitted them to the editors of *La Revue nouvelle* and showed them to other poets. On one notable occasion, des Essarts read Mallarmé's verses at the salon of Cazalis's cousin Valentine Lejosne, which was frequented by Édouard Manet, Jules Barbey d'Aurevilly, and Charles Baudelaire. Des Essarts reported to his friend in the provinces that Baudelaire had listened "without disapproving, which is a great sign of favor."[15] He assuaged Mallarmé's skepticism at the great man's reaction by assuring him, "If he had not liked them, he would have interrupted."

In the spring of 1864, Marie announced that she was expecting a child. It suddenly occurred to the poet, who had been fascinated by happy accidents of birth, such as the issue of a poet of genius from the coupling of the intensely dull couple in the poem "Sonnet," that the opposite was also possible. "I tremble at the idea of becoming a father," he wrote to Cazalis that April 25. "What if I were to have an half-wit or a homely child?"[16] Marie suffered from morning sickness in the first months of pregnancy and left the miserable climate of

Tournon to visit a friend who owned a farmhouse outside Vienne, a nearby town, also on the Rhône. In her absence, Mallarmé inexplicably spent a few days in the monastery of the Grande-Chartreuse, writing to Cazalis, "I almost took the habit."[17] Then, escaping Tournon in a whirlwind of travel, he visited des Essarts, who had been transferred to Avignon, his stepmother, Anna, in Sens, the Desmolins in Versailles, and Cazalis in Paris.

Geneviève Mallarmé emerged on November 19, 1864. Stéphane wrote proudly to his grandmother to remind her that she had been born on his mother Élizabeth's feast day. Despite his initial fear of birth defects, he wrote to Cazalis that the newborn was "ravishing, big and beautiful, *for her age*."[18] He was surprised at the disruption to his writing introduced by care for an infant and his temporarily taking charge of housework. Nonetheless, Geneviève's birth marked the beginning of a productive period for the poet, who began *Hérodiade*, a dramatic poem whose ostensible subject is the biblical story of Herodias, Salomé, and John the Baptist, and *Afternoon of a Faun*, an erotic soliloquy whose typographical alternation between the meditative parts in Roman type and the narrative parts in italics prefigured the wild graphic newness of "One Toss of the Dice."

The poet brought *Afternoon of a Faun* to Paris, hoping to arrange a dramatic reading at the Comédie Française. Though France's most prestigious theater refused to present the work of the neophyte poet, the trip was by no means a loss. In the course of his stay in the capital, he made new acquaintances, some of whom would be of lasting value. He met the Cuban-born poet José-Maria de Heredia, the novelist Léon Cladel, and the writer François Coppée.

Heredia was the leader of the Parnassians, formalist poets who, in the wake of Romanticism, were the foremost proponents of art for art's sake in the second half of the nineteenth century. One of the several of Mallarmé's friends who would enter the Académie Française, Heredia ended his life as director of the Arsenal Library, a post that carried some measure of social surface and prestige. The Franco-Cuban poet loved to entertain, and many eligible young artists would visit his apartment on the rue des Moines for the pleasure of admiring his three beautiful daughters, two of whom would marry writers in his immediate circle. Cladel, a regional poet and novelist from the southern town of Montauban, had at first attracted the attention of no lesser light than Charles Baudelaire, who wrote the preface for his first novel, *The Ridiculous Martyrs*. François Coppée worked as a librarian in the French Senate and became the archivist of the Comédie Française, ending his career, like Heredia, among the *immortels* of the Académie Française.

While in Paris, Mallarmé reunited with two writers he already knew, and who would become fast and reliable friends, Auguste de Villiers de l'Isle-Adam and Catulle Mendès—to the extent, that is, that anyone as vain as Mendès or as wacky as Villiers could be reliable.

Villiers de l'Isle-Adam was the son of an impoverished Breton marquis who further ruined one of the aristocratic lineages of France with various get-rich schemes. Villiers's father was convinced that at the time of the Revolution wealthy families had buried treasure near their castles and country houses. He thus bought land and excavated, selling it afterward if the subsoil yielded no valuables. After the Restoration in 1815, the marquis developed the equivalent of a real estate agency, Agence Villiers de l'Isle-Adam, whose main activity was to research and to restore to its rightful owners land that had been wrongfully misappropriated after 1789. Villiers de l'Isle-Adam *père*'s highly litigious character was inherited by his son, who also pursued get-rich schemes, including a frivolous suit against a playwright who, he claimed, had insulted one of his ancestors. For the most part, however, he was obliged to work for a living. Villiers had been employed at a funeral parlor, as a sparring partner and boxing instructor in a gymnasium, as, in his own phrase, "comptroller of the waggonage of the cattle transported from the South to Paris," and as a planted "cured madman" whose job it was to sit calmly in the waiting room of a doctor specializing in mental illness.

In October 1862, two years before the reunion with Mallarmé in Paris, the Greek king Otto I had been deposed as a result of a coup d'état ending the constitutional monarchy and rule of the German-linked Wittelsbach dynasty in Greece. With no candidate in line, Russia, Great Britain, and France were the protectorate powers responsible for ensuring succession. Villiers, possibly misled by a friend who planted false rumors that Emperor Napoleon III had him in mind, put himself forward for the sovereign post. He applied for a loan from the Rothschild Bank, which had financed many loans to Greece at the beginning of Otto I's rule. He sought an audience with the emperor, and presented himself at the imperial residence in the Tuileries, only to be ushered out as a madman. There is no way of knowing, of course, whether or not this implausible story, which was not the maddest of Villiers's capers, was true. However, as Mallarmé emphasized in a portrait of his lifelong friend, "the credible legend, was never, by the one involved, denied."[19]

Catulle Mendès, son of a Sephardic Jew from Bordeaux and a Catholic mother, was one of the great rakish literary intelligences and promoters of the second half of the nineteenth century. By the age of twenty, he had founded his own literary journal, *La Revue fantaisiste*, and published poems by Baudelaire, Villiers, and Théophile Gautier. Mendès was also an early and avid follower of Wagner, to whom he wrote as a nineteen-year-old to request an article with *La Revue fantaisiste* in mind. In 1866, at the age of twenty-five, he was admitted to the editorial circle of the Parnassian poets, joining Gautier, Heredia, and the older Charles Leconte de Lisle as editors of *The Contemporary Parnassian*. In a decision that many in Paris of the 1860s could not understand, the journal refused to publish Mallarmé's *Afternoon of a Faun* in its second issue.

Catulle Mendès met Judith Gautier, daughter of Parnassian poet Théophile Gautier, at a Wagner concert. The attraction between them was immediate. He was extraordinarily handsome, adventuresome, capricious, and self-absorbed, yet he radiated energy, wit, and talent. Mendès was also an epic womanizer, addicted to pornography as well as laudanum, and had spent a month in prison in 1861, a victim of the tight censorship under Napoleon III, for inserting obscene lines in his verse drama, *The Novel of a Night*. Judith Gautier, a fitting complement, was ravishingly beautiful and passionate. She was also a talented writer with a deep interest in Asian culture. At twenty-two, she would translate an anthology of poems from the Chinese, *The Book of Jade*. She sent a copy to her father's friend Victor Hugo, who had lived outside of France since she was a little girl, with an inscription: "To the triumphant exile who walks with solemnity, saying immortal things." Hugo responded, "I see my name as written by you, transformed into a luminous hieroglyph, as if by the hand of a goddess."[20] Three years later, Judith Gautier published her first novel, *The Imperial Dragon*.

Catulle was drawn to Judith because of her beauty and her literary gifts, but also because of her father's prominent place in the Parisian literary scene. An invitation to the Gautiers' house in Neuilly must have struck to the root core of his ambition. As he smoked a cigarette down to the butt on that first visit, she warned him, "Be careful, Catulle, you'll burn your claws."[21] On his third visit, Mendès brought his friend the decadent Catholic writer Jules Barbey d'Aurevilly along as a decoy to occupy the attention of Théophile, while he, alone with Judith, proposed marriage. The imperious Catulle demanded an immediate answer, but matters were not so simple. Before attaining majority, a woman might not marry without her father's consent. At first Théophile agreed but then, having looked into his future son-in-law's background—his philandering as well as the financial situation of his parents—he withdrew his approval. The lovers had a choice between eloping and biding their time until Judith's twenty-first birthday.

Catulle became increasingly frustrated by waiting for Judith's heretofore indulgent and mild-mannered father to change his mind. He published an announcement of their forthcoming marriage, which Théophile, furious, forced him to withdraw. Meanwhile, Judith became increasingly unsure of her unofficial fiancé's intentions. He treated her badly, provoking scenes of jealousy, questioning her love for him, threatening to leave. At one point, she suggested that they take laudanum together, which apparently cemented the bond between them, at least for her. This was something that Gautier *père* might have understood. Upon his first visit to the Club des Hashischins, Gautier reported that the master of before-dinner ceremonies informed him that time spent in the presence of the mustard-colored paste on a spoon the size of his thumb "would be deducted from his time in paradise." Gautier thought that hashish was paradise itself: "Nothing material was mixed with such ecstasy; no earthly desire could alter the purity. Love itself could not increase it. Romeo on hashish would have forgotten Juliet."[22]

Judith did not forget Catulle. They were married in 1866, with Villiers de l'Isle-Adam and Gustave Flaubert as their witnesses. Théophile Gautier, whose own marriage had unraveled over his wife Ernesta's more favorable attitude toward their daughter's betrothal, refused to attend.

Before, during, and after his marriage to Judith Gautier, Catulle Mendès maintained a liaison with the composer Augusta Holmès. Born in Versailles of Irish parents, Holmès, who added the accent to the "e" in her name after the Franco-Prussian War, shared Mendès's passion for Wagner, and, she too, had visited the musical master at Tribschen on Lake Lucerne. Like Judith, Augusta was a femme fatale, and she attracted the attention of Henri Cazalis after his relationship with Ettie Yapp had ended. Composer Camille Saint-Saëns had asked her to marry him. César Franck wrote his Piano Quintet with her in mind. Augusta, however, remained loyal to Mendès, with whom she had five children, three of whom are pictured in Renoir's 1888 painting *The Daughters of Catulle Mendès*. Judith, after a period of mysterious illness in the first years of marriage, gradually detached from Catulle. After his return to France in 1870, Victor Hugo, in the fullness of his glory, became infatuated with Judith Gautier and they became lovers after Théophile's death in 1872. Hugo was only the beginning. When Judith and Catulle separated in 1878, she drew closer to Richard Wagner, initiating him to the mysteries of oriental religion, and becoming almost certainly the last mistress of the dominating German composer, who died in 1883.

During his time in Paris in the summer of 1864, Mallarmé visited Henri Regnault, whom he had met at the Carrefour des Demoiselles. Regnault, the son of noted chemist and physicist Victor Regnault, was only twenty-one at the time. Yet he had already gained a reputation as a talented painter, who, two years later, would win the coveted Prix de Rome, a grant from the French government to paint at the French Academy in Rome. Regnault's studio on the rue d'Enfer was already a gathering place for artists and musicians and may have offered the visiting poet from the provinces a first taste of what a Parisian artistic salon might be. On the studio piano, Mallarmé heard music played by Charles Gounod, Camille Saint-Saëns, and Augusta Holmès.

The whirlwind trip to Paris sent Mallarmé's head spinning with notions of living in the capital among like-minded artists who also appreciated his ideas about poetry, painting, and music. The return to Tournon must have seemed like even more of an exile. He delighted in Geneviève's—he and Marie nicknamed their daughter Vévé—first words and steps. But the time he spent teaching at the lycée, to judge by reports of the inspectors sent annually to evaluate his performance, had little to suggest competence or interest. Mallarmé's year of study in London had produced no visible effect upon his mastery of English. The end-of-the-year appraisal for 1866 noted that M. Mallarmé, despite his intelligence and his learning, had up until now obtained only poor results from his teaching. His pupils pronounce English very badly and do not know the most common words. "In the first year of special Classes, fourteen students, pooling their efforts, were not able to translate for me, 'Give me some bread and water.'"[23] Mallarmé was criticized not only for the poor performance of his pupils but for seeming distracted in class and, acting on complaints from concerned parents, for publishing poems in disreputable avant-garde journals. Because of his publications, he was removed from the classroom in the outlying school district of Tournon and sent summarily, in November 1866, to Besançon, which was almost as far from the capital and arguably harsher and drearier than Tournon.

The move to Besançon provoked a crisis that had a determining effect upon the poet's life. For some months, he must have been withdrawn, in a deeply meditative state. Then, in something like a trance or syncope, he seemed to have lost consciousness for several days. "All that . . . my being has suffered during this long agony is unspeakable, but happily, I am perfectly dead, and the most impure region to which my Spirit, this regular loner in its own Purity, has ventured is Eternity, which not even the reflection of Time obscures."[24] In this state of altered consciousness, Mallarmé experienced a vision of God in the form of an enormous bird, which bore him under "the bony wing of his old and menacing plumage" to a "realm of Shadows." There, the poet and the godhead engaged in a frightful struggle from which he emerged victorious, having wrestled God to the ground. Mallarmé awoke three days later—the Christological three days?—from this otherworldly experience in front of the Venetian mirror that he and Marie had purchased

Venetian mirror.
Photograph by author.

together. The mirror itself was a frightening bronze tangle of foliage and serpents with the haunting head of a man, crowned by what could be a laurel leaf, the traditional sign of victorious poets, on top. The transfigured poet recognized the face he had forgotten several months earlier. Like a saint after conversion, he became a vessel of truth. He wrote to Cazalis, "I am no longer the Stéphane whom you have known—but a capacity of the spiritual Universe to look at itself and to develop itself through what was once me."[25]

Insofar as Mallarmé considered himself to be "a capacity of the spiritual Universe," he took himself to represent all of humanity. The crisis of his young adulthood was in some deep sense that of the age in which he lived, the period of "the great upheaval," which he also helped to make.

Modernity, as it took shape in the second half of the nineteenth century and the first quarter of the twentieth, was synonymous with rupture, melancholy, skepticism, anxiety, self-criticism, spiritual failure, nihilism, and despair, alongside the perceived loss of individual autonomy as well as the failure of science and technology and of liberal democratic institutions. To philosophers of the mid- to late 1800s, Enlightenment faith in reason seemed less and less plausible. German philosophy—beginning before but, most powerfully, after Nietzsche—was deeply pessimistic. The key catalyzing sentence of the end of the century was, of course, Nietzsche's famous declaration in 1882 of the death of God, which left man suspended in a world without any fixed point to moor human values: "God is dead. God remains dead. And we have killed him. Yet his shadow still looms. How shall we comfort ourselves, the murderers of all murderers?"[26] Martin Heidegger would drive the stake of pessimism even further into the heart of spiritual value with the question "What if in truth the nothing were indeed not a being but also were not simply null?" In which case, "Nihilism would be the essential nonthinking of the essence of the nothing."[27]

The development of the social sciences at the end of the nineteenth century went hand in hand with philosophical despair. Already in Marx, the evolution from feudalism to capitalism was sensed as a passage from authentic use-value, in the direct relations between men and the things they make and consume, to less authentic market-value, where human relations are mediated—that is to say, debased—by money. Max Weber, writing in the early 1900s, traced a similar loss of human wholeness in the rationalized forms of social relations that took hold in the Protestant work-oriented countries of northern Europe. "The fate of our times," Weber intoned in a speech delivered at the University of Munich in 1918, "is characterized by rationalization and intellectualization and, above all, by the 'disenchantment of the world,'" a phrase that coursed richly through the twentieth century.[28]

Mallarmé may have thought himself a vessel of the crisis of faith as it worked itself out between the Enlightenment and the end of the nineteenth century. Yet, he emerged in the 1860s from the psychological and moral extremity of his midtwenties not disenchanted but invigorated. On the other side of his three days of illumination, he had caught a glimpse of the great universal undefined infinite, which he would henceforth characterize as his "dream" or "ideal," and which gave direction and meaning to the rest of his life. From that point on, Mallarmé sought to capture that ideal in a book. "I just, in the hour of synthesis, laid out the work. Three poems in verse . . . of a purity that man has not yet attained and will perhaps never attain, for it could be that I am only the plaything of an illusion, and that the human machine is not perfect enough to arrive at such results."[29] Mallarmé struggled for the next three decades to transform the pure Idea, eternal and abstract, into writing. The result, imagined as a book, would culminate in "One Toss of the Dice."

For Mallarmé, this beautiful world-book was no mere metaphor, but a real project. "As for me, I have worked more this summer than in my entire life," he wrote to the poet Théodore Aubanel on July 16, 1866. "I have laid the foundation of a magnificent work. Every man has a secret within him, many die without ever finding it. . . . I am dead and resurrected with the jeweled key of the ultimate treasure chest of my mind. It is now up to me to open it in the absence of any impression borrowed from elsewhere, and its mystery will spread out into a most beautiful heaven. I need twenty years during which I am going to retreat within myself, avoiding any publicity except for some readings to my friends."[30]

The idea of a single book, an epic poem of humanity, would be surrounded by a vocabulary of mystery, magic, miracle, alchemy even. Mallarmé spoke of it in the most hyperbolic terms. He described *The Book* as a hymn, "all harmony and joy," and as "an immaculate grouping of universal relationships come together for some miraculous and glittering occasion." Man's duty in this world is to observe with the eyes of the divinity, and the only way of expressing what he observes is through the pages of a book.[31]

Like the Romantics of the first quarter of the century, and like Baudelaire, who reached his poetic peak in the 1850s, Mallarmé believed in the great universal harmony and connection of all things. In almost everything he wrote, poetry is infused with the burden of spirituality that once belonged to religion. The very sight of a book summoned the spirit—from the Latin *spiritus*, meaning "breath," "breeze," "air"—in a secret, silent communication between letters and the world, even in the absence of any human presence. He imagined a book lying outside on a garden bench, pages blowing in the breeze, as an infusion of life into the inert bound object. "The foldings of a book," he noted, "form a tomb in miniature for our souls."[32]

Mallarmé's virtual *Book* was also pictured as a real printed volume. He spoke, even in his twenties, in a second letter to Aubanel, of a project comprising five volumes. In the autobiographical sketch for Verlaine of 1885, it was a question of "a work of many tomes." The poet René Ghil, writing in 1923, claimed that Mallarmé confided that *The Book* would be composed of twenty volumes that together would make for a Philosophy of the World. However many tomes Mallarmé imagined would be required for the Poem of Humanity, the book that "would explain all earthly existence," was unclear. Much clearer was that the poet felt as if he were in a race against time and that, if he originally thought in terms of twenty years, by the time of the letter to Verlaine, "a lifetime would not be sufficient."[33]

Mallarmé's dream of the world as book was in some mundane way rooted in the technology and the spirit of the times. Beginning in the late 1700s, monumental advances were made in the realm of printing and book manufacture, a full three hundred years after Gutenberg's invention of the printing press, which in its primitive way had dominated bookmaking until then. Smoother and more easily printable vellum paper began to replace the older wire-laid rag paper, whose supply was limited by the supply of disposable cloth. More efficient mechanical means of making paper came into being, as production shifted away from the single sheet and toward the continuous roll. After the fall of Napoleon I, certain improvements in the actual process of mixing the paper "paste" made it possible in France for factories to produce 1,000 kilos of paper per day instead of the previous 100 produced by hand. It was after the 1840s, however, that the real boon to papermaking came about in the form of paper made from a mixture of pulverized tree pulp bonded chemically (this was the acid paper whose disintegration was not at first foreseen). To the increased capacity of paper manufacture were added immense advancements in the efficiency of the printing press, which had, in fact, changed very little since the invention of printing in the fifteenth century. By the middle of the 1800s, four-cylinder steam engines were driving the presses of France's major newspapers and print houses. Mechanically driven rollers had replaced, in the phrase of Honoré de Balzac in his novel about print culture, *Lost Illusions*, the old leather "groaning balls," originally used for applying ink. The ink itself, once handmade out of organic material, was replaced by industrially produced chemical dyes.

The print industry, thus, grew phenomenally after the Consulate of 1799 to 1804, and during the Restoration, which lasted from 1815 to 1848. The number of print shops increased by 150 percent, or twice as fast as the population, such rapid growth slowing only with the tighter surveillance of the press during the Second Empire and the reign of Napoleon III. The number of Parisian booksellers grew proportionally, as did the sheer mass of printed material, from newspapers and magazines, to advertising brochures, posters, and books. The rate of book publication, which was estimated at fewer than 2,000 titles per year before the Revolution of 1789, grew, according to the Bibliothèque de France, to 2,547 titles in 1814, 8,237 titles in 1826, and 12,269 titles in 1869. Such an exponential increase reflected the growth of literacy among a burgeoning urban intellectual and upper-middle class, with historical reverberations that would play themselves out throughout the nineteenth century.

François Guizot, minister of education under the July Monarchy of 1830, called for French scholars, in a race with their German and English counterparts after the Napoleonic wars, to track down as many documents related to French history as they could find. Guizot submitted an increased budget request of 120,000 francs for fiscal 1835 in order "to accomplish the great task of a general publication of all the important and unedited materials having to do with the history of our country."[34] He proposed editing himself a thirty-volume *Collection of Documents Relative to the History of France from the Foundation of the French Monarchy up to the Thirteenth Century*. Fifty years later, Prime Minister Jules Ferry, father of the French system of public education, proclaimed in a speech to Parliament, "For us, the book, do you hear me, the book whatever its nature, is the fundamental and irresistible means of freeing the intelligence."[35] The Belle Époque brought changes in written communication equivalent to the current explosion of electronic media. Mallarmé's project of *The Book* was, then, part and parcel of the times, and it was, as we shall see by way of conclusion, so far in advance of its time as to set the agenda for today's digital revolution.

Mallarmé's total book, which laid the groundwork for "One Toss of the Dice," was more than a reflection of advances in book manufacture and means of communication. The ambition reached back to the roots of the Western tradition, and it served to put the poet in touch with a long classical and medieval legacy of imagining the

world as a book. The Bible, both Old and New Testaments, is filled
with metaphors of the Book. God writes in the "Book of Life"
(Exodus 32:32). The Tables of the Law are "written with the finger
of God" (Exodus 31:18). The Prophet Isaiah's eschatological vision
(Isaiah 34:4) predated the advent of the book as codex, which was
part of a revolution in written culture between the third and the
sixth century C.E. It promised nonetheless that "the heavens shall
be rolled together as a scroll."

In the High Middle Ages, one of the dominant metaphors for
the earthly realm was the Book of Nature. Alain de Lille, in the
twelfth century, and Jean de Meun, in the thirteenth, linked writing
to the natural world. "Sitting in Audience before Goddess Nature,"
Jean wrote in the *Romance of the Rose*, the most copied vernacular
manuscript of the Middle Ages, "the willing priest recorded the
images (representational figures) of all corruptible things, which he
had written in his book, as Nature gave them to him."[36] Dante, at
the end of his journey through the underworld and Purgatory,
arrives at the highest point of Paradise where he has a vision of the
eternal light of the entire spiritual universe:

> In its depth I saw contained,
>
> by love into a single volume bound
>
> the pages scattered through the universe:
>
> substances, accidents, and the interplay between them,
>
> as though they were conflated in such ways
>
> that what I tell is but a simple light.[37]

For the astronomer Galileo at the end of the sixteenth century,
"philosophy is written in this grand book, the universe, which stands
continually open to our gaze."[38]

Mallarmé was naturally fascinated by the Middle Ages, which he
considered, in the wake of the Romantic turning away from classical

antiquity and embrace of the indigenous medieval roots of France, a period of authenticity in which man was conjoined with the world, this vision thus celebrated in all the arts. When the poet was not boating or fishing, one of his activities once he started spending summers at Valvins involved amateur theatricals. In fact, he wrote a version of the late medieval comic drama *The Farce of Maître Pathelin* and played the role of Pathelin, a clever lawyer who tricks a cloth merchant out of his wares. When in Paris, Mallarmé was also taken by the survival of the Middle Ages in the Cathedral of Notre-Dame, which had been restored by the architect Viollet-le-Duc between 1847 and 1863. "Close your eyes," he suggested in "Magic," an essay, "you cannot miss . . . Notre Dame" which "refuses to fall."[39]

Mallarmé was also captivated by the look of medieval manuscripts, whose varied visual layout, with room in the margins for annotation, historiated and floriated initial letters, miniature illuminations and drolleries, resonate with the multidimensional appearance of "One Toss of the Dice." Alongside William Morris's turn to the Middle Ages in the Arts and Crafts movement in England, the French poet was seduced by the medieval arts of the book, a seduction that would come to the fore in the course of a visit to Belgium in April 1890. In Brussels, he dined with several admirers— the poets Iwan Gilkin, Albert Giraud, and Valère Gille—who showed their guest a volume of his own poems, written on parchment in a Gothic hand, bound like a medieval prayer book, with illuminations, decorated letters, and *culs-de-lampe* (tailpieces). Highly impressed, Mallarmé borrowed the handmade book, which he brought back to Paris and, after showing it to family and friends, returned with a poem added to "this book of hours."[40] The manuscript spoke to the organic, spiritual quality that, having disappeared from contemporaneous uniformly printed books, Mallarmé nonetheless found in medieval handwritten volumes.

Soon, Mallarmé would have occasion to come into contact with a living medieval poetic tradition. From the start of his stay in Besançon, the poet had complained of health problems related to the town's "black, humid, and glacial climate." In October 1867, he received a letter from the minister of public education transferring him to the Lycée Impérial of Avignon. Mallarmé was familiar with the medievally significant Avignon, having made several visits to the Mediterranean coast. In the course of one such trip, the poet made it as far as Cannes, where his friend Eugène Lefébure, an aspiring poet who had worked as a postman in Auxerre and who would eventually become one of France's most accomplished Egyptologists, was living comfortably in a villa as a result of an inheritance that had come his way. Together, Mallarmé and Lefébure spent an evening at the casino in Monaco, which is the only evidence of contact between the author of "One Toss of the Dice" and the real world of gambling. Mallarmé wrote home to his wife at eleven p.m. on the night of April 4, 1866, "I will tell you about all my doings when I get back, I am satisfied with informing you only that the excursion to Monaco was delicious, and that at roulette I won a few sous with which I bought you a pretty little. . . . I won't tell you what, which surprise will go marvelously with the dress that you will buy this summer!"[41]

Mallarmé's stays in southern France, with its more limpid weather, had brought temporary relief from the deeply depressive atmosphere of Tournon and Besançon. He had written to Cazalis as early as 1864, "Ah! My friend, how I would love to be in Avignon! Pray for it to the gods who put the pen pushers in the ministry offices."[42] And, when he heard of his new appointment, he wondered whether someone had uncovered the "intimate and ancient secret" of his dreams. Des Essarts had introduced Mallarmé to his poet friends in Avignon, which was the center of one of the most important indigenous cultural movements in nineteenth-century France. The Félibrige association, founded in 1854, took as its goal

the restoration of the Occitan, or Provençal, language and its literature to their rightful place among the arts. Provençal, the language
of the first vernacular poets, or troubadours, could trace its origins
back to the early twelfth century—that is, to a time before music
and verse were distinct from each other. The ambitions of the
Félibrige poets to revive medieval lyric thus coincided with Mallarmé's vision of an integrated work of art. For the young Mallarmé,
the revivalist Provençal poets of Avignon—including Frédéric Mistral, Joseph Roumanille, and Théodore Aubanel—may not have
been as exciting as the cosmopolitan writers and painters he had
encountered in Paris, but in Avignon he joined a circle of active
poets with whom he remained lifelong friends.

While in Avignon, Mallarmé began work on *Igitur*, a semiautobi-
ographical dramatic poem in four acts: "Midnight," "The Stairs,"
"The Dice Throw," and "Sleep on the Ashes, after the Candle Is
Snuffed Out." Some elements of this enigmatic work cast back to
the poet's struggle to free himself from his family: "The infinite at
last escapes the family, which has suffered from it—old space—no
chance." Some are rooted in the psychic crisis of 1867, right down to
the poet's battle with monsters, the attainment of a state of absolute
purity, and the disappearance and reappearance of the self in a mirror. Without the visual innovation of "One Toss of the Dice," still
other elements of *Igitur* anticipate Mallarmé's last work: the Hamlet-
like figure up against a midnight deadline when, "Midnight
sounds—The Midnight when the dice must be cast"; an obsession
with chance, and, more precisely, the abolition of chance: "having
denied chance, he concludes from it that the Idea has been necessary. Then he conceives that there is, to be sure, madness in admit-
ting it absolutely: but at the same time he can say that since through
this madness, chance was denied, this madness was necessary";[43]
and, of course, a dense, elliptical, unruly syntax that, even in a prose
poem, is difficult to decipher.

Toward the end of his three years in Avignon, where he lived within the walls of the medieval city and within walking distance of the fourteenth-century Pope's Palace, Mallarmé received a letter from Catulle Mendès informing him of the existence of "a new art, which is neither poetry nor music, but which is both music and poetry." Mendès was referring to the operatic total works of art of Richard Wagner. Mendès and his wife, Judith Gautier, were the chief proponents of Wagner's music in France. Incredibly, in the summer of 1870, on the eve of the Franco-Prussian War, the Mendèses, together with Villiers de l'Isle-Adam, traveled to see Richard and Cosima Wagner in their house on Lake Lucerne. They were there when the news of the outbreak of war arrived, which did not interrupt the plan also to visit Mallarmé.

Mallarmé read *Igitur* out loud to his guests in the course of their short stay in Avignon. They reacted with embarrassment and shock. "What!" Mendès would write of the incident many years later. "Is this work, whose subject is difficult to identify and in which words are never used in their proper sense, what Mallarmé ended up with, after such a long effort?"[44] Villiers burst out laughing. M. and Mme Mendès beat a hasty retreat: after a quick visit with the Félibrige poets, they left for Paris. Villiers, who never lacked get-rich schemes, stayed on and tried to get Marie Mallarmé to help him translate articles from German newspapers that he intended to publish in the French press. The two poets discussed what Villiers, despite his initial outburst, sensed to be the immense ambition of *Igitur*. Finally, completely out of money, the impoverished aristocrat borrowed train fare to return to the capital which would be severely disrupted, both physically and existentially, from the time of Kaiser Wilhelm's capture of Napoleon III at the Battle of Sedan in September 1870 to the defeat of the Commune in May 1871.

Three

ENCHANTING A
DEVASTATED WORLD

Perhaps no single event in the entire nineteenth century trauma-tized the French nation as profoundly as the invasion by Ger-many in the late summer of 1870. In fact, just as Catulle Mendès, Judith Gautier, and Villers de l'Isle-Adam listened to Mallarmé read *Igitur,* the early version of what would become "One Toss of the Dice," the German Confederation, led by the Prussians, was massing and moving west. After several preliminary battles, the German army on September 1, 1870 routed the French in the Ardennes at the northeast town of Sedan, a name that still resonates with infamy in the national conscience. It was a date that would live yet again in infamy almost seventy years later, when the Germans invaded Poland on September 1, 1939, and Great Britain and France declared war on Germany two days later. At Sedan, 17,000 French troops were killed and some 100,000 taken prisoner, among them Napoleon III, who was unceremoniously removed to the castle of Wilhelmshöhe, before going into exile in England. Like so many fellow Frenchmen, Mal-larmé was touched by Sedan. Jean-Auguste Margueritte, his cousin by marriage, had been promoted to the rank of divisional general on the morning of September 1 and later that day was wounded by a bullet that passed through both cheeks and his tongue. Unable to speak, he nonetheless gestured with his sword for his men to charge against the advancing wall of German troops who decimated the French First Division Cavalry Reserve. He died four days later.

From the distance of Avignon, Mallarmé recognized the absurdity of the struggle between Kaiser Wilhelm I and Napoleon III. He wrote to Mistral two days after Sedan, "There is in today's atmosphere an unknown dose of suffering and insanity. And all this because a fistful of fools . . . thought they were insulted and failed to recognize that modern history contains something other than such puerile old stuff."[1] Indeed, the war had begun as a crisis over the succession to the Spanish throne and a series of perceived diplomatic sleights. When Prussian Prince Leopold of Hohenzollern-Sigmaringen was offered the Spanish kingship after the Spanish Revolution of 1868, the French feared being trapped by an alliance between her neighbors to the northeast and the south. The prince's candidacy was withdrawn under pressure from the French, but Napoleon III demanded a formal apology from Kaiser Wilhelm. The wily Otto von Bismarck, prime minister of Prussia, released Wilhelm's telegram. The Ems Dispatch, as it came to be known, rejected the French demands, but the ambitious Bismarck, always eager to manipulate the emperor, had also altered the text of the message to make it sound as if the Prussian king had insulted the French ambassador, a move calculated to lead to war.

By the time Villiers arrived in Paris two days after the colossal defeat at Sedan, the Second Empire had been replaced by a Government of National Defense. Kaiser Wilhelm of Prussia, Field Marshal Helmuth von Moltke, and Prince Albert of Saxony continued to move toward Paris, and, by the middle of the month, had encircled the capital, which by this point was paralyzed by fear. In his short story "A Duel," Guy de Maupassant captured the mood of France in the wake of the German victory: "The war was over; the Germans were occupying France; the country was trembling like a beaten warrior beneath the foot of the conqueror."[2]

The siege of Paris lasted through the terribly cold winter of 1870–71, a winter so severe that the Seine actually froze for three weeks. Cut off from the surrounding countryside, Parisians suffered devastating shortages of food, firewood, coal, and medical supplies. The novelist Alphonse Daudet wrote to Frédéric Mistral on December 31, "It is cold, it is dark, we are eating horse, cat, camel, and hippopotamus."[3] Risking starvation, Parisians emptied the zoo. A Christmas menu marking the ninety-ninth day of the siege included stuffed donkey's head, elephant consommé, fried gudgeon fish caught locally, camel roasted with an English sauce, wolf thigh with venison, kangaroo stew, antelope terrine with truffles, bear ribs with peppers, and cat with rats. De Maupassant took the measure of the situation: "Paris was starving, panic-stricken, in despair."[4]

Though communication with the outside world had been interrupted, ingenious Parisians foiled the blockade via an early avatar of airmail, if not Twitter. Messages of twenty words or less were grouped together, photographed, and flown to the outside world in multiple copies via carrier pigeon. The photographer Nadar, who was no doubt involved in processing the images, also happened to be a noted balloonist, and he organized a series of regular flights out of the besieged city. The Yapp sisters were trapped in their Parisian apartment at the time of the German invasion, yet they transmitted to London dispatches published in *The Queen: The Lady's Newspaper* under the rubric "Shut Up in Paris" and the pseudonym Eliane de Marsy. "This morning a balloon containing from thirty to forty thousand letters ascended from the heights of Montmartre, and disappeared from thousands of gazing eyes in the direction of Chartres," they wrote on September 23. The Yapp sisters' reports from the center of the siege were particularly concerned with the plight of families: those displaced from the outskirts of Paris, "men, women, and children of the family tramping with baskets, bundles, and bags"; and those, like Monsieur and Madame Jules Legendre, who "lost their daughters, Alice, aged thirteen years and a half, and Clémence, aged eight, *both struck by a Prussian bomb.*" The war would touch the Yapps more directly. Ettie's younger sister Isabelle succumbed to the hardships of life in Paris under siege, the first to die of the young girls in flower of the Carrefour des Demoiselles.

After three and a half months of encirclement, the standoff between the Germans and the Parisians appeared interminable. The invaders were not fully supplied for the long winter, and tuberculosis began to spread among the besieging troops. The German high command decided to increase the bombardment of Paris. Beginning in early January, 1871, 300 to 600 shells per day rained down upon the city. Around the middle of the month, the Yapp sisters wrote that "for more than forty hours we have heard the long detonations, bursting forth with fierce explosion and rolling away in sullen thunder, at intervals of one or two minutes with more rapid successions at times."

On January 18, 1871, Wilhelm I was declared German emperor, a regal promotion of sorts that was designed to instill patriotic fervor in the newly unified nation. That very evening Augusta Holmès hosted a musical gathering with Auguste de Villiers de l'Isle-Adam, Henri Regnault, and her lover Catulle Mendès. Regnault was known for his beautiful tenor voice and had led a combined singing of holiday songs—Adolph-Charles Adam's "Cantique de Noël" in French and the "Choral of Luther" in German—across enemy lines on Christmas Eve. Villiers recounted that at Augusta Holmès's soirée Regnault sang a war hymn that she had composed in a "moment of savage hesitation" with the noise of shells in the background. All three men wore their soldier's hats. Then, around midnight, Reg-

nault sang an impressive melody by Saint-Saëns, which began, "Near
this white tomb, we mix our tears." Upon arriving home, he found
an order to join his battalion in the morning. The pressure of the
large-caliber Krupp siege guns had provoked the army of the
National Guard to attempt to break out along the western fortifications of the city. Heading toward the seat of the government, which
had retreated to Versailles, the French troops got as far as the castle
of Buzenval, seven miles west of Paris, where they were turned back.
Regnault is reported to have said to his comrade in arms, fellow
painter Georges Clairin, "just one more shot, and I'll be back." Come
back he never did. Having taken a bullet in the head, he was among
the four thousand killed in this final push to lift the siege of Paris,
and among the last to die in the Franco-Prussian War. Anticipating
death, he had pinned a note to his shirt, "Henri Regnault, painter,
son of M. Victor Regnault, of the Institut [of France]," along with
letters addressed to his fiancée. Within days of the Battle of Buzenval, a vanquished French President Adolphe Thiers and a triumphant
Chancellor Otto von Bismarck signed an armistice at Versailles.

When Camille Saint-Saëns heard of his friend's death, he finished composing his *Funeral March*. And, as the news spread through
Paris that hostilities with Germany had ceased, he played it for the
first time at the solemn mass for Henri Regnault at the Church of
Saint-Augustin. "The poor young painter's friends were well nigh
countless. Truly, I rarely saw mourning so deep as among that
crowded concourse, in which even men shed bitter tears," Ettie
Yapp reported to her readers in London. Ernest Meissonier, then a
legend among mid-nineteenth-century French painters, delivered
the eulogy, and, in the midst of low chanting, a military command
was heard. The trumpeters of Regnault's unit burst forth with a bril-
liant fanfare. Geneviève Breton, the dead soldier's fiancée, who had
searched alongside his comrades for his body on the field of Buzenval, left the church on the arm of his older brother and only remain-

ing relative. In Meissonier's historic painting *The Siege of Paris, 1870–71*, a wounded Regnault is depicted leaning against a pedestal in the center, beneath the statuesque fierce figure of Marianne, national symbol of the Republic, holding a tattered tricolor French flag triumphantly high.

As many as half a million middle-class Parisians had fled the city by the time the siege ended. The French army was in shambles. The eastern provinces of Alsace and Lorraine had been lost to the German Empire, and France found itself obliged to pay an indemnity of 200 million francs. In reaction to the defeat, a sizable proportion of the population in the working-class neighborhoods of Belleville, Montmarte, La Villette, Montrouge, Faubourg Saint-Antoine, and Faubourg du Temple rose in revolt against Thiers and the government of Versailles. Some were dedicated revolutionaries, for whom the memory of the failed uprisings of 1830 and 1848 was still alive; some were disgruntled workers seeking better living conditions; some were dedicated patriots who felt France's surrender to Germany to be a betrayal, "a fever of powerless patriotism," in Guy de Maupassant's phrase;[5] and some, like the poet Paul Verlaine, who became head of the press bureau of the Central Committee of the Commune, joined for the promise of artistic liberation that a direct democracy of the people seemed to hold.

Even while the armistice of Versailles was being negotiated, members of the National Guard, no longer loyal to the defeated regime, surrounded the Hôtel de Ville with the demand that the military be placed under civilian rule. By the middle of March, the Communards had requisitioned four hundred cannons, originally paid for by a subscription of Parisians, and which represented a credible means of self-defense. The army of Versailles tried to seize the cannons on March 18, but their troops were turned back. Their leaders, Generals Clement-Thomas and Lecomte, were beaten to death by angry mobs. Thiers ordered all regular army troops to regroup in Versailles and all government offices to evacuate the city, which now belonged to those loyal to the Commune in what Karl Marx and Friedrich Engels would refer to as the "dictatorship of the proletariat." The National Guard occupied the Ministries of Finance, Interior, and War, with headquarters in the Hôtel de Ville, which now flew the red flag of revolution.

In early April 1871, the Communard troops of the National Guard marched out of Paris with the intention of capturing Versailles. Roundly defeated, they retreated within the wall of Paris, which meant that there would be fighting in the streets. Barricades were erected along the *grands boulevards*—the rue de Rivoli, the rue de l'Opéra, and the other streets that had been widened and straightened by Baron Haussmann's urban renewal of Paris under Napoleon III. In the weeks following the definitive withdrawal of the government to Versailles, an atmosphere of exultation reigned among the Communards, for whom the future seemed open to a general repeal of the economic inequality, social repression, and arbitrary rule associated with the Second Empire. In the account of photographer and chronicler of Paris Maxime Du Camp, who was not sympathetic to the urban uprising, life for the worker had never been so enjoyable. "Regularly paid, as was the National Guard, the worker always had 'pocket change,' which lacked sometimes when he had a regular job in the workshop; he received an allowance for his wife and for his children; the State or local canteens distributed sufficient food: never had he drunk so much wine, never more spirits, than during this period of general scarcity."[6]

The mood of gleeful triumph was broken, however, when, on May 10 the armistice of Versailles was ratified by the Treaty of Frankfurt, officially acknowledging the terms of the agreement struck between Thiers and the German chancellor in January. Two days later, the Communards sacked Thiers's home, offering the works of art in his collection, including bronzes by Leonardo da

Vinci and Michelangelo, to the Louvre. On May 16, by a decree of
the Central Committee of the Commune, the Vendôme Column
was toppled to the singing of "La Marseillaise." The painter Gustave Coubet, president of the Commune's Art Commission, had
declared this monument to Napoleon's victory at the Battle of Aus-
terlitz a "work of barbarism . . . devoid of all artistic value."

While the makers of revolution celebrated in the streets, in caba-
rets, and in newly founded political clubs, or *parlottes*, the French
army advanced toward Paris, shelling the neighborhoods of Auteuil,
Passy, and Trocadero, and capturing the defensive Fort d'Issy, one
of the sixteen fortifications built between 1840 and 1845 to defend
the city from attack. On May 19, the forces of Marshal Patrice de
MacMahon further penetrated the southwest walls of Paris, and
began filing into the city. Maxime Du Camp reported that on the
night of May 21, he leaned out of the window of his apartment on 62
rue de Rome and heard the baritone voice of a young man of about
twenty-five singing in unison with the crowd a popular tune, "The
Proletarian," the defiant words "God, Workers, People" repeated
like a refrain:

> Did God make the world so broke,
> That in the walls of workhouses,
> Vitriol, tallow, soot, and smoke
> Pierce the heart with their deadly gases
> Under the eyes of a nasty boss? . . .
> They have their arms, and we have ours:
> What's one more hole in the rags we wear![7]

As the Communards sang in the streets, sixty thousand army troops
passed through the Porte de Saint-Cloud and the Porte de Versailles.
They spread out over the city in what was to be the beginning of
"Bloody Week."

Many of the Communards had been convinced that the troops
of Versailles would not fire upon fellow Frenchmen. Surprised by
MacMahon's rapid penetration of the city walls, they scrambled to
build more barricades out of paving stones and sandbags. Fighting
broke out along the quai d'Orsay and the boulevard de la Madeleine, and around the Tuileries Palace, Napoleon III's former residence. The advancing French forces, with the memory of the brutal
deaths of General Clement-Thomas and Lecomte still fresh in their
minds, took no prisoners, but shot National Guardsmen and resist-
ers, men and women, on the spot. In return, the Communards
executed the prisoners held in the prison of La Roquette, among
them the archbishop of Paris. When the rebels killed Saint-Saëns's
superior at the Church of the Madeleine, the composer, who had
served in the National Guard, escaped into exile in England. The
Communards burned public buildings, an order carried out in part
by the *petroleuses*, women carrying oil cans. The Tuileries Palace, the
Richelieu wing of the Louvre, the Palais de Justice, the Prefecture
de Police, and the Hôtel de Ville all went up in flames. On May 28,
the army cornered what remained of the defenders of the Commune in Père-Lachaise Cemetery. By nightfall, 150 National
Guardsmen had surrendered, and were lined up and executed
against the southeast wall of the burial park. At the end of "Bloody
Week," between 10,000 and 20,000 Communards had died. More
than 40,000 had been taken prisoner; and, of these, after military
trial, 13,500 were found guilty. One hundred were sentenced to
death, 250 were sent to forced labor, 5,000 to deportation, 3,500 to
prison, and the rest were eventually released. "A desperate Paris,"
in Maxime Du Camp's phrase, "had withdrawn into its walls and
ended by devouring itself."[8]

Mallarmé opened the newspaper on February 2, 1871, to read the
news of Henri Regnault's death, "this first hole among us," as he

wrote to Cazalis, referring to the bond between young poets and a painter that had been forged at the Carrefour des Demoiselles almost ten years earlier. But the loss of a friend, the source of "unknown suffering," produced several unforeseeable effects. Regnault's early death filled Mallarmé with resolve to finish his own life's work in order to fulfill the artistic promise that his dead friend had left behind. "There is only one way of avenging our brother," he wrote to Cazalis, "that is, to let him live in the two of us."[9] The poet vowed to finish *The Book* born in the crisis of his midtwenties, which had quickened in *Igitur*, and which would reach its final form in "One Toss of the Dice."

Regnault's death had another, more tangible effect. The dead painter's fiancée, Geneviève Breton, who was the granddaughter of the founder of the reigning twenty-first-century Hachette publishing empire, took it upon herself to bring Mallarmé from Avignon to Paris, as if it were the realization of one of the last wishes of Henri. Cazalis, who served as intermediary in the exchange, wrote to the poet in the provinces to ask what kind of work he might do at Hachette. Mendès also informed Mallarmé that a representative of Hachette would be dispatched to Avignon to interview him, as knowledge of English might be of service to the firm either in Paris or in London. The incredulous poet replied that he would be of little use to a large business enterprise because "he was only familiar with the English words contained in the verse of Edgar Allan Poe."[10]

While his supporters in Paris worked to secure him a position, Mallarmé went to work on his own. He lobbied Frédéric Mistral, who had friends in high places, to write to the Occitan poet's admirer Saint-René-Taillander in the Ministry of Public Education, in order to ask that he be transferred from Avignon to a teaching job in Paris. If no teaching job were available, the poet in exile would be willing to put his English-language skills to use as a librarian or archivist. Meanwhile, Villiers de l'Isle-Adam tried to secure for his friend in the provinces a contract writing for the *Illustrated London News*. They discussed the possibility of his undertaking a series of translations of nineteenth-century English poets, beginning with Poe, always a favorite in France, and of writing plays. For a brief moment, Mallarmé even considered taking a job as the English tutor on a steamboat, a measure of his desperation to be in the capital, for he concluded that the long months at sea would only have kept him away from where he wanted to be.

Several days before the beginning of "Bloody Week," Mallarmé wrote to Mistral to ask whether he and des Essarts might come to visit Mistral at his home outside of Avignon the following Sunday, Pentecost, which fell that year on May 28. He added that he "would be leaving the next morning, Monday, for the North."[11] Mallarmé had decided that, even without a job, he would try his fortunes in the capital, which had "devoured itself" and was still burning.

On Monday morning, May 29, as the last victims of the Commune began to be counted and buried in mass graves, and as the captured resistance fighters marched under army guard to Versailles, the Mallarmés left Avignon for the north. Marie was expecting a second child. She planned to give birth at Anna's house in Sens while Stéphane looked for work. When he arrived to stay with Catulle Mendès and Judith Gautier, Paris still looked like a battle zone, with burned-out buildings, whole blocks decimated, and walls scarred by rifle and artillery fire. The debris of barricades still littered torn-up streets. The Mallarmés moved north with little money. Stéphane, who had inherited money directly from his mother, had also counted on receiving what remained of the Desmolins' estate when his grandmother, who had no other heirs, died two years previously. But Fanny had left only debts. In a letter to José-Maria de Heredia, the poet Leconte de Lisle noted the precarious situation of the young poet with "a wife and two children, one still to come into this world, and not a *centime*."[12]

With the birth of Anatole Mallarmé on July 16, 1871, the need for money was such that the poet accepted to work as a journalist for the newspaper *Le National*, which sent him to London to report on the International Exposition of 1871. Housed on Alexander Square by a colleague of Ettie Yapp's father at the *Daily Telegraph*, he reconnected with the magical young woman of the Carrefour des Demoiselles, who had weathered the siege of Paris and the Commune. They spoke in confidence of Ettie's unhappy relationship with Henri Cazalis, which had continued for six years after their meeting in 1862. She asked the poet to intervene on her behalf to persuade her former fiancé to burn her letters. Later that year, Ettie Yapp would marry the Egyptologist Gaston Maspero. Two years after that, she would die in childbirth at the age of twenty-seven.

For the French of the mid-nineteenth century, England—Manchester as much as London—was the place where industrially produced art had been most successfully integrated into everyday life. According to the Belgian poet Georges Rodenbach, Mallarmé hoped to do for France what Dante Gabriel Rossetti, the poet and painter, had done for England when he had cofounded the Pre-Raphaelite Brotherhood in 1848; or what William Morris, the textile and book designer, and Walter Crane, the illustrator of children's books, had accomplished as leaders of the British Arts and Crafts movement: that is, to make more beautiful the useful objects found in every bourgeois home.[13] Thus Mallarmé wrote a series of letters from London, which appeared in *Le National* on October 29, and November 14 and 29, 1871, under the pseudonym L.-S. Price (no doubt a play on the English "priceless" or "list price"). The poet's English letters showed France to be a worthy rival of its neighbor across the Channel. His descriptions, a blend of nationalism mixed with aesthetics, bestowed a patina of poetry on the French luxury goods— clocks, lamps, furniture, jewels, accessories, vases, table settings, tapestries, carpets, paintings, a Pleyel-Wolf grand piano—on display at the fair in London just six months after the Treaty of Frankfurt.

At the time of his move from Avignon to Paris, Mallarmé reaffirmed his literary calling and dedication to the *Grand Oeuvre*, no longer a myth, but a version of *The Book*. As outlined to Cazalis, his life's work would contain three parts: "a volume of Tales, dreamed," by which the poet referred to his longer poetic dramas that tell a story, *Hérodiade, Afternoon of a Faun*, and *Igitur*; "a volume of Poetry, glimpsed and hummed," by which he referred to the rest of his poetic output, thus far, "The Azure," "Windows," "The Clown Chastised," "Summer Sadness," "Sea Breeze," "Apparition," "Weary of Bitter Rest," a series of sonnets, and, of course, the juvenilia written while still in high school; and "a volume of Critique, that is, what used to be called the Universe, considered from a strictly *literary* point of view."[14] This last component—"the Universe, considered from a strictly *literary* point of view"—can be understood only as the other side of the project of *The Book*. If the *Grand Oeuvre* would capture and change the world, "Critique" would reinscribe the world as it exists with the magic power of poetry.

Mallarmé made poetry out of the industrially produced goods that were part of every middle-class life—"this elusive spirit that presides over the manufacture of the familiar decor of our daily existence."[15] Thus, the world, no matter how difficult, or grim, or filled with the foolishness of political leaders bent on destroying each other, might partake of some of the charm that belongs ordinarily only to the realm of art. Eventually, he would transfer this fascination with luxury from home furnishings to clothes via his writings on feminine dress for a ladies fashion magazine, *The Latest Fashion*, and he would literally reinscribe the world with beauty and meaning by writing poems on the surfaces of a variety of everyday objects. The poet once confided to a journalist that "the world was created in order to end in a beautiful book."[16] In waiting for *The*

Book to take shape, the poet would capture and catalogue the hidden, indeed the ineffable, poetry in things. Far from the frivolous musings of a late-nineteenth-century dandy or a fashionable flâneur, his writings on furniture, accessories, and fashion raised the most expensive playthings of human vanity to the power of an idea.

Mallarmé meditated on the banality of human time versus the eternal attributes of art in describing a "solemn furnishing, the clock," manufactured by Ferdinand Barbedienne, whose foundry, obliged to forge cannons during the Franco-Prussian War, had returned to manufacturing luxury goods by the time of the poet's London sojourn. "This gross exaggerated watch, as if made for the infantile eye of an Indian nabob, is trimmed with arabesques incised into burnished silver, and playing round about a frame, in which yellow and black enamel are married with white enamel."[17] The poet turned cultural reporter found a certain absurdity in late-eighteenth-century and Empire-style clocks, whose allegorical figures sit upon a marble base, but "the manufacture of lamps, differing from that of clocks, has never bordered on the absurd; and for this reason—that the shape has been preserved by that of the vase."[18] As for the jewels of the Maison Froment-Meurice, "such bracelets! A vine of virgin gold;—a succession of clasps, panels and arabesques, pearls and diamonds, burnished gold and emeralds. And these necklaces! One of enamel, pink like flesh, but colder, suspending precious stones of a pale tone, nonetheless alive."[19]

Mallarmé was equally fascinated by the relationship of originals to reproductions and by the modern combination of industrially produced objects and handmade fine arts, especially in the manufacture of ceramics and of cloth. MM. Soupireau et Fournier's renderings of the elaborate Renaissance pottery of Bernard Palissy, in particular, captured the poet's attention. He noted that the spiny and twisted fish necessary for remarkable fish soups can be found mixed with fanciful salamanders and blazons in the high relief of

majolica soup bowls. "I admit that, before these admirable reproductions, the word *authentic*, frequently pronounced by the exacting
collector, oddly loses its meaning."[20] As obsessed as he was by the
coincidence of actual things with their artistic reproduction, the
poet delighted in the miniature porcelain fish, eels, shellfish, and
mollusks swimming in the actual broth that they have made.

Upon his return to Paris in the fall of 1871, Mallarmé was greeted
with what finally seemed like welcome news. Through the efforts of
Geneviève Breton, who knew Jules Simon, the minister of education, he was appointed to a part-time teaching position at Paris's
Lycée Condorcet, with a secondary appointment at the Lycée Saint-
Louis. Though working at two institutions meant a long commute,
between the rue du Havre and the upper boulevard Saint-Michel,
the full salary meant that the family of four might just make ends
meet. The Mallarmés moved into a fourth-floor apartment on the
rue de Moscou. Their first Parisian home was not far from some of
the most contested lines of urban combat of earlier that spring,
within walking distance of the hill upon which Sacré-Coeur would
be built as a national penance imposed upon Paris's most rebellious
neighborhood. Four years later, Mallarmé would move to the rue de
Rome, within earshot of the spot on which the young Communard
with a baritone voice had regaled his neighbors with "The Proletarian" at the beginning of "Bloody Week."

The onerous task of teaching in those first years in Paris did not
prevent Mallarmé from socializing whenever he had the chance,
especially if there were the opportunity of talking about poetry or
meeting other poets. He was convinced, perhaps because of his contact with the Félibrige movement in Provence or his knowledge of
the Pre-Raphaelite Brotherhood in England, that all poets were
spiritually connected. He had the idea of forming an international
poets' union, and even wrote about such a project to John Payne in
England and to Mistral, who was uninterested. On one of his eve-

nings out, Mallarmé met the poets Arthur Rimbaud and Paul Verlaine at a dinner of the Vilains Bonhommes (Bad, Bad Boys), a monthly gathering of Parnassian poets, advocates of "art for art's sake," who read their latest compositions and discussed verse.

At the age of sixteen, Rimbaud had boarded a train without a ticket in the northern town of Charleville, in the Ardennes. Arriving in Paris on September 6, 1870, just five days after the French defeat at Sedan, he was immediately imprisoned and sent home. Ten days later, he was on the road again, drinking, stealing, and composing poems along with a letter, sent in May 1871 to one of his high school teachers, about achieving a higher poetic vision through a "long, gigantic and rational derangement of all the senses."[21] Rimbaud dreamed of returning to Paris, and began sending his poems to Verlaine, among which a sonnet, "The Sleeper in the Valley" ("Le Dormeur du Val"), which depicts a sleeping soldier lying in the grass, and who turns out, like Henri Regnault, to be dead—"Tranquil. He has two red holes in his right side"—one of the victims of the Franco-Prussian War. Verlaine was so taken with Rimbaud's verse that he sent the young poet a reply, with a one-way ticket to Paris—"Come, dear great soul. We await you. We desire you." How much he desired, he had little idea.

Rimbaud arrived in Paris in September 1871 and lodged at first with Verlaine and his seventeen-year-old wife, who was pregnant. In short order, the Verlaine-Rimbaud couple displaced the married couple. The two poets stayed out all night or did not come home at all, consumed large quantities of alcohol, absinthe, and hashish, and scandalized the Parisian literary scene—Verlaine because of his unconventional marital arrangement, and Rimbaud because of his unsettling behavior. The younger poet stole from those who housed him and disrupted poetic meetings that, by the standards of this enfant terrible from Charleville, were not disruptive enough. In March 1872, Rimbaud's repeated cries of "shit!" during one of the readings at the Vilains Bonhommes ended with the young poet's striking the photographer Étienne Carjat with a cane, and his exclusion from future gatherings. During this period, Mallarmé met Rimbaud, who impressed the older poet with the country redness of his face, his steely blue eyes, and the swollen roughness of his hands, which had "signed beautiful unpublished verses," though his mouth, "with a sullen and mocking fold, had recited none."[22]

In September, Verlaine abandoned his wife and infant son. The lovers—"two poets in ferocious pain," in Mallarmé's phrase[23]—left for London, where they lived "in orgiastic misery."[24] Throughout the affair, Verlaine supported his new couple by offering English lessons, and was supported by his mother, who repeatedly urged him to return home. Verlaine did come back to Paris in June 1873, but the period of renewed domestic respectability was short-lived. A month later he telegraphed Rimbaud to meet him in Brussels, where he and his mother traveled together; and, on July 10, the older poet, jealous and furious at his young lover's threats to leave, shot him twice. Verlaine was originally indicted for murder, a charge reduced to assault with a firearm. He served two years in prison, during which time he converted to Roman Catholicism. Rimbaud, on the other hand, left France and poetry before he was twenty, landing first in Indonesia, where he enlisted in and deserted the Dutch colonial army, and then in the Horn of Africa—Yemen and Ethiopia—where he sold weapons, coffee, and apparently slaves as well, before dying of bone cancer at the age of thirty-seven.

Upon his release from prison, Verlaine returned to England, and then immigrated briefly to Boston, where he taught English, Latin, and Greek. He would return definitively to Paris in 1877. There, he and Mallarmé resumed a relationship of mutual respect for each other's poetic gifts. According to Mallarmé, Verlaine divided his time in two equal halves. He wrote poetry, and he drank. When in misery, with a couple of difficult months ahead, Verlaine would write to the director of a hospital he frequented, as if it were a hotel, to announce that he would arrive on such and such a day. But, Mallarmé observed, "certain verses of Verlaine to Rimbaud are so beautiful!"

Mallarmé showed no evidence of the desperate agony, none of the excesses or scandalous capers, the bankruptcies and binges of so many of the Romantic, Parnassian, and Symbolist poets. If he had a vice by today's standards, it was smoking—cigarettes, cigars, and a pipe. The flume from his cigar in Manet's portrait of the poet, completed in 1876, is one of the great captures of smoke in all of Western art. In one of those Belle Époque parlor games, which involved completing a questionnaire to be shared with others, Mallarmé indulged in a game of "confessions." His response to the question of "Your idea of unhappiness," which Marcel Proust once famously answered with the plaintive "being separated from Maman," was, simply, "doing without cigars."[25]

Mallarmé's appetites and afflictions were remarkably plain. Although he liked fine wine and eventually became known for his toasts at literary banquets, he was modest in his consumption of alcohol. The poet suffered from chronic insomnia, for which he took analgesics, and wore a prosthetic dental device, yet he indulged in none of the artificial paradises synonymous with the circles in which he moved. Unlike many of the writers of the nineteenth century— who sought, via exotic travel, escape from what was among the Romantics "the sickness of the century" (*mal du siècle*), "boredom and spleen" (Baudelaire), or Europe's "bad blood" (Rimbaud)— Mallarmé, having raised some of the money to send Paul Gauguin to Tahiti, himself traveled no farther than London, Oxford, Cambridge, and the Côte d' Azur.

The poet's reports from the London International Exhibition had, however, given him a taste for and a knowledge of luxury goods. So, six months after his return to Paris, he wrote to fellow poet José-Maria de Heredia of his dream of editing a magazine devoted to the decorative arts. "I am gathering, now, in various parts of Paris the necessary subscriptions to found a beautiful and luxurious review, the thought of which obsesses me: *L'Art Décoratif, Gazette Mensuelle*, Paris, 1872." He sought Heredia's help in encouraging his friend Claudius Popelin, a well-regarded history and portrait painter, to design the cover.[26] The moment, too, seemed right for such a venture. With the memory of the war and the Commune fading, French industry and commerce flourished in what was the beginning of a period of intense consumerism, aided by the extension of railway lines, the continued migration of rural population to large cities, improved techniques of advertising, and the building of shopping arcades and department stores in the capital.

Together with a friend, Charles Wendelen, who lived just up the street on the rue de Moscou, Mallarmé published eight issues of a biweekly ladies' magazine, *The Latest Fashion* (*La Dernière Mode*). He was meticulous about the appearance, and even the feel, of his guide to the arts of gracious living. Elegance of dress and decoration went hand in hand with elegant writing, paper, illustration, and printing.

When it came to fashion, cooking, and household management, Mallarmé ironically picked up where Isabella Beeton, the author of *Mrs Beeton's Book of Household Management* (1861), had left off. From his time in London, the French poet would surely have known about the ubiquitous English guide to running a Victorian household, which, like *The Latest Fashion*, began as a serialized magazine and was only later collected into a book. Isabella's husband, Samuel Orchart Beeton, had founded *The Queen: The Lady's Newspaper*, where the Yapp sisters published their dispatches from Paris. It is inconceivable that the Yapps, in whose London and Paris homes Mallarmé was a frequent visitor, did not possess a copy of *Mrs Beeton's Book of Household Management*, a work that helped define domestic

Victorian mores. The English book was enormously successful, selling nearly two million copies by 1868, even though Isabella Beeton died in 1865, as Ettie Yapp would eight years later, of puerperal fever. Mallarmé had also read copies of *The Queen*, which contained the latest society gossip from the court of Queen Victoria alongside advice about the latest in fashion, decoration, cooking, and entertaining. Upon his return from London to Paris, the poet must have seen the publication of a magazine for upper-class ladies as a means of getting rich.

Mallarmé, perhaps sensing that such pieces would mar his reputation as a poet, wrote the entirety of every issue of *The Latest Fashion* under a variety of pseudonyms, each with a different specialty in the arts of living: Marguerite de Ponty for ladies' fashion; Miss Satin for fashion houses; Ix, a male, for book and theater reviews; the Chef de Bouche de chez Brébant for cuisine; Madame de P. for education; Toussenel for naturalist activities and sports; and "A Grandmother" when it came to tried-and-true home remedies—"A Syrup to cure a cold," "Ointment for chilblains"—that have been "practiced for generations." In case such obvious disguise might raise suspicion, Mallarmé assured his readers of the reality of the fabrication: "Have full confidence, Mesdames, in the foreign pseudonym of a well-known Parisian lady: Miss Satin."[27] It was not so much that the poet had inverted traditional gender identities, but he was capable of identifying with women, of imagining their sensitivities to decoration and dress. He spoke in the voice of a woman.

The persona adopted for food suggestions, the Chef de Bouche de chez Brébant, summoned the luxury dinners of the real Paul Brébant, who, in 1863, had purchased Chez Vachette, 32 boulevard de la Poissonière, the restaurant frequented by Paris's intellectual, journalistic, and literary elite. It was at Chez Brébant where dramatist Alexander Dumas *fils* honored his novelist father with a nineteen-course meal, not counting cheese or fruit. In *The Latest*

Fashion, Mallarmé's fictitious chef proposed a comparatively modest seven-course "menu for a luncheon by the seaside," and a midnight supper consisting of Ostend and Marennes oysters, for a first course; consommé of plovers' eggs, black pudding à la Richelieu, fillets of sole with Montpellier butter, saddle of Nîmes lamb with asparagus tips, for an entrée; truffled bartorelles, thrush pâté with juniper berries, new peas française, and buisson of crayfish with Ribeauvillé wine, for the main course; and louvers in pastry with chocolate, for dessert.

Mallarmé's recipes for a less luxurious home-cooked meal tended still toward the exotic. Instructions for cooking chicken gumbo, an excellent bisque and a spicy dish, were attributed to a "a Creole Lady," and a recipe for coconut jam to Zizi, a mulatto maid from Surat. The ingredients and all the spices "can be found at 5, boulevard Haussmann, at the shop of an old friend of our Readers."[28] Mallarmé was quite taken by the advertising industry that blossomed in the late 1800s in France, and the last pages of *The Latest Fashion* contained a series of advertisements accompanied by what look like business cards of recommended purveyors of luxury goods and services: "Marliani—Carpets and Decoration," "Henri Laudron, S—Luxury Gloves," "Mathilde Leclerc—Marie-Antoinette Style Corsets," "Carjat—Photographer," "Anchor Line Steam Ships —Paris to New York."

The Latest Fashion was filled with tips for home decoration, some of which are so curious that one wonders how serious Mallarmé could have been. The poet saw no contradiction, in any case, between his goal of "purifying the words of the tribe," on the one hand, and making upper-middle-class households more beautiful, on the other. Thus, he provided instructions for adapting Jewish Dutch lamps (by which I assume he referred to menorahs) to gas, and for "the application of leather on leather: an afternoon occupation."[29] He offered advice for creating a movable false ceiling for a rented apartment with the same concern for the ideal space behind openings in the sky that are an obsessive theme in his most serious verse. For those who live in flats, "the obstacle to the realizing of many a dream is inevitably the ceiling: for the wall, with its wallpaper is hidden, and doors can be painted; but white as a sheet of paper without a poem, only larger, or veiled with cloud on a sky-blue background at so much the yard, is the Sky offered to the tenant's eyes, as he looks up from his armchair."[30]

Flowers were an integral part of the Belle Époque decorative arts and would culminate in the organic aesthetic of Art Nouveau. *The Latest Fashion* included monthly advice on flower arrangement. In the issue of December 20, 1874, Mallarmé outlined instructions for decorating an "ordinary Christmas tree": "Acclimatized in France from the North (especially since the war) by patriotic efforts, the Christmas tree, once reserved for rich cosmopolitan children, is now accessible to all." Mallarmé provided his readers with cultural hints about noteworthy events at Parisian theaters and opera, about new volumes in bookstores, and about museum and gallery exhibitions in the world of fine arts. *The Latest Fashion* featured counsel from "a professor in one of the Parisian lycées" on which books and educational methods are worthy of maternal attention.[31] The leisure class, which the poet targeted as his readers, summered away from Paris, and *The Latest Fashion* was filled with vacation suggestions—commentary on railways and stations, a list of suitable bathing resorts in Normandy, Brittany, south of the Loire, and along the Paris–Lyon–Mediterranean line. The poet, who had just begun to spend his summers in Valvins, made recommendations about keeping busy in Paris during the indolent summer months. Fall, of course, was hunting season, and Mallarmé, under the pseudonym of his gaming expert Toussenel, described in *The Latest Fashion* of October 4, 1874, a "Lark-hunt, with a Draw-net."

The Latest Fashion aimed to please the ladies, and women's clothes were its defining topic. Mallarmé acted as a permanent fashion advisor, answering questions from subscribers about particular questions of style. To Mme D. in Toulouse: "Yes, Madame, you may safely trim a plum-colored silk dress with light blue: but you must confine it to borders and rouleautés [a portion of material rolled round on itself], or the effect will be simply ugly: and it must be a very pale blue." To Mme Marie de L., who had asked about wedding dresses in the issue of December 20, 1874, Mallarmé first extended "smiling congratulations." In the matter of the latest bridal fashion, however, the poet urged caution. Wedding dresses are the last to change in style. So: "There would be something not quite proper—particularly in your case, living so far from the capital as you do—in a bride's wishing to be in advance of fashion."[32]

In a tradition that stretches all the way back to the early fathers of the Church, Charles Baudelaire famously believed that a woman's dress was part of her body. "What poet would dare," he asked, "in the portrayal of pleasure caused by the apparition of a beauty, separate the woman from her clothes?"[33] Mallarmé, on the other hand, not only distinguished between the body and its dress, but he was capable, unlike Baudelaire, of dreaming of the dress alone. Miss Satin's article in the issue of November 1, 1874, featured a "blue-of-dreams" outfit by Charles Worth, who dominated French fashion in the second half of the nineteenth century. "We have all of us been dreaming of that gown, without knowing it. M. Worth, alone, has the art of creating a toilette as elusive as our own thoughts. Picture (you can if you try) a long skirt with a rep train, of the most ideal sky-blue silk—that blue so pale, with gleams of opalescence, that one sometimes sees, like a garland, round silvery clouds."[34] Years later, Mallarmé admitted to Paul Verlaine that certain of his works had been written out of economic necessity, "of which it is better not to speak." His essays on style, however, were another matter. His writings on women's dress, in the poet's phrase, "still make me dream for a long time."[35]

Anticipating astonishingly "One Toss of the Dice Never Will Abolish Chance," Mallarmé maintained in *The Latest Fashion* that the correct choice of garments and accessories and just the right department store—Paris's flourishing Bon Marché—will abolish chance. Miss Satin promised, "No more long hours or days hunting for a particular ribbon! It is not just chance that makes us write down, before all others, the name of the Bon Marché. We have a deep conviction that the Lady Reader who, when she gets into her carriage, utters the words 'rue du Bac' or 'rue de Sèvres,' will not return dissatisfied either with our advice or her own journey." The poet went on to sing the praises of the department store, which, unlike the specialty boutiques that sold only one type of good, umbrellas, gloves, ribbons, furs, or cloth, might meet all of a woman's consumer needs—"yours, Madame, yours Mademoiselle, and those of all you Mademoiselles and Mesdames."[36] Eight years after the rise and fall of *The Latest Fashion*, Émile Zola published his great shopping novel, *Ladies' Paradise*, which chronicles the devastating economic struggle between Paris's new department stores, "cathedrals of commerce," and the old shopkeepers in and around the Bon Marché in the capital's seventh arrondissement.

Mallarmé recognized that poetry may never change the world, as one toss of the dice never will abolish chance. The poet might, however, reinvest the world with meaning and magic by literally covering it with writing, by making the world rhyme. If the Book of Nature is no longer visible to be read, nature and all its contents were nonetheless available to be written upon, and so he wrote poems on surfaces that ordinarily do not contain verse as well as on surfaces that do not ordinarily contain writing. In waiting to write *The Book*, Mallarmé wrote upon the physical world as if it were a giant notebook.

Almost twenty poems written on fans—from a mere couplet dedicated to his confidante Méry Laurent, to five quatrains to his daughter—attest to Mallarmé's predilection for objects associated with the Far East. The fan in particular attracted the poet because of the comparison, present in almost every example, between the opening of the fan and the outstretching of wings. In the Mallarméan spiderweb of meaningful connections, he associated wings with angels, and with sails, which are the equivalents of the pen with which one writes and the paper on which one writes.

Mallarmé made the fan-wing-sail metaphor explicit in the fan poem dedicated to his daughter:

> O dreamer, that I might
> Plunge into pure delight,
> Learn through a subtle stratagem
> How to guard my fragile wing in your hand.
>
> Crepuscular breezes blow
> Their freshness out to you
> As lightly each imprisoned stroke
> Presses the whole horizon back.[37]

As in the constellation at the end of "One Toss of the Dice," where the layout of type takes the shape of the Big Dipper, Mallarmé's fan poem to Geneviève is one of those instances in which form and content coincide. The poem about the fan's breeze is inscribed on a fan, which makes the breeze. The poem says and is what it does.

Mallarmé maintained that the shape of an envelope reminded him of a poetic quatrain, and he addressed more than a hundred letters with such four-line strophes to friends, fellow artists, and his publishers. Not a single one of the poet's rhymed labels failed to reach its destination, the postmen of France having become readers of his verse.

> Their laughter will expand
> in harmony should your way wend
> Chez Monsieur Whistler and Madame,
> Old Rue Bac, number 110.

> At the Villa des Arts, near the Avenue
> De Clichy, paints Monsieur Renoir
> Who gets something other than all blue
> In front of a shoulder with no peignoir.

> Halt, postman, at the tones
> Groaned by the cellos: it's well
> The home of Monsieur Ernest Chausson,
> 22 Boulevard de Courcelles.[38]

Mallarmé regularly dispatched books and photographs with rhymed inscriptions in the flyleaf or on the surface of the image. Each new year, he sent baskets of candied fruit to friends. Over sixty of the poems accompanying the traditional offerings survive. On January 1, 1897, Mallarmé accompanied his yearly gift of a box of candied fruit with a note to Julie Manet, the daughter of Eugène Manet and Berthe Morisot:

> To flee the ice floe and avalanche
> Julie or cold reckless fools
> It is enough to remain good as gold
> With your interior innocence.[39]

This would be the next-to-last gift that Mallarmé sent to his orphaned protégée, and Julie Manet noted in her journal, "M. Renoir came to see us together with M. Mallarmé who brought each of us [Julie and no doubt her cousin Jeannie Gobillard] a box of candy with a charming quatrain, as he has done for the past nine years. This one is very beautiful, and very 'Mallarmé.'"[40]

When birthdays came around, the highly domesticated poet sent his family and friends presents inscribed with poems. Easter brought red colored eggs bestowed upon Méry Laurent, Mme Mallarmé, or Geneviève, each inscribed with a verse in gold ink, and numbered to ensure in which order the eggs were to be read. Asked by the journalist Alidor Delzant to compose an inscription for the shelves of his library, the poet complied: "Here lies the noble human span / Remnants bending with these tomes / In order that you give them homes / You must take one in your hand." And on the mantle of his fireplace: "Here is where fire is reborn / Long lasting, and then charming / Like its master's friendly chord / Oak with vines all entwining."[41]

So attentive was Mallarmé to his family that he inscribed couplets on stones found on the beach at Honfleur, the town in Normandy where Geneviève and Marie vacationed with the Ponsots, family friends. "To Françoise, who serves at table / Many a plate delectable," he wrote on a stone to the Ponsots' cook to thank her for her culinary gifts; and, to wife and daughter, "Mesdames, the ladies of Batignolles [the neighborhood of the Mallarmés's apartment] / Here become lazy and unprofitable."[42] While in Normandy, the home of Calvados liqueur, Mallarmé also inscribed a number of pitchers of this apple brandy. "Friend, drink this apple cordial / You will feel yourself amply male"; "I hold the secret of what men think / Who drain my belly with their drink."[43]

The poet was not without humor in his inscription of the things around him. He left a little poem on the wall of the communal out-

Outhouse wall inscription.
Photograph by author.

house in Valvins to discourage the local villagers from befouling it: "You, who often relieve your tripes / Can in this act hidden from all / Sing or smoke your pipes / Without smearing fingers on the wall."[44] Mallarmé sent a copy of the original, which was taken down and is now exhibited at the Mallarmé Museum in Valvins, to his friend Édouard Dujardin, with a note: "I offer you the following inscription, which I was obliged to post this morning in order to surprise the farmers because they frequently do just this."[45]

Mallarmé had no illusions, of course, about ever covering the world with words, making of the world a book. But his overwhelming goal, which became a formula for living, was to make life rhyme, whether in the everyday or in the marking of important events, whether in the shape of finished poems or of occasional verse, whether on paper or on the common objects around us. Investing the world with poetry and inscribing our presence on things were ways of situating ourselves in the universe and of affirming what makes us most fully human. Mallarmé recast the famous phrase of Descartes "I think, therefore I am"—which many consider the foundation of modern philosophy—in terms of the activity that made him feel most at home and most powerfully alive: "I write, therefore I am."

Four

TUESDAYS IN THE
"LITTLE HOUSE OF SOCRATES"

For Mallarmé, the move to Paris in the summer of 1871 meant living amid a vibrant community of artists for whom the rebirth of formalist poetry among the Parnassians, the glorification of the everyday among Impressionist painters, and the formation of a Société Nationale of composers to promote French music were part of the national recovery from the devastating blows of the Franco-Prussian War. The move to the capital also offered the poet a new and wider arena in which to accomplish the *Grand Oeuvre* in the form of a book.

The great rivalrous model for such an undertaking was, of course, the operas of Richard Wagner, who had written *Rienzi* and *The Flying Dutchman* during his first sojourn in Paris, from 1839 to 1842. The German composer sought to synthesize music, drama, architecture, song, and dance in an all-embracing total artwork, which would restore the ritual function of art that had existed among the Greeks but was lost with the advent of Christianity. "Only the great Revolution of Mankind, whose beginnings erstwhile shattered Grecian

Tragedy, can win for us this Artwork," Wagner announced in his 1849 essay *The Artwork of the Future*. Nothing thus far came closer than Wagner's *Gesamtkunstwerk* to the purity of an Idea, nor pointed more powerfully toward the restoration of the true role of art in the remaking of human community, its "future Spectacle," in Mallarmé's own phrase. An earthshaking work of poetry, however, might surpass music by exposing the "music of perfect fullness and clarity, the totality of universal relationships," a pure Idea without the material means of sound, or the often disappointing trappings of stage sets, costumes, and makeup. "Our present task," Mallarmé claimed, "is to find a way of transposing the symphony to the Book: in short, to regain our rightful due. For, undeniably, the true source of Music must not be the elemental sound of brasses, strings, or wood winds, but the intellectual and written word in all its glory."[1]

Wagner, however, had had his setbacks in Paris. The debut of *Tannhäuser* on March 13, 1861, in a specially revised version for the Paris Opera House, caused an uproar. The Parisian *Tannhäuser* had come at the request of Napoleon III. Performance at the Paris Opera required, according to the traditions of the house, a ballet, which Wagner had not written into the original Dresden premiere of 1845. The composer's insertion of the ballet in Act I, however, violated another custom, which was an obligatory ballet in Act II. In this way, the wealthy members of the Jockey Club, having dined previously, might arrive in time to see their mistresses, many of whom belonged to the Opera Ballet, dance. In what was an inversion of the trope of the crude Teuton and the refined Frenchman, the aristocratic clubmen interrupted the Parisian *Tannhäuser* with whistles and catcalls, some lasting for as long as fifteen minutes. Wagner withdrew his opera after only three performances. Although influence of the Jockey Club hardly spread to the general cultural elite, the German composer became unpopular in some quarters, as would the German-born Paris transplant Jacques Offenbach. A Jew who

had converted to Catholicism, Offenbach, whose favor with Napoleon III earned him French citizenship and the Legion of Honor,
was forced to flee to Spain during the Franco-Prussian War, and was
then reviled by the French public as a result of his adopted country's
defeat of 1870–71.

The Paris *Tannhäuser* was a dramatic failure, but Wagnerism
defined artistic, social, and even political affinities for at least two
decades in France. The poets whom Mallarmé most admired wor-
shipped Wagner. Charles Baudelaire, upon leaving a Wagner concert, announced that he had had "the most joyous musical experience
of his life." Auguste de Villiers de l'Isle-Adam proclaimed Wagner
"a genius such as appears on earth once every thousand years."
Catulle Mendès had originally informed Mallarmé of the new art
from Germany when he and Judith Gautier stopped in Avignon on
their way back from visiting Wagner in Lucerne, Switzerland. The
Mendès-Gautier couple would found the *Revue wagnérienne* in 1885,
and, when they officially divorced three years later, the legacy of
Wagner was one of the contested articles in their settlement.

In his early days in Paris, Mallarmé frequented the salon of the
pianist Nina Gaillard, whom he had met at the Carrefour des Demoiselles in 1862. Having hosted too many of the vehement supporters of the Commune before 1871, the flamboyant Nina left France
for Geneva, but returned when government reprisals died down. In
the presence of painters Édouard Manet, Paul Cézanne, and Jean-
Louis Forain and poets Charles Cros and Villiers de l'Isle-Adam,
Mallarmé listened to Augusta Holmès, Villiers, or Nina herself play
the revolutionary, modernistic-leaning music of Wagner. The poet
Maurice Rollinat, a member of the circle who called themselves the
Hydropaths, maintained that Nina's salon, "from dinner until late
into the night, was a coterie of young minds in revolt, whipped up
by alcohol into all possible mental debauchery . . . , in a state of
hyperexcitation presided over by a slightly demented muse."[2]

Mallarmé, far more modest in demeanor than Wagner but equally ambitious, sought to do for poetry no less than what the German composer had done for opera. In a holiday greetings letter sent at the end of 1877 to the English poet Arthur O'Shaughnessy, who was part of the Pre-Raphaelite circle, the French poet stated his ambition: "I am working like crazy; and I am studying everywhere the fragments of a new Theater which is being prepared in France and that I am working on too; something that will astonish the sovereign people as never a Roman emperor or an Asian prince has been able to do. This is the goal; it's difficult: it will take time."[3]

Time was the one thing that, in the first few years of life in the capital, Mallarmé lacked. The commuting in horse-drawn omnibuses or on foot between the Lycées Condorcet and Saint-Louis was so grueling that the poet was obliged to give up the second post. Thanks to the good offices of Charles Seignobos, father of his former student in Tournon and a deputy from the Ardèche, his situation at Condorcet was regularized to a full-time position and his salary raised sufficiently for the Mallarmés to survive. Even without the cross-town commute, however, teaching consumed an inordinate amount of time that otherwise might have been devoted to art. So, while waiting to write *The Book*, Mallarmé described and inscribed the things of this world as poetry. He wrote a few poems, notably, the first of his famous literary homages, or *"tombeaux"*: "Funerary Toast," upon the death of Judith Gautier's father, poet Théophile Gautier, and "The Tomb of Edgar Allan Poe," which appeared in a memorial volume to Poe published in the United States. And he began to live as if life itself could be crafted into a work of art according to the natural cycles of summer and winter, and even the days of the week.

For Mallarmé, the secret of living in a disenchanted, increasingly mechanized, and affectless world meant locating the rhythms in the everyday that resonated with the larger rhythms of nature—daily, weekly, and seasonal changes. Even the most mundane existence might participate in the wondrous ritual that once had belonged to the sphere of religion but, with the disappearance of religion, now belonged to art. Gustave Flaubert famously confided to his lover, Louise Collet, that "one must make two parts in one's life: live like a bourgeois and think like a demigod." Even though Mallarmé may have thought like a demigod and written like a genius, he lived joyfully as a bourgeois. In fact, he did not distinguish between the two. He, like James Joyce, who would follow, found poetry in the most prosaic experiences amid the familiar objects in his immediate surroundings, as it was to be found in the most abstract ideas, inaccessible to any material expression. He undertook to make the most fundamental natural cycles no less part of everyday life.

In the early summer of 1874, Mallarmé visited the area of Fontainebleau with the art critic Phillipe Burty, who, as an editor of the *Gazette des beaux-arts*, had promoted *japonisme* in France, and would play a role in the promotion of the Impressionists. Mallarmé and Burty called upon the prominent engraver Alfred Prunaire, whose nearby summer home was a gathering place for poets, painters, and musicians. Prunaire pointed out to the poet a house for rent in Valvins at a modest price. Mallarmé quickly arranged to occupy the ground floor and two rooms on the first floor, one of which would be his study, with a window looking out over the water. Behind the former boatman's cottage was a large garden filled with apple, pear, and cherry trees, a reminder that the local economy along this particular stretch of the river still depended upon the sale of fruit. From the outset in Valvins, the poet would be surrounded by Burty, Prunaire, and the composer and violinist Léopold Dauphin, whose comic opera, *The Chinese Wedding* (*Le Mariage de Chine*) had played at Paris's Opera Bouffe the previous year. The poet and the musician would enjoy boating excursions and long walks in the woods. For Mallarmé, renting near the Forest of Fontainebleau restored some of the magic of the glorious day in the summer of 1862 at the Carrefour des Demoiselles. Eventually, other artists would come to summer near Mallarmé in what was a country version of a Parisian salon along the banks of the Seine.

In the mind of the poet, the yearly cycle of the sun was captured in the movement between Paris in the winter and Valvins in the summer, which corresponded to an innate difference between writing styles. Summer was the season of poetry, a time for verse. "Winter," however, was for prose. "With the autumnal burst, verse stops, which makes way for theater [*le geste*] and a miraculous withdrawal." What Mallarmé meant by "withdrawal" (*recul*) was a leaving off of the truest and purest human activity, poetry, in favor of a more active life in the city. Insofar as autumn brought the poet back to Paris, the place of human invention and artifice, it was dramatic play, and occasioned visits to the playhouse. "Far from everything, Nature, in autumn, prepares her Theater, sublime and pure, waiting to illuminate, in solitude, moments of meaning and prestige, so that a lucid eye may penetrate their sense (and it's a notable one, the destiny of man)." In winter, in the city, "a Poet is recalled to mediocre pleasures and cares."[4]

A ritualized weekly rhythm accompanied the yearly rhythms and rites of summer and winter, country and city. Off and on between 1875 and his death, the poet spent Wednesday evenings at the home of Catulle Mendès, Thursday *chez* Émile Zola, Fridays with Léopold Dauphin, and Saturday afternoons at the salon of Charles Leconte de Lisle or José-Maria de Heredia. Sundays, however, were reserved for afternoon concerts at the Salle Lamoureux, which was one of the halls in which Wagner's music continued to be played in France. The ritual significance of Mallarmé's visits to the *Concerts Lamoureux* did not escape his daughter. "Each Sunday in winter he put aside—for this, by himself—an afternoon of work to go to the Lamoureux concert. 'I'm off to vespers,' he said to us in leaving the house."[5] Poet

Henri de Régnier reported seeing Mallarmé seated in the concert hall, taking notes. He found there, de Régnier confided, "a secret analogous to nature."[6] De Régnier was married to de Heredia's daughter and lived one of the famously public *ménage à trois* of Belle Époque France. Both he and his close friend the novelist Pierre Louÿs loved Marie de Heredia and had made a pact that neither would ask for her hand without asking the other first. When Louÿs was away visiting his brother, a diplomat in Egypt, de Régnier broke their agreement. As he was the wealthier of the two suitors and de Heredia *père* had run up gambling debts, it was agreed that Marie would be his. She, however, was furious, and apparently kept Louÿs on as a lover, naming her son Pierre de Régnier after Pierre Louÿs, the presumed father. Louÿs eventually married Marie de Heredia's younger sister, Louise, a marriage that ended in divorce.

The poet Paul Valéry described his mentor delighting in the music of Beethoven or Wagner: "Mallarmé left the concerts full of a sublime jealousy. He sought desperately ways of taking back for our art what too powerful Music had stolen from it by way of marvels and significance."[7] The religious terms in which others perceived the poet's going to, attending, and leaving the Sunday rites of the Lamoureux orchestra, this "Sunday cleansing of banality," were confirmed by Mallarmé's own description in a work called *Offices*, under the subheading "Sacred Pleasure," of the concert as a holy ceremony, the equivalent of a church service. For the poet, "music was the last and full human cult."[8]

Mallarmé, now installed in Paris and increasingly at the center of a vibrant artistic circle, dreamed of hosting his own salon. He did not have the means to entertain in the grand style of many literary and political salons of the Third Republic. In and around cultural discussion, the host might be expected to offer elaborate dinners, musical performances, occasional balls, and excursions to the theater or opera. In contrast, the Mallarmés' desperate need for money upon arrival in the capital led to a plan to conduct a salon for profit. The poet had supplemented the family income in Avignon by giving private English lessons. The idea of reviving the old institution of the salon, where the bourgeois art of conversation had replaced the wit that belonged to the courts of France's ancien régime, seemed in Paris like a way of making ends meet. The poet printed and circulated a prospectus advertising lessons in culture and charm:

> Monsieur Mallarmé, Professeur de l'Université, receives, 29 rue de Moscou, at two-thirty, Tuesdays and Saturdays, young people whose parents desire them to acquire familiarity with ancient and contemporary literature. . . . The price of the course is *twenty* francs payable at the beginning of the month. . . . Literary taste, once so developed in women, was the source of the charm and renown of our old salons. One cannot hide the fact that such taste is being lost by the lack of necessary culture. . . . This course features one particularity: that it encourages the participation of young people and prepares them for the first secret of conversation, destined to recapture its old luster.[9]

There is no evidence that Mallarmé's "literary afternoons" for young people ever attracted the fifteen students he had calculated were necessary to supplement his income in the first few difficult years in Paris.

Beginning with the Mallarmés' move from the rue de Moscou to the rue de Rome, Tuesdays meant weekly gatherings after dinner for the purpose of listening to the poet hold court on a wide range of topics—from poetry, painting, and music to politics, religion, and fashion—with a freshness, in the phrase of André Gide, that made it appear that "he had just in that instant invented each new proposition."[10] The poet may have written poems that were difficult to understand, but he was famous as a master without equal of the art of conversation. For a quarter of a century, almost everyone who was anyone in the world of the arts in France visited of a Tuesday in winter the "little house of Socrates" on the rue de Rome.

The poet issued written invitations to those whom he knew, sometimes sent with the *coquetterie* of one of his poetic envelopes with the address in the form of a quatrain. Other times, he would invite an artist to visit him at another hour and day of the week and, at the end of the conversation, suggested that the visitor return on Tuesday after dinner. Climbing the four flights of stairs, the *Mardists* would knock. The master opened the door to his modest sitting room, filled nonetheless with exquisite paintings on the walls, ceramic pitchers and pewter plates on a long rustic sideboard, and thickly upholstered chairs. Mallarmé would sit in a rocker when he was not standing next to the fireplace, with its open brass louvers under the mantel piece topped by a pair of candlesticks and a small pot of dried flowers. In the center of the room stood a table covered with books, a red lacquer inkwell, a Chinese porcelain bowl, tobacco, and a lamp that cast a low light over the hushed intimacy of the inner sanctum of Paris's most rarefied literary salon.

The *Mardists* included such well-known poets and novelists as William Butler Yeats, Paul Verlaine, Auguste de Villiers de l'Isle-Adam, André Gide, Paul Claudel, and Paul Valéry; composers such as Claude Debussy; and painters such as Édouard Manet, Claude Monet, Edgar Dégas, Paul Gauguin, James McNeill Whistler, and Auguste Renoir. Georges Clemenceau, the physician, journalist, statesman, and future prime minister, attended several Tuesdays on the rue de Rome.

A number of lesser literary lights left accounts of their Tuesday time with Mallarmé, as if they were in competition with one another to exhibit their closeness to the master. Camille Mauclair, an avid proponent of Wagner, wrote a roman à clef about Mallarmé's circle,

Mallarmé at home on the rue de Rome.
Bibliothèque littéraire Jacques Doucet, Paris, ms MNR 1848.

The Sun of the Dead (*Le Soleil des morts*). Playwright and poet Édouard Dujardin, editor of the *Revue indépendante* and one of the cofounders of the *Revue wagnérienne*, left a memoir entitled *Mallarmé by One of His Own* (*Mallarmé par un des siens*). Bernard Lazare, the poet, journalist, and anarchist, who was one of the first defenders of Dreyfus, compiled an account of literary figures in fin-de-siècle France, *Les Contemporains*, in which he compared the Tuesday evenings with his mentor to the philosophical schools of classical tradition. The Belgian Symbolist Albert Mockel, author of *Stéphane Mallarmé: A Hero*, honed in on Lazare's thought when he observed that classical philosophers were given to expressing general ideas and that, in Mallarmé's salon, the feelings of a solitary dreamer were raised to the level of universal truth. The essayist and novelist Henry Roujon worked in the Ministry of Education. There, he was able to support

Mallarmé's career in lycées despite the poet's flagging devotion to teaching as he became increasingly well-known in the world of literary lights. In his assessment of late-century literary life, *Gallery of Busts* (*La Galerie des bustes*), Roujon, who later became a member of the Académie Française, devoted a chapter to Mallarmé, whom he described as "full of enchantments, while pretending to live out his mortal destiny as an English teacher."[11] Henri de Régnier left two accounts of gatherings *chez* Mallarmé, *Our Meetings* (*Nos Rencontres*) and *Figures and Characters* (*Figures et caractères*), in addition to a long journal of literary life, which reproduced in detail the words of the master on specific Tuesdays.

Of the *Mardists* who could not wait to get home from the rue de Rome in order to write down what had happened there, the most loyal was Edmond Bonniot, who, as a law student with poetic aspirations, entered the inner circle in 1892. He left a log of the *séances* he had attended, an assessment of the state of mind of the host, an inventory of topics discussed, along with various anecdotes and aphorisms for which Mallarmé became famous. On the night of January 17, 1893, for instance, Bonniot reported that the poet had the impression that the mothers who waited for their sons outside of the lycée at the end of the school day were angry at him for not teaching the boys enough of what they needed to know about the English language. One day one of his students came up to him, tapped his elbow with a knowing air, and began, "M'sieu, my mother knows what you are up to. Really! You know what I mean, at night." "How's that?" Mallarmé asked. "That's right, M'sieu, I would like to come sometime to hear you sing at the concert of the decadents."[12] Tuesdays *chez* Mallarmé had apparently entered the popular imagination in the form of nightclub entertainment.

Oscar Wilde appeared once or twice on the rue de Rome and, having spoken at length, incurred the disapproval of all by exercising his wit in the presence of the master. Édouard Dujardin condemned "the abominable Oscar Wilde, who should have known by our mute reprobation that one does not come *chez* Mallarmé to discourse about oneself."[13] James McNeill Whistler, who was convinced that Wilde had mocked him in *The Picture of Dorian Gray*, went so far as to ask Mallarmé to insert a copy of an article denouncing Wilde in the *American Register*, a newspaper owned by Dr. Thomas Evans, whom the poet knew through his confidante Méry Laurent. The poet responded on January 5, 1890, urging Whistler to send along his "fabulous article. You're becoming a regular James Mac Neill [sic] Buffalo Bill Whistler."[14] The painter wrote to Mallarmé to excuse himself from the gathering of Tuesday, November 3, 1891, since his enemy would be present. "I realize it is a little ungrateful of me not to stay to denounce Oscar Wilde in front of your disciples tomorrow night." On the day itself, Whistler sent a telegram: PREFACE PROPOSITIONS WARN DISCIPLES PRECAUTION FATAL FAMILIARITY HOLD TIGHT TO YOUR PEARLS BONNE SOIREE—WHISTLER.[15] Mallarmé wrote to assure Whistler that the evening had been "as dull as could be."

Mallarmé intervened on both sides as an unofficial negotiator in the French state purchase of Whistler's masterwork, known at the time as *Arrangement in Grey and Black*, and now as *Whistler's Mother*. On November 11, 1891, he informed the American painter that Minister of Fine Arts Antonin Proust "seeks, in a spirit of pure admiration for your work and sympathy for you, to buy and present to the State, to put in the Luxembourg Museum, the masterpiece that is that portrait of your mother: this as a French demonstration of the honor in which it holds Whistler."[16] Whistler responded two days later, *"Bravo! O! Ministre Mallarmé!"* and suggested a price of 25,000 francs. Mallarmé eased the blow of the state's offer of only 4,000 francs, which he had learned of in a telegram from the minister. He informed Whistler that the painter would receive the Legion of Honor the following year, thanks to the intervention of

Georges Clemenceau. "Yes, you have released the fairies," Whistler responded, "Clemenceau's influence kept things moving along."[17]

Relations between the Tuesday men were not always easy or gracious. Rivalries for the attention of the master was keen, and, in several instances, led the more intensely vain *Mardists* to risk their lives. Catulle Mendès was enraged over an article published by fellow *Mardist* Francis Vielé-Griffin in which the American Symbolist poet insinuated that Mendès had somehow intervened with the editors of *Le Figaro* to remove the name Vielé-Griffin from among a list of poets mentioned by Mallarmé in a newspaper interview published in 1891. Catulle Mendès sent Mallarmé a telegram asking him to intervene: IMPOSSIBLE TO TOLERATE PHRASE OF VIELE-GRIFFIN ABOUT ME, ENTRETIENS LITTERAIRES—PLEASE DECLARE TELEGRAPHICALLY AND PUBLICLY THAT YOU KNOW ME TO BE ABSOLUTELY INCAPABLE OF SUCH A MANEUVER.[18] Mallarmé wrote Mendès a personal note, confirming that he was, indeed, "incapable of such a maneuver." Unsatisfied, Mendès demanded that the offender publish a retraction affirming that "M. Mendès is an honest man." And, when Vielé-Griffin published in response, "I do not know M. Mendès. I cannot therefore say if he is or is not an honest man," Mendès challenged him to a duel.

Mallarmé tried to stop the quarrel among his *Mardist* "children," but the two combatants met to settle their difference with swords. Mendès engaged the playwright Georges Courteline and Félix Rosati as his seconds. Vielé-Griffin fought with the historical novelist Paul Adam and Félix Fénéon at his side. All assembled on the morning of Sunday, September 20, 1891, on the Île de la Grande-Jatte. (A few years previous to the quarreling Symbolists's armed confrontation, Georges Seurat had captured a much quieter *Sunday Afternoon on the Island of La Grande Jatte*, his painting filled with leisurely picnickers, strollers and bathers.) On the field, his shirt open to show his chest, sword in hand for the *"mise en garde,"* Mendès was smoking a cigar. "Permit me," Vielé-Griffin said, and he strolled to the nearest tree where his jacket was hanging, and pulled out a pipe, which he stuffed and tranquilly lit. As the duelists fought and smoked, Mendès, the more experienced swordsman, wounded his opponent in the stomach.[19]

Mallarmé was saddened by the quarrel between his followers. In a letter written on September 29 to Henri de Régnier, who was caring for the injured Vielé-Griffin, the poet noted that "this story cast a pall over my last days of vacation. I thought that as far as Mendès was concerned, the thing would end with my response to his demand for a public statement."[20] Six years later, Régnier himself would meet *Mardist* Robert de Montesquiou to settle differences between them with swords. In a report on duels, *L'Annuaire du duel*, Édouard Dujardin had recorded two thousand such incidents between 1880 and 1889. "Unable to eat us," the realist Émile Zola commented disdainfully on the quarrels among the Symbolists, "this band of sharks fed on one another."[21]

Though the majority of Parisian literary salons were hosted by women who, like Mme. Verdurin in Proust's *Swann in Love* or the real-life Nina Gaillard, were the center of attention, women were remarkably absent from Tuesdays *chez* Mallarmé. Mme Mallarmé and Geneviève sat sewing in a room adjoining the salon. They appeared at an appointed hour with grog, then retired for the night. The sculptor Camille Claudel, sister of Paul and the mistress of Auguste Rodin, and the composer Augusta Holmès were exceptions. Each had attended at least one of the weekly meetings. Berthe Morisot apparently once teased the poet by offering to dress as a man and to show up at his door one Tuesday night. On the eve of his departure for a lecture tour at Oxford and Cambridge in February 1894, Mallarmé invited Morisot to come with her daughter, Julie, "like students to sit on the bench of my friends." "We'll smoke as little as possible," he promised. Morisot refused, claiming the bench of friends "too intimidating."[22]

It would have been difficult to refrain from smoking. The poet, whose idea of unhappiness was "doing without cigars," kept a bowl of tobacco on the table in the center of his sitting room. The room bathed in low light, the incense of cigar, cigarette, and pipe smoke, and the ritual grog served at ten o'clock were all integral parts of Mallarmé's "intimate gala," which the *Mardists* experienced as a religious rite, a mass for their time. Bernard Lazare remembered Tuesday evenings "in the discreetly lit salon whose corners of shadow gave off the atmosphere of a temple, or an oratory."[23] Geneviève remarked that young poets behaved as if in the confessional: "Few among them simply recited their verses—they confided them, as at confession, to father."[24] Édouard Dujardin sensed that he had somehow spoken too freely or out of turn on the evening of Tuesday, January 11, 1887. He excused himself in a letter of January 17, acknowledging the "unique magnificence" of his host's thought, which troubled him emotionally. Dujardin recognized what went on in the Mallarmé apartment as a "serious and gigantic religion." "It was thus," Dujardin confessed, "that I saw something like 'we will raise a tower to the heavens,' something like 'we will be like gods,' something like 'I will destroy the temple . . . , and stone will not remain on stone.'" The abject acolyte, quoting the Gospel of Matthew 16:18, compared Mallarmé with Saint Peter. "What quartet of evangelists will recount this Jesus?" Dujardin asked.[25]

Albert Mockel spoke of the "religious joy of the spirit" in the atmosphere of Mallarmés' apartment. André Fontainas, who was a student in Mallarmé's English class and later joined the inner circle, claimed to have left the rue de Rome on the night of December 21, 1897, "comforted, illuminated."[26] Paul Adam noted that Mallarmé "was more than a hero, he was a saint."[27] Catulle Mendès observed

Mallarmé as "the prophet of a messiah without advent."[28] For Camille Mauclair, poetry "was a religion to which we brought the seriousness and the fervor of catechumens."[29]

The effects of Mallarmé's papal-like authority were not always appreciated. The "instrumentalist" poet René Ghil, who practiced a metaphysical materialism combining the scientific writings of Charles Darwin with Buddhism, claimed that a "smiling Mallarmé of the Tuesdays on the rue de Rome liked to remind the gathering that, up until the age of twelve, he had no other ambition than to become a Bishop."[30] Mallarmé wrote the introduction to Ghil's essay on Symbolism, *Traité du verbe* (1886), but Ghil broke with the older poet two years later, when, "one Tuesday in April, discoursing on the Idea as the only representative of the truth of the World, he turned to me, and, with some sadness perhaps, but a clear intention, said: 'No, Ghil, one cannot do without Eden!' I responded softly, but just as clearly: 'I think one can, dear Master.'"[31] Ghil, who never returned, sensed the incident as something on the order of an excommunication from the ecclesiastical atmosphere of Tuesdays *chez* Mallarmé. Such an exercise of worldly power was, Ghil maintained, "the true instinctive expression of Mallarmé's soul."

Sitting in audience in his salon on the rue de Rome, as a high Church official would in Rome, Mallarmé presided "as the supremely bishoplike representative of an occult art, his look fixed in contemplation on the large and magic violet stone set in the sacred ring."[32] The banished poet's remarks were bitter. They associate Mallarmé's overwhelming authority to pronounce and to exclude in the realm of pure art with the corruption of the Church's meddling in worldly affairs. Ghil's critique did not stand alone, however. Max Nordau, the Hungarian physician turned social critic, attacked the Symbolist poets for the difficulty of their verse. He associated Mallarmé's "flood of incoherent words" with a propensity for mystical, medieval, neo-Catholic thought—the result of contact with the English Pre-Raphaelites.[33]

Mallarmé was not a practicing Catholic in the traditional mode of Paul Claudel or Paul Valéry, or in the extreme mode of the novelist Léon Bloy, who was convinced that the Virgin had actually appeared to two children at La Salette, near Grenoble, in 1846, and that the end-time was near. And Mallarmé did not adopt the perverse Catholicism of, say, Joris-Karl Huysmans, who equated decadence with holiness and finished his life in a monastery, or of Jules Barbey d'Aurevilly, who considered the French Revolution a work of the Devil against God. Nor did he practice the satanic Catholicism of Charles Baudelaire, who wrote blasphemous inversions of the mass. In fact, Mallarmé explicity addressed only once the question of the Catholic mass, in an essay entitled "Catholicism": "Our communion or sharing of one with all and of all with one, thus, abstracted from the barbaric feast designated by the sacrament—in the consecration of the Host, nevertheless, affirms itself the prototype of ceremonials—despite its uniqueness—within an artistic tradition: the Mass."[34]

Mallarmé did not seek to bring back the power of the Eucharist to radically secular Third Republic France. Rather, he looked to the religiously gripping effects of Tuesdays on the rue de Rome to reverse the decline of religion and the rise of capitalism and rational science, which, since the end of the Middle Ages, had reduced the mystery and the meaning of everyday life, or of just being alive. Without recourse to Baudelaire's "artifical paradises," and escape into opium and hashish, or Rimbaud's "unleashing of all the senses," a self-induced synesthetic excess, or Verlaine's addiction to alcohol and absinthe, Mallarmé found yearly and weekly rituals a way of reviving the intensity of belonging and purpose that religion once provided. He brought to all he did or said some of the meaningful mystery and communal force of the mass. Through poetry, but also through living wisely, he sought to enchant the universe that so many of his contemporaries found joyless and devoid of sense.

Mallarmé's annual migration between Paris and Valvins and his weekly gatherings on the rue de Rome were punctuated by daily meetings with Édouard Manet, whom he had first met at the salon of Nina Gaillard. Weekdays, on his way home from school, he would make a slight detour to Manet's studio on the rue de Saint-Pétersbourg. There he encountered other painters, such as Edgar Dégas, Auguste Renoir, Claude Monet, and Berthe Morisot, who was married to Édouard's brother Eugène. There, too, the poet first ran into the woman who would become his lifelong confidante and his muse, Méry Laurent.

Daughter of a laundress from Nancy, married at the age of fifteen, and divorced within months, Méry Laurent had moved to Paris to try her fortunes as an actress. According to Antonin Proust, she visited Manet's studio, which had been rearranged as an exhibition gallery after the jury of the official Salon of 1876 had refused to include his paintings *The Artist* and *The Laundry* in that year's offerings. The forty-four-year-old Manet, standing in an adjoining room, overheard Méry, in front of *The Laundry*, exclaim, "That's very good, this one!" In and of itself, the exclamation was not remarkable, but Manet, taking it as portentous revenge against the Salon jury from the mouth of a seductive woman, befriended Méry Laurent, who modeled for at least four portraits and may, for a time, also have been the painter's mistress.

More famously, Méry Laurent was, over a period of decades, the mistress of Napoleon III's American dentist, Thomas Evans, whom she first met in the course of having a tooth fixed. The dashing Dr. Evans was one of the pioneers in the use of the amalgamated fillings and of nitrous oxide in his lucrative dental practice on the rue de l'Opéra. In the years following his arrival in Paris in 1847, Evans, who was fluent in French, worked on the teeth of many European heads of state, and it is thought that the intimacy of the dental office, where he found himself alone with patients whose open mouths elsewhere might change the map of Europe, made Evans an unofficial ambassador between France and its neighbors.

In the summer of 1864, the emperor sent Evans as his emissary to Abraham Lincoln to assess the chances of the Union's winning the Civil War. He returned from Washington and from General Ulysses S. Grant's headquarters near Richmond with firsthand knowledge of surgical field hospitals, one of which he reconstructed at the Universal Exposition in Paris in 1867. There, both German and French military planners observed the new technology. It was put to good use in the Franco-Prussian War, in which Evans, after the French defeat at Sedan, played a minor but crucial role. On the night of September 5, 1870, with Napoleon III the prisoner of Wilhelm I, the accommodating dentist smuggled Empress Eugénie out of Paris in his carriage amid angry crowds declaring the end of the Second Empire and the beginning of the Third Republic. They eventually reached Deauville, where "the Doctor" chatted up an English "yachtsman," who carried Eugénie to England, where she was eventually reunited with Napoleon III in exile at Chislehurst. In addition to his editorship of the *American Register*, Evans published books in French and in English based on his experiences abroad: *History and Description of an Ambulance Wagon, Constructed in Accordance with Plans Furnished by the Author* (1865), *History of the American Ambulance Established During the Siege of 1870–1871* (1873), and, posthumously, a fascinating memoir of Napoleon III and Eugénie.

While living in Paris, Thomas Evans became enormously wealthy. His fortune came neither from his dental practice nor from sale of "Dr. Evans's celebrated dental preparation, in powder, paste, or elixir form," but from advanced knowledge—the emperor's open mouth?—of Baron Haussmann's plans for the urban renewal of Paris, and smart investment in real estate. At the time of his death in 1897, Evans was worth 25 million francs (by contrast, Mallarmé's retirement pension brought in only 5,000 francs per annum). A native of Philadelphia, the wealthy dentist left his fortune to found the Thomas Evans Museum and Dental Institute, which eventually became the Dental School of the University of Pennsylvania. He also made a special provision that 1 million francs be set aside to erect a monument in his honor. Julie Manet recorded in her journal that Auguste Renoir, upon hearing of Evan's bequest, asked, "Of what could such a monument consist? Dentists' offices covered with rhinoceros teeth?"[35]

While he was alive, Thomas Evans was extremely generous to his patient turned mistress, and she was openly generous to Mallarmé. On at least two occasions, the three vacationed together at the spa of Royat. This must have been a merry threesome. There is evidence that Evans was not particularly faithful to Méry Laurent, and she claimed that she preferred to deceive him rather than to leave him. Laurent entertained Mallarmé and friends in her Paris residence, Villa des Talus, on the boulevard Lannes. The poet and his muse dined companionably in restaurants, attended concerts together, and exchanged gifts on annual and special occasions. When Mallarmé was not in Paris, they wrote to each other almost every day. In the famous picture of Mallarmé taken by Nadar in 1896, he was wearing a Scottish cashmere shawl that Méry Laurent sent him.

Leo Tolstoy, who claimed not to be able to understand Mallarmé's verse, maintained in *War and Peace* that Napoleon I lost the Russian campaign of 1812 because his butler brought him the wrong pair of boots, and the emperor caught cold before the Battle of

Mallarmé and the painter Henri Gervex *chez* Méry Laurent.
Bibliothèque littéraire Jacques Doucet, Paris, ms ING 32.

Borodino. A similar law of unintended consequences might be applied to Mallarmé, who, despite his exquisite taste for luxury goods and his appetite for fine foods, participated in whatever few of the expensive pleasures of the Belle Époque he did because Napoleon III had bad teeth.

Relations between Méry Laurent and Mallarmé were those of an intimate friendship that may at one time have been amorous, though the novelist Joris-Karl Huysmans claimed that Laurent once confided to him over dinner, "and between two cigarettes," that Mallarmé had made advances, but that she had never slept with him for reasons of personal hygiene. "She spoke of his moth-eaten flannel shirts and collars. He slept once in a room at her house, the sheets were black. The housekeeper raised her arms in despair."[36] Nonetheless, the wealthy courtesan and the impecunious poet grew closer after tragedy struck the Mallarmés in the fall of 1879. Méry Laurent would then offer the kind of joyous affirmation of life and intellectual sustenance that inherently stern Marie, who rarely left home after that diffucult time, was unable to provide.

Having left for London and the International Exposition of 1871 shortly after Anatole was born, Stéphane had not been fully aware of how sickly his son was as an infant. By the time he was two months old, Anatole's respiratory difficulties had reached a crisis, and Marie wrote, "My Stéphane, we are awaiting his last moment at any time."[37] But the infant did not die. He recovered as mysteriously as he had hovered near death, and was to his parents all the more precious for having nearly disappeared.

In the spring of 1879, however, just as the Mallarmés were preparing to travel to Valvins, Anatole seemed pale, listless, and to suffer rheumatic pain in his joints. Marie decided to stay in Paris with him, while Stéphane and Geneviève boarded the train for Fontainebleau. The specter of rheumatic fever, which had been fatal in the case of his sister, and probably his mother as well, must have filled the poet with apprehension. Marie assured him that Tole, as the boy had come to be known, was cheerful but did not seem to be getting any better. The poet returned to the rue de Rome to supervise the medical visits and to seek freelance editorial work to pay the doctors' bills. A diagnosis of rheumatoid inflammation of the joints would require a period of long recovery. Little by little, Anatole's condition grew worse. Swelling of the face and stomach was accompanied by nausea, rapid heartbeat, and a persistent dry cough, attributed, finally, to a pericardial infection. Mallarmé began to correspond with his old friend Henri Cazalis, who had become an eminent physician near Grenoble. Cazalis arranged for a consultation with one of France's foremost cardiologists, a member of the Academy of Medicine, who confirmed the diagnosis of endocardia.

Against the advice of the doctors, the Mallarmés decided that the fresh air of the country would do Anatole good, so they left together for the country, where the local doctor was no more encouraging than the Parisian specialist. The only bright spot was the arrival at Valvins of an exotic bird in a Japanese cage, the gift of poet and sometimes *Mardist* Robert de Montesquiou. One of the great dandyish eccentrics of the Belle Époque, Montesquiou had become attached to Anatole and had visited the rue de Rome to play with the sick child in Stéphane's absence.

The Mallarmés took the suffering child for rides in the little donkey cart along the banks of the Seine and tried to amuse him as best they could. Meanwhile, the cough and joint pain and swelling in the stomach persisted. At the end of September, the family returned to Paris, where a lancing of Anatole's swollen stomach attested to the seriousness of his condition. Mallarmé found himself in a state of desperation. "Yes, I am quite outside of myself, like someone swept by a terrible and long wind," he wrote. "No work for a long time now! I had no idea this terrible arrow had been launched at me from some indiscernible shadowy corner."[38]

Surrounded by his mother and sister, eight-year-old Anatole died two days later. The poet had left the house briefly to mail a letter. "Just as I was taking a word to you to the post office," he wrote Montesquiou, "our dear child left us softly, without knowing it. . . . The poor little adored child loved you well."[39] Together with a few close friends such as Catulle Mendès and Léopold Dauphin, the Mallarmés made the sad journey to the cemetery of Samoreau adjoining Valvins, where Anatole was laid to rest, along with many of the poet's aspirations. "This charming and exquisite child has captivated me to the point where I associate him with my projects for the future and all my dreams," he wrote to the English poet John Payne.[40]

The poet's grief was such that he probably took little note of the France all around him, events like the resignation of president of the Third Republic, Patrice de MacMahon, the military officer who had finally vanquished the Commune in 1871, and a general amnesty declared for the Communards in 1880. MacMahon was replaced by Jules Grévy, who would himself be forced to resign in 1887 as a result of the scandal surrounding his son-in-law's illegal sales, often negotiated in houses of prostitution, of national decorations like the Legion of Honor. The poet would probably have been indifferent to the adoption of "La Marseillaise" as the national anthem, the declaration of July 14 as the national holiday of France, or the appearance on July 14, 1880, of the motto "Liberté, Égalité, Fraternité" on the pediments of all French national buildings.

For a long time after Anatole's death, Mallarmé wrote little verse. He offered for publication several poems written earlier, including "This Virginal Long-Living Lovely Day" ("Le Vièrge, le vivace et le bel aujourd'hui") and "What Silk with Balm from Advancing Days" ("Quelle Soie aux baumes de temps"), and he managed to finish two works of nonfiction that he had begun before his son took sick. The poet had hoped that they would be commercial successes. The first, *The Ancient Gods* (*Les Dieux antiques*) was a translation and adaptation of the English anthropologist William Cox's *Manual of Mythology*, which was itself based upon the linguistic writings of the philologist and orientalist Max Müller. A second significant writing project put forth a curious study of the English language, *English Words* (*Les Mots anglais*), which was related to the anthropological material. Both contributed conceptually to "One Toss of the Dice" in ways that will be clearer when we begin actually to analyze Mallarmé's masterwork.

In the wake of Anatole's death, Mallarmé pursued a mysterious project that, in consonance with *The Ancient Gods* and *English Words*, foreshadowed "One Toss of the Dice." Tuesdays on the rue de Rome resumed in 1881 after a pause of almost two years, and rumor circulated among the *Mardists* that the master would, finally, strike the spark of *The Book*. In a volume on contemporary poets he published in 1884, Paul Verlaine alluded to Mallarmé's "gigantic effort" in the making of a book. The following year, Verlaine requested biographical information for a volume he was editing on *The Men of Today* (*Les Hommes d'aujourd'hui*). Mallarmé made it clear that the poems and prose he had published thus far did not live up to the promise of the "magnificent book." "I have always dreamed and attempted something else, with the patience of an alchemist, ready to sacrifice all vanity and all earthly satisfactions, as once upon a time, one burned the furniture and the rafters of the roof, to feed the furnace of the *Grand Oeuvre*."[41]

The poet imagined that his work would surpass the traditional limits of verse. It would use words to exceed words—that is, to make the jump to things themselves, to change the world, in the catalytic way that has for so long been imagined in the West: in the formulas of alchemy, the Kabbalah, hieroglyphs, the philosophy of Hermes Trismegistus or Nostradamus, the secret rites of Freemasonry, the mysterious cartography of Poe's "The Goldbug," the esoteric wisdom of Helena Blavatsky, or, in our own time, the physically and metaphysically altered world of Jorge Luis Borges's *Tlön, Uqbar, Orbis Tertius*.

So, like an alchemist working in the secret of his laboratory, Mallarmé began to write under cover a series of notes—sketches, really—in soft pencil, on loose pages, full of smudges, crossed-out words, and scattered lines; these came as close as anything thus far to *The Book* as it was conceived after the crisis of his midtwenties.

Throughout, the notes, some of which are presented here, attest to the incredible pain that Anatole's death had caused his parents:

> child sprung from
> the two of us—showing
> us our ideal, the way
> —ours! father
> and mother who
>   sadly existing
> survive him as the two extremes—
> badly coupled in him
> and sundered
> —from whence his death—o-
> bliterating this little child "self"[42]

Anatole's death had upset the natural succession of the generations, which frames and surpasses the ritual cycles of the year or of the week.

> child our
> immortality
> in fact made
> of buried human
> hopes—son—
> entrusted to the woman
> by the man de-
> spairing after youth
> to find the mystery
> and taking a wife
>   ___[43]

———

Mallarmé's early awareness of the life cycle, no doubt inspired by the death of his sister when he was fifteen, can be seen in a poem written two years after Maria's death, "Everything Passes!": "Man flows, pushed along by the man who follows / like the wave!"[44] It would come back in "One Toss of the Dice" as the boat captain's "legacy amidst disappearance."

Should he not complete *The Book* as he had imagined it, the poet had counted on his son to pursue it after his death. Now that Anatole was no longer there to carry on, the natural cycle has been interrupted. It has been reversed: The son will live on through the father:

> no—nothing
> to do with the great
> deaths—etc.
> —as long as we
> go on living, he
> lives—in us
>
> —
>
> it will only be after our
> death that he will be dead
> —and the bells
> of the Dead will toll for
>
> him[45]

Anatole's life would be extended nearly a century later by the appearance of a monumental literary work, which took the shape of notes. *Pour un tombeau d'Anatole*, published by the Éditions du Seuil in 1961, reveals many of the defining characteristics of Mallarmé's masterwork. The loose pages, translated into English in 1983 by Paul Auster as *A Tomb for Anatole*, were filled with syntactical inversions, as if the reversal of ordinary word order might somehow undo the

A Tomb for Anatole, folio 46.
Bibliothèque littéraire Jacques Doucet, Paris, ms 46022.

unnatural sequence of a father surviving his son. The notes lacked orientating markers of punctuation and line breaks, some words were separated in places other than at the end of a syllable, and some verses were separated by a series of hyphens or other diacritic indicators, such as + signs and "x's," horizontal ampersands, vertical brackets covering several lines, underlinings, and ellipsis marks. The notes for *A Tomb for Anatole* contained great compacted jumps that make for difficult understanding, even when the words are arranged in familiar patterns. Most of all, the notes displayed the early signs of a break with the uniform visual appearance of traditional poetry. They were laid out graphically with unjustified lines, empty spaces between lines and between words in a single verse, and rhythmic starts and stops that would be fully developed only in "One Toss of the Dice."

Five

"THERE HAS BEEN AN ATTACK ON VERSE!"

In the long dormant period of the early 1880s following Anatole's death, Mallarmé was discouraged by a lack of progress in creating a total and transformative work of art rooted in poetry and not in music. At times, he seemed aware of the immensity of the undertaking and uncertain that he would ever write this work in its entirety. "I don't know who could!" he wrote to Paul Verlaine. "I can nonetheless prove by the portions already done that the book exists, and that I was aware of what I could not accomplish."[1] Because of the mystery surrounding the project, it is hard to tell exactly how it happened, or when, but the contents and the physical appearance of the notes for Anatole did morph, over a period of years, into notes for *The Book*.

Like *A Tomb for Anatole*, the folios for *The Book* took the shape of disjointed writing, jottings, lines, dots, arrows, isolated arithmetic calculations (addition, multiplication, and division), and, again, great blank spaces like those of "One Toss of the Dice." They were interspersed with computations of all kinds—of page numbers, of print layout, of the print runs of editions, of potential book sales, of the cost and potential earnings of this great poem of Humanity that "would explain all earthly existence."

Always tempted by stage performance, rivalrous with the overweening figure of Wagner, Mallarmé imagined *The Book* along dramatic lines as a "new theater," a "future spectacle." It was the poet's deepest desire that literature would provide a theater, one whose performances would be the true modern religion, providing an "explanation of man, sufficient to our most beautiful dreams."[2] The specificity of his planning could have been a page taken from a Wagner score. He pictured, on the model of theatrical Tuesdays *chez* Mallarmé, how the performances of the *Grand Oeuvre* would take place, the quantity and pacing of sessions during which *The Book* would be read aloud, the number of attendees, their seating arrangement. The poet envisioned a series of readings or presentations. Each sitting would involve twenty-four participants, divided into three groups of eight, each participant reading a prescribed number of folios. Mallarmé's own role in the performance was ambiguous. He sometimes referred to himself as a "simple reader," the "first reader," "me, the twenty-fifth," or the "operator."

The poet laid out a plan for the publication of two editions of *The Book*, one for an elite public, presumably the twenty-four readers plus the "operator," the other for a general readership. Given that the whole would contain twenty volumes, he planned to print 24,000 copies, for a total sale of some 480,000 books, an enormous printing by the standards of late-nineteenth-century France. In the kabbalistic calculation of the relationship between print runs and money, the final folio of Mallarmé's notes for *The Book* was key:

The Book, folio 258.
Harvard University, Houghton Library, ms Fr 270.

4000, printing × 4 = 16000 copies × 3 at 1 f = 48000 ex.

3 f. per vol. = 12000 × 4 = 48000 f

× 5[years] 240 000 f

96 attendees × 5 = 480 (+ 20. my 20 v.)

manuscript

the 480 cop.

not printed replaced by 500 f. rehearsal)

to make can appear 48 000 cop. 240 000 cop.[3]

In order to increase the revenue of the alchemical project, which was
to turn printed words into gold, Mallarmé proposed using the blank
spaces of *The Book* for "the insertion of newspaper advertisements."[4]

Here is where the poet's fantastical printing adventure revealed, alongside "One Toss of the Dice," the influence of the poster art of the Belle Époque, with its varied type sizes, forms, and irregular spatial layout. Folios 166, 167bis, and 168 (217–219), for example, were presented as if they were a cross between a commercial billboard and daily tabloid sheet:

```
                              ----- ----- --- poster

                        advertisement        gibberish

                        pays for printing     folio

              and paper

      hunting      yacht        burial     baptism

            war                                marriage---

            ---                                war

                                               gu

      ball --- meal               bomb

                                               theft

      ball         meal         dessert    fire works.⁵
```

Mallarmé computed the revenue from advertising in the overall calculation of the cost of the "orphic explanation of the earth" on folio 182 (234): "Advertising pays for printing and paper (lottery)—and the price was to be shared between the seller and the author."[6] It seemed that as long as the *Grand Oeuvre* was pure and isolated from the world, there would be no author; but, as soon as money was involved, the author reappeared to share in the profit.

Beginning in the summer of 1889, six years after Wagner's death in Venice, a number of events conspired to affirm Mallarmé's resolve to finish *The Book*. Some came in the form of a warning, and others as a challenge.

That spring of 1889, Auguste de Villiers de l'Isle-Adam had come down with a mysterious ailment, and Mallarmé, through the good offices of Méry Laurent, arranged for him to see a doctor. The destitute aristocrat had moved from Paris to a less expensive apartment in the eastern suburb of Nogent-sur-Marne with Marie Dantine, his cleaning woman and the mother of his son, Victor, known as Totor. A diagnosis of stomach cancer prompted Mallarmé, together with Joris-Karl Huysmans, whose conversion to Catholicism stood him in good stead with the Church, to arrange for Villiers to be moved to the Maison des Frères Saint Jean de Dieu on the rue Oudinot in central Paris. There, Villiers expressed the desire to marry Marie Dantine in order that she not be listed on the death certificate as a common charwoman, but as Mme Villiers de l'Isle-Adam. In this way, too, their son might benefit from state assistance to the children of deceased artists. Given that the shortness of the time left would not permit the publication of banns, given that Marie was from Luxembourg and not French, and given that all this took place in the middle of August when most Frenchmen were away from their desks in Paris, a timely marriage seemed nearly impossible. Yet, with the aid of a neighbor on the rue de Rome, Paul Beurdeley, a lawyer who was also mayor of the eighth arrondissement, Mallarmé managed to expedite the paperwork.

On August 15, 1889, Villiers on his deathbed, exclaimed, "I'm getting married today, we'll drink a bottle of champagne, and all the commotion will finish me off."[7] When the time came to sign the marriage certificate, however, it became painfully clear that the wife of one of France's greatest literary geniuses could not even write her own name. "I'll sign," she said to the embarrassment of all, "as I did in my first marriage." Huysmans and Mallarmé apparently helped her with the required signature, and the priest, after administering the last rites, arranged for Marie to spend the night among the brothers of Saint Jean de Dieu. Villiers de l'Isle-Adam died four days later; his last words were "I'm leaving so many beautiful things."

Unlike Henri Regnault's death, which could be attributed to the folly of war, and unlike that of Anatole, which struck a singular cruel blow, the disappearance of Villiers de l'Isle-Adam impressed Mallarmé as part of the natural cycle of life and death. The poet, who was forty-seven years old at the time of Villiers's death at the age of fifty-one, surely thought to himself that he might be the next to go. In fact, he had an accidental brush with death just before that of Villiers. Coming back to Valvins after visiting his ailing friend, Mallarmé missed his step descending from the train, which was still moving as it came into the Fontainebleau station.

"It was nighttime, I was thrown the length of my body with a wild violence, and dragged under the running board, which grabbed me by the shoulder, for seven or eight meters. I felt close to my last hour, just like Villiers," he wrote.[8] Reminded of his own mortality by the dying Villiers and by his fall, Mallarmé did not want to leave Marie and Geneviève in the kind of financial straits that befell Marie Dantine and Totor. He, in fact, tried to ease the difficulties of Villiers's dependents even before death by organizing a subscription of five francs per month from various of his literary friends. After Villiers's passing, Mallarmé advised his widow and son about how to hold on to the small sum collected in the face of creditors' demands to be paid. And, again, Mallarmé recognized that the most worthy homage to the writer he considered without equal would be to complete his own life's work, with however little time he might have left.

Public life in Paris during the summer of 1889 was taken up by the Universal Exposition to commemorate the Revolution of 1789. It attracted 32 million visitors to the area of Trocadéro, the quai d'Orsay, and the Champs de Mars, on which the Eiffel Tower had been erected. Given his experience reporting on the London International Exposition of 1871, Mallarmé should have been interested in its French avatar. We know that he visited it quickly. "I looked in on the Exposition," he wrote to Henri Cazalis. "I was asked to write an article, but I only came up with these words: 'The Eiffel Tower surpasses my expectations.'" Much of his effort and time that summer had gone into traveling back and forth between Valvins and Paris to care for Villiers. Still reverberating from his loss, the poet vacationed with Méry Laurent and Dr. Evans at Royat in early September. He could not have failed, however, to be aware of at least one of the major events of the celebration of the centenary of the French Revolution, one where the Wagnerian project of the total work of art found its most stunning expression to date.

Augusta Holmès, the longtime mistress of Mallarmé's friend Catulle Mendès and one of the few women to attend one or more Tuesdays on the rue de Rome, had composed a *Triumphal Ode* to the French Revolution. Holmès's *Ode* was performed on September 11, 1889, in the lavishly decorated Palace of Industry, an enormous hall built to celebrate machines. The epic composition called for 900 singers and 300 instrumentalists on a stage that measured 197 feet across, 164 feet deep, and 148 feet high. The hall, located between the Champs-Élysées and the Seine, held 22,000 spectators. The staging had been modeled on Wagner's innovative design of a sunken orchestra pit at Bayreuth, and the split curtain opened to reveal painted forests, mountains, and cities in the background. Incense burned around an altar to the Republic in what was a clear mix of elements from Christian, nationalist, and Masonic traditions. The first choral entry was that of the winemakers of France, who chanted, "This wine is the blood / Hot and turning red / From the earth which made us!" They were followed by the harvesters: "This bread is the flesh / Of the three-times cherished soil / That the plow tears and penetrates!" To the invocation of the bread and wine of the mass, soldiers and sailors called on France to fulfill its colonialist ambition of conquering the world. Lady Republic appeared, as lightning accompanied a call to prayer from the people, to which she replied:

> O people, here I am!
> > the heights of the heavens
> Where I rule forever your
> > glorious destiny
> I come at your call, and
> > surrounded by flames,
> I appear to your eyes.[10]

By the late 1880s, Wagnerism in France had waned, and there was no visible rival to Mallarmé's project of *The Book*. Yet the staggering aspiration of Augusta Holmès's *Triumphal Ode* to reproduce in Paris the combined effects of ancient Greek drama and the Catholic mass must have awakened in Mallarmé some sense of the dramatic power of the "future spectacle" that he still hoped to capture in *The Book*.

In February 1890, Mallarmé honored the memory of Villiers with a lecture delivered in Brussels. He spoke in the loftiest terms of the sacred calling of the poet. "A man used to dreaming comes before you to speak of another who is dead. Ladies and gentlemen, Do you know what it is to write? An ancient and very vague but jealous practice, whose meaning lies in the mysteries of the heart."[11] The lecture was not universally acclaimed. A retired general exclaimed audibly, "This man is drunk or crazy," then left the room, where, in the phrase of one witness, "his word is law."[12] The reviewer for the Belgian newspaper *La Patriote* reported that "you had to be

drunk to understand what remains, nonetheless, a beautiful meditation on literature, written in mourning for Villiers six months after
his death."

Even those sympathetic to Mallarmé found the lecture difficult.
Henri de Régnier reported having trouble reading it, but he also
observed that when the poet read it out loud before invited guests
chez Berthe Morisot later that spring, the homage to Villiers became
comprehensible. This was not the case for Edgar Dégas, who apparently threw his hands up in despair, blurting, "I don't understand, I
don't understand." The painter claimed once to have asked Mallarmé how he would speak to a maid, to which the poet replied, "No
differently." On the night of Mallarmé's reading in honor of Villiers,
Dégas might still have been smarting from the poet's reaction to his
own attempt to write sonnets. "It is not with ideas that one writes
verse, Dégas" Mallarmé reminded him, "it is with words."[13]

The lecture in honor of Villiers de l'Isle-Adam was Mallarmé's
first public address. It would not, however, be his last. In 1893, he
received an invitation to speak at both Oxford and Cambridge,
which was only natural, given his occupation as an English teacher,
his previous trips to London, and his growing reputation among
British poets.

The Times of London of February 23, 1894, published an article on
the current state of French letters, with special reference to the
Académie Française. Lamenting the conservatism of this venerable
institution for the preservation of the French language, *The Times*
noted, "Literary fashions die hard. The tradition of grace and perfect form which has so long attached to French Academical work
will not disappear just yet, even though much of the new production will be mediocre and common." The editors declared, "Still,
the Academy is advancing. It has nearly elected M. Zola; who
knows whether it may not soon take M. Stéphane Mallarmé, the

Symbolist—or is it Luminist, or Décadent?—who is just about to lecture at Oxford? Then it may come to be the turn of M. Paul Verlaine himself. We move quickly nowadays; we adore today what we burned yesterday; schools and creeds in the arts follow one another with bewildering rapidity; and even the French Academy, that most conservative of bodies, is affected by the spirit of change."[14]

By the time *The Times* had published its report on official literary France, Mallarmé was already in England, having hosted his regular Tuesday on the rue de Rome on the evening of February 20. The poet's first stop was Sussex Bell, Haslemere, Surrey, the estate of Mr. Charles Whibley, a literary journalist and Whistler's brother-in-law. He wrote to Marie and Geneviève that he was working on his English with Whibley, and that in two days, "I will no longer know French, except to write to you."[15] As things turned out, the French poet became terrified at the idea of reading his talk in what he referred to delicately as "the local clause" (*la clause locale*), a requirement of the Taylorian Association, which sponsored his Oxford visit. The night before he was to speak, he had it retranslated by Frederick York Powell, Regius professor of modern history—"my friend for three days now and forever." Powell would first read the English version, then Mallarmé, the French.

The poet was astonished by the beauty of Oxford, with its medieval cloisters in the middle of parks and water, fields with cows and stags, and a dinner in a refectory "as beautiful as a cathedral." Amid the high wood-paneled walls with portraits of distinguished graduates, he indulged in afterdinner drinks with the professors, who may have taken off their robes, but who retained their bizarre hairstyle, "a cross between the *chapska* and a blotter."[16]

Mallarmé's lecture at Cambridge, however, met with bad luck. It was scheduled to take place at the same time as the performance of a visiting theater troupe. Tickets for both events had been available at a local bookshop, but only twenty people paid five shillings apiece for the privilege of hearing Mallarmé's "proper French," which many in France would have considered far from proper. He reported to Marie and Geneviève that the audience of Pembroke College listened religiously and applauded tactfully as he read his notes by the light of two high silver candelabra. "The lover of rare things in me was seduced."

Mallarmé concluded that Oxford and Cambridge were worlds of study and sport, where, "like peacocks adorning a garden, a select breed of men received salaries just for being charming people."[17] Democracies, the poet reflected, ought to create such cities for poets. Upon his return, he published a plan for doing just that in *Le Figaro*, on August 17, 1894. Young struggling poets were, Mallarmé reasoned, the true heirs of the successful writers who had preceded them. They should therefore share in the royalties earned by publishers of works in the public domain, such profit sharing to be supervised by a Ministry of Poetry with offices in the National Library.

At Oxford, Mallarmé encountered the essayist, art critic, and novelist Walter Pater, who taught classics and philosophy, and who shared the poet's belief that "all art constantly aspires towards the condition of music." At Cambridge, where Poe once lectured to Whistler, Mallarmé was interviewed on the topic of the present state of French men of letters. His interviewer, R. A. Neil, a librarian at Pembroke College, was struck by the poet's unassuming manner, describing him as "a man of modest height, casual in his dress, who speaks English badly, completely simple and *liebenswürdig* (*amiable*), full of anecdotes and wit, intensified when he lifts his eyebrows."[18] They must have discussed Paul Verlaine's visit to England the previous year. Mallarmé recounted to Neil the story of the difficult beginning of a public lecture that Verlaine had delivered, the location unspecified. With the audience all gathered in the absence of the lecturer, someone asked the security guard if he had not seen someone who looked like Verlaine. "Oh," the guard replied, "a man who matches that description tried to get in, he said he was supposed to give a lecture, but I found he was not presentable and didn't let him enter."

Mallarmé's Oxford lecture was also poorly attended, yet he was reassured by how well behaved the two or three professors, a few students, and the ladies were, with "correct and long applause at the end." But, the poet feared that his lecture has been on too high an aesthetic plane, and he lamented that he could have delivered it without preparation, "on an empty stomach, during the day in a frock coat." He wondered if it was worth the trouble to have made the long trip in order to distract sixty people from the world of studies or to provide an occasion to hear spoken French.[19] Mallarmé may have wondered about the context of these English lectures, but "Music and Letters" and "Crisis in Poetry" remain among the most important literary essays of the nineteenth century.

Like a messenger from the Greek gods warning of impending doom or a newsboy selling the *Daily Sun* with headlines proclaiming the outbreak of war, Mallarmé arrived in Oxford and Cambridge to announce, "I bring the most surprising news. Nothing like it has ever been seen. There has been an attack on verse! Governments change; yet prosody has always remained untouched: either because in revolutions, it passes unseen, or because the revolutionaries fail to convey the belief that it might ever change."[20]

When the French poet proclaimed an "attack on verse," he was referring to traditional alexandrine verse, inherited from the neo classical seventeenth century and, beyond that, from the High Middle Ages, where it first appeared in the thirteenth-century *Roman d'Alexandre*. The alexandrine, a twelve-syllable line, usually divided by a caesura between the sixth and seventh syllables, was every bit as strong an organizing principle of French national identity as the flag, the national anthem, or the constitution. Yet, increasingly, as the long nineteenth century began to sound a drumbeat, at first faint but ever louder with the approach of modernity, the alexandrine was threatened by the *vers libre*, or free verse: poetry that does not respect regular patterns of rhythm or rhyme, and which may involve irregular line length. Heinrich Heine, Walt Whitman, and Arthur Rimbaud had experimented with free verse earlier in the century, as had Jules Laforgue, the Symbolist poet who was impressed by *Leaves of Grass* and who, in turn, would influence Ezra Pound and T. S. Eliot. The *Mardist* Gustave Kahn, a Jew from Lorraine and ardent Dreyfusard, claimed in the 1880s to have invented the looser form.

However much earlier or contemporaneous poets may have experimented with free verse, none attacked the alexandrine more violently than Stéphane Mallarmé, who worked quietly on the notes for *A Tomb for Anatole* and for *The Book* until "One Toss of the Dice" would take the shape of an attack—yea, an annihilation—of traditional poetic form. The beginning of the process of the dissolution of uniform meter, with justified lines of poetry singly spaced in stanzas separated by a double space, began shortly after Mallarmé's proclamation of an "attack on verse." In writing to Charles Bonnier, a teacher of French at Oxford who had initiated his English tour, Mallarmé spoke of a decision to "put in a line of poetry only very short whole phrases, interrupted on purpose, solely to counterbalance other long sentences; to erase duration, only to restart."[21]

It would be some time before Mallarmé's announced assault on verse would come to fruition. In the meantime, much of the poet's time was taken up tending to his day job, taking on freelance assignments to supplement his income, and in helping others.

Shortly after his return from England to France, the poet began to play a material role in the protracted legal battle between Whistler and Lord William Eden (father of the future prime minister Anthony Eden). The painter had agreed, upon the recommendation of novelist George Moore, to paint a small portrait of Lady Eden for a fee of between 100 and 150 guineas. Lady Eden began sitting for the portrait in early February 1894. On Valentine's Day, Lord Eden showed up at Whistler's door, and informed him he was leaving for India on a hunting trip. He handed the painter a sealed envelope with a check for 100 guineas and a message: "Herewith your valentine. . . . The picture will always be of inestimable value to me, and will be handed down as an heirloom as long as heirlooms last! I will always remember with pleasure the time during which it was painted. My thanks."[22] The painter responded with irony: "My Dear Sir William—I have your valentine. You really are magnificent— and have scored all around." Of course, he also cashed Sir Eden's check, keeping the painting. He not only kept it but also exhibited it in the annual Salon on the Champs de Mars with the title *Portrait of Lady Eden: Brown and Gold.*

Back from his hunting trip, Lord Eden demanded delivery of the painting. When Whistler refused, he sued him in court for the painting, return of the check, and one thousand francs damages in recompense for the time spent in Paris while Whistler worked on the portrait of his wife. Whistler turned to Mallarmé, who again turned to his neighbor Maître Paul Beurdeley, who had expedited Villier's deathbed marriage. The quite public trial was complicated by the fact that when *Portrait of Lady Eden: Brown and Gold* was brought into the courtroom, the face of Lady Eden had been effaced and another appeared in its place. Whistler explained that, since he had another lady's portrait to do, he simply sat her down on the same canapé in front of the same golden curtain. She had a brown dress about the same color as the other, the same fur collar, the same muff, and assumed the same pose. In the place of Lady Eden, *Portrait in Brown and Gold* now depicted an American named Mrs Herbert Dudley Hale, "and the painting now belonged to my new model," Whistler concluded.[23]

On the day of the unveiling of the disputed portrait, Whistler had the "genial idea," in his own phrase, to invite Mrs Hale to be present in court along with Lady Eden. The painting of Lady Eden/Mrs Hale, brought into the courtroom as evidence, was covered in glass. The lawyer for the other side, Maître Bureau, demanded that the glass be removed and that a portion of the face as well as of the dress be rubbed with a cloth. The not completely dry surface of the face was irrefutable proof of Whistler's alteration of the prime piece of evidence. On the evening of March 11, 1895, between the concluding arguments and the verdict, Beurdeley, Mallarmé, and Whistler dined together.

Whistler lost the first round in the court, which ordered him to deliver the portrait, return the check, and to pay the thousand francs in damages as well as court costs. When he appealed, Paul Beurdeley argued in favor of the inherent unfairness of Lord Eden's keeping both the painting and the check. At one point in the proceedings, Beurdeley introduced into evidence a letter Whistler published in the *Pall Mall Gazette*: "I will read you a translation of his letter, made, not by a sworn translator, but by his intimate friend, the distinguished man of letters, Stéphane Mallarmé."[24] The letter, which was read to the appeals court, showed the fine hands of Whistler and Mallarmé, who compared the product of artistic endeavor to that of a cobbler. A shoemaker had every right to refuse delivery of a pair of boots to the client who had not paid the asking price for his work. On the defensive, Whistler claimed that he was merely being ironic, to which Maître Bureau unleashed irony of his own: "The translation I used at the first trial is said to have been very inaccurate. . . . I much regret, however, that this letter was not translated by M. Stéphane Mallarmé, like the other. What would have been the meaning of an ironical letter on this occasion?"

The final verdict of the appeals court was that, inasmuch as the agreement between Whistler and Lord Eden was "in no sense a contract to sell, but merely an obligation to execute, so that the portrait had never ceased to be the artist's property," the painter had the right to retain his work. However, since Whistler altered only Lady Eden's face and not the overall "harmony given to his composition," his right was not absolute, and he "may not make any use of it, public or private." He was also obliged to refund the hundred guineas with interest to Lord Eden along with the thousand francs damages. Whistler was ordered to pay the costs of the first trial, and Lord Eden those of the second.

In a less protracted episode, Mallarmé came to the assistance of art critic and *Mardist* Félix Fénéon. Fénéon's mother had asked the poet to intervene after her son, who worked in the War Office, was accused of involvement in the anarchist bombings of the mid-1890s, which traumatized not only Paris but the nation as a whole. Fénéon was arrested after a bomb went off at Foyot's Restaurant on April 4, 1894, blinding the poet Laurent Tailhade in one eye. Tailhade's injury was particularly poignant since he had declared, upon hearing the news of an explosion in the Chamber of Deputies in late 1893, "What do the victims matter, if the act is beautiful?" Symbolist poets, associated by some with verbal anarchy, were often thought to be allied with the anarchist movement in politics. And, so, Mallarmé, who believed deeply in the power of poetry to shape the mind and therefore the deeds of others, was interviewed by the popular newspaper *Le Soir*, where he famously quipped that for Fénéon "there was no better bomb than his articles, no more efficient arm than literature."[25] The notorious "trial of the thirty," one of whom was Fénéon, was not lacking in irreverent repartee. Accused by the judge of having been spotted speaking to a known anarchist behind a lamppost, Fénéon asked the judge "which side of a lamppost was its behind?" Mallarmé testified that neither he nor any of the others attending Tuesday meetings in his apartment had ever heard Fénéon speak about anything other than art. The defendant was acquitted. Many years later, Félix Fénéon, in whose office dynamite capsules had been found, was discovered in fact to have been involved in the bombing at Foyot's.

Almost twenty years after Rimbaud left France, Mallarmé was approached by the painter Paterne Berrichon, a sometime vagabond and anarchist who had spent time in prison, for a letter-of-character reference to Rimbaud's mother in support of his marriage to her daughter, the poet's sister, Isabelle. "She is very strict, you know, Mme Rimbaud, frightfully severe, but I have told her everything about my past," Berrichon confided. Mallarmé wrote to Mme Marie-Catherine-Vitalie Rimbaud, "Everything . . . bears witness in Paterne Berrichon to an inflexible desire to live according to established order.[26] The marriage was concluded.

Stéphane Mallarmé, one of the great abstract thinkers of the late nineteenth century, was clever, practical, and resourceful, the man to whom friends turned when in need. *Mardist* Henry Roujon recounted that one night, between two and three o'clock, a racket disturbed the poet's peaceable dwelling. Mallarmé jumped out of bed, grabbed a candle, and, half-naked, went to the door to see who was there. It was a giant and affable Englishman, who explained in a few guttural phrases that he had seduced a woman of high social standing. The lady was now downstairs, in a carriage, beset by labor pains. Not knowing where to turn, the seducer thought that the poet, who was always so gracious, might help the two embarrassed lovers find a midwife favorable to clandestine births. Mallarmé, candle in hand, lowered his eyes and said, "I am all yours."[27]

Among the poet's friends, Méry Laurent occupied pride of place. Mallarmé had put to use his considerable taste and knowledge of the Parisian purveyors of luxury goods, acquired first at the London exposition, then honed through his solo edition of *The Latest Fashion*, to help Méry Laurent furnish her Parisian home. Whether it was a question of where to eat or where to shop, Mallarmé knew the best addresses in town. He wrote to Méry Laurent from school on May 17, 1893, to recommend that she visit the Grande Épicerie Anglaise on the avenue Victor-Hugo, where they serve "breakfasts." He counseled her about what furnishings and decorations to buy, where, and for what price, and worried whether his choices would please Dr. Evans, who paid the bills. "Don't let the two Saxon porcelain flowerpots at the antique dealer's get away. . . . You can have them for 75 f., they are marvelous and are worth four times as much. Be careful, the dealer will talk them up."[28] Mallarmé influenced not only Méry Laurent's choice of what to buy but how the knickknacks, which were such an integral part of the home decoration of the Belle Époque, were to be arranged. To make an interior unified in tone, he advised her to have the glass paneling of her little salon case covered by an upholsterer, on the rue des Martyrs, in an antique fabric, preferably Louis XIV or XV. He specified that she should "run along the edge of your shelves, in the long direction, a braid of old gold, to be had *chez* Madame Kahn. . . . This will be just right, and pretty."[29]

To those within his circle, Mallarmé was generous to a fault. Not only did he come to the aid of Whistler in his legal struggle against Lord Eden; of Villiers in his dying and of his widow and son after his death; of Félix Féneon in his defense against the terrorist charges against him; of Paterne Berrichon in his suit to marry Isabelle Rimbaud; of the anonymous Englishman in his quest for a discreet midwife; of Méry Laurent in her decoration of Les Talus; but the poet was almost always available to host literary banquets, to contribute to the erection of monuments, to compose verse tributes, and to edit memorial volumes to such worthy dead poets as Baudelaire, Banville, Villiers, and, eventually, Verlaine. All contributed to the deferral of the project of *The Book*.

In the years of his growing reputation, Mallarmé continued to teach a full load at the lycée. His evenings and weekends were still filled with Tuesdays on the rue de Rome, Sunday afternoons at the Lamoureux concerts, and the events that he attended as a cultural reporter. The poet wrote regular reviews of musical and dance performances for *Le Mercure de France*, *La Revue blanche*, and London's *National Observer*. He was especially taken by the American Loïe Fuller, whose whirling veil dances at the Moulin Rouge took Paris by storm in the early 1890s. He attended his first live Wagner opera, *Die Walküre* at the Paris Opera in May 1893, followed by Maeterlinck's *Pelléas et Mélisande* a week later. Mallarmé dined out several nights a week, with Méry Laurent, Berthe Morisot, and her American friend Mary Cassatt, Dégas, Renoir, or other of his widening circle of friends.

Mallarmé's literary production in this period was minimal. He received five hundred francs for rewriting *Tales and Legends of Ancient India* (*Contes et légendes de l'Inde ancienne*) of the historian and orientalist Charlotte Foucaux, who wrote under the pseudonym Mary Summer. The project was paid for by Dr. Edmond Fournier, Méry Laurent's new lover, who thought the poet might improve the style of certain of these anthropological stories published in 1878. The poet worked assiduously on an anthology of his own works, *Vers et prose*, which contained verse written prior to 1893, prose poems, translations of several poems of Edgar Allan Poe, and the lecture on Villiers, as well as those delivered at Oxford and Cambridge. The frontispiece of *Vers et Prose* displayed Whistler's lithographic portrait of the poet.

Distracted by a whirlwind of social activity and of lesser literary production, reviews of the work of others and the painstaking edition of his own work, Mallarmé sensed in the early 1890s that time was running out for completing the *Grand Oeuvre*. He undertook to remove the most obvious impediment to realizing his dream—his day job teaching English. In late 1892, he wrote to the poet and journalist Jules Boissière, who had married one of Geneviève's childhood friends from Avignon, "A new year is beginning, my last, I think, of teaching: I have so much to do and, though aged, have not really given enough to my dream, except a gesture here and there, to those willing to listen."[30] So, the poet submitted a request for a reduced teaching load, and, in the spring of 1893, he filed for early retirement with a well-fashioned letter from his doctor attesting to neurasthenia, heart trouble, dyspepsia, and chronic insomnia.

Minister of Public Education Raymond Poincaré, a cousin of the celebrated mathematician Henri Poincaré, granted the poet's petition, effective the beginning of the fall semester. He would receive a supplementary grant from the state, in what amounted to a subsidy for artists, of 1,200 francs a year, which meant that early retirement carried no financial penalty. Mallarmé, in his own phrase, was now finally free to "launch a literary career." On November 8, 1893, he wrote to Méry Laurent:

> Bonsoir, petit paon; ça y est
>
> Mr Mallarmé
>
> rentier[31]
>
> Good evening, little peacock, all is OK
>
> Mr Mallarmé
>
> rentier

The freedom to write might have seemed exhilarating, yet Mallarmé also knew that there would be no more deferrals of this last chance to reach the goal he had set for himself almost three decades earlier. "I don't live in Paris, but in a room," he wrote in May 1894, "it could be in London, San Francisco, or China. . . . Writing a book today is to write one's last will and testament."[32]

As the poet contemplated retirement, the Panama Canal scandal swirled all around him. Some eight hundred thousand French men and women had invested in stock in the Panama Canal Company, which went bankrupt in 1889, and many lost their life's savings. Beginning in 1892, however, the news began to emerge that numerous ministers (including *Mardist* Georges Clemenceau), members of the Chamber of Deputies, and financial middlemen took bribes from the head of the building project, Ferdinand de Lesseps, to allocate government funds to aid the failing French venture as well as to hide its true financial condition. In the trial that unfolded while Mallarmé negotiated his retirement, Lesseps, his son Charles, engineer Gustave Eiffel, and Baron Jacques Reinach, who had negotiated the bribes, received long jail sentences, which were later annulled. Some historians consider the Panama Canal crisis a source of the social unrest that motivated the anarchist bombers, including Félix Féneon, of the early 1890s. Still others, among them Hannah Arendt, see in the Panama scandal an early phase of the Dreyfus affair, since the chief financial advisors of the project, Jacques Reinach and Cornelius Herz, were both Jews of German origin. Reinach fled to England, where he committed suicide in November 1892. In one of the great ironies of history, his cousin the journalist and politician Joseph Reinach would be one of the earliest and most ardent defenders of Captain Alfred Dreyfus immediately after his false conviction in December 1894.

Throughout his poetic career, Mallarmé had sought to reclaim for poetry what poetry had lost to music, especially to Wagner's seductive integration of music, visual spectacle, and words. Augusta Holmès's *Triumphal Ode* had gone as far as possible in the direction of the Wagnerian epic spectacle. Beginning around the time of the poet's retirement, however, a new specter loomed on the horizon, one that threatened to surpass even Wagner, and which was arguably closer to *The Book* in its potential to "alter the nature of the human community" than the operatic *Gesamtkunstwerk*.

Mallarmé, who was a contributor to and a daily reader of *Le Figaro*, was no doubt aware of an article by his friend Octave Uzanne that appeared on May 8, 1893. On the first page, Uzanne recounted his recent visit to Thomas Edison's workshop in Menlo Park, New Jersey, where the inventor, "with the air of an old baby," revealed his latest invention, the kinetograph. "The kinetograph will be for the eye what the phonograph is for the ear. In two years, when it is perfected, Talma, Rachel, Sarah Bernhardt . . . all will continue to live." Mallarmé was also sensitized to Edison through Auguste de Villiers de l'Isle-Adam's 1886 novel *Tomorrow's Eve* (*L'Ève future*), in which the wizard of Menlo Park created an artificial woman—Halady—to replace his friend Lord Ewald's difficult mistress, Alicia. In Villiers's account, the synthetic human being, which speaks and can be seen, was a prophetic example of what Edison would reveal to Octave Uzanne seven years later as an imminent possibility: "Thanks to this new system, one will see an opera, a play, or a person at the same time as one hears it."

Edison, whose outsized ego was more like Wagner's than Mallarmé's and whose gift for self-promotion was rivaled only by that of P. T. Barnum, made his new machine available to the public in New York, and by 1894, at least seven kinetoscopes, as the device was now known, were up and running in Paris as well. Antoine Lumière, the photographer father of two inventors, who had made a fortune in the 1880s from the production of fast photographic film, purchased one of the new machines, and brought it back to Lyon. There, Antoine and his sons, Auguste and Louis, disassembled it in order to study the mechanism for making a series of still images appear to move. The kinetoscope was not all they imagined it could be. Only one person at a time could peep into Edison's viewing apparatus, the images seen through the binocularlike device were disappointingly small, and, while it was true that the figures in the kinetoscope did move, their movement still retained the jerky quality of an animated flip-book.

Inventors working on cinematic devices knew that the key to smoothing out movements captured in successive individual images lay in the phenomenon of retinal retention. The physiologist A.-M. Bloch noted in 1887 that we have no consciousness of the present moment. By the time we think we know the present, or say "I see lightning, or I hear a sound," the sight or sound has already passed. However, if two strong sensations follow each other in rapid succession, "they melt into a single one, and appear synchronous."[33] For two sounds, the interval is $\frac{1}{82}$ of a second; for two flashes of light, $\frac{1}{25}$ of a second; and for two taps of fingers on the hand, $\frac{1}{42}$ of a second. When it came to the viewing of moving images, the emission of light through photographic film had to be shuttered such that it would not hit the individual image as it was being drawn into place, or as it was being withdrawn to allow the positioning of the next image in the sequence. The situating and shuttering of individual images must occur, furthermore, some fifteen times a second in order that the process of sequential projections does not become apparent, and that the movement of things and people, photographed in rapid succession, appears, when projected upon the screen, in seamless array. This mechanical problem had eluded all the inventors working on projected moving images until late one night in the fall or winter of 1894.

Auguste and Louis Lumière had married two sisters on the same day, and the two couples lived with their children in a large house near the factory where their famous fast Etiquette Bleue film was manufactured. That night, Louis Lumière, on his way to bed, stopped to chat with the family seamstress when he experienced an extraordinary breakthrough—a "eureka!" moment. The mechanism capable of making the individual still photos of the film band stop long enough for the light to pass through it, and then move on, was that of the sewing machine, whose technology, within a matter of months, the Lumière brothers had adapted to the photographic shutter.

The Lumière brothers had solved the problem of the intermittent-stop-motion shutter, which allows the projected picture to fade while the retina still retains its image, causing the viewing eye to experience simultaneously both an instant in time and the aftereffects of a previous instant. However short the persistence of luminous impressions on our retina may be, the overall sensation is one of temporal duration, the passage of time as a continuous stream and not a succession of separate points. Further, by reversing the relationship between the light source and lens of the traditional camera, Auguste and Louis Lumière also managed, using the older technology of the magic lantern, to project moving images so that more than one person could view them at the same time.

While their lawyers worked on patents, the wizards of Lyon shared their invention with the members of the Congress of Photographic Societies in June 1895. A filmshot of congress attendees disembarking from a boat in the morning was processed and projected that very night. And, on December 28, 1895, in the Salon Indien du Grand Café on Paris's boulevard des Capucines, the Lumière brothers offered to the world the first public movie projection.

The event created an immediate sensation, which resonated with Mallarmé's calculations of the interactive sessions for the *Grand Oeuvre*. On the model of the Tuesday gatherings in his home, which was within walking distance of the Salon Indien, the poet imagined an audience guided by a leader or "*opérateur,*" which is the French term for projectionist. He spoke in the preface to "One Toss of the Dice" of an "implicit guiding thread" (*fil conducteur latent*—a more literal translation would be "latent conducting wire"); and he foresaw, in the performances of *The Book*, electrically projected images along with the commercial trappings of the movies—ticket sales and advertisements. And, as we shall see, Mallarmé's ambitions for *The Book* coincided uncannily with the vitalizing effects of moving pictures.[34]

Newspaper reports stressed the animating power of film. In what may be the first movie review ever, *La Poste* reported in its edition of December 30 on a Lumière film called *Exit from the Lumière Factory in Lyon*. From the workshop door that opened poured forth a sea of workmen and women, with bicycles, dogs that run, and cars. "It all moves, it swarms. It is life itself, movement captured live." Someday, the reviewer predicted, these machines will be available to the public. Then we can all photograph those most dear to us, no longer in their immobile form, but in their movements, with their familiar gestures, with speech on the tip of their tongues. At that moment, "death will cease to be absolute. . . . Life will have left an indelible trace." *Le Radical* of the same day noted that man had already captured and reproduced words, and now one has reproduced life. "We will be able to see our loved ones move long after we have lost them."[35]

By sheer coincidence, on the same day that the world learned of the Cinématographe, as the Lumières called their device, in Paris, Wilhelm Röntgen published in Würzburg, Germany a paper announcing the discovery of X-rays. The actual experiment had taken place two months earlier. In the first focus upon a human subject, Röntgen X-rayed the hand of his wife, Anna Bertha, who, looking at the ghostly image of the bones of her hand, declared, "I have seen my death!" If the moving pictures made the dead come alive, the still shot of the skeleton reminded the living of their mortality.

In the imagination of the first moviegoers, the Cinématographe seemed to conquer death and to offer the possibility of time travel.

Journalist Henri de Parville had noted only a month before the Lumière brothers revealed their invention to the public, "It is clear that from now on any historic scene can be reproduced. Up until now all we had were paintings and photographs. Henceforth, we will have kinétogrammes. Our descendants will be able to attend the marriage of their grandmothers. They will see the fiancés approach the altar, the maids of honor present their velvet and satin purses. . . . They will all be alive, gay, young, and primped . . . *secula seculorum.* 'O Time! Suspend your flight!'"[36] This last line, quoting Alphonse de Lamartine, was especially appropriate, appearing as it had in "The Lake" ("Le Lac"), an elegiac evocation of the Romantic poet's dead lost love, an attempt to make her live again. Who knows if Romanticism, a poetic movement based upon lost and dead loves, would have come about in a world with Cinématographes, and the possibility of attending one's grandmother's wedding?

Mallarmé was clearly aware of the advent of cinema. In April 1896, the poet Charles Morice delivered a lecture on France's new "Prince of Poets." Mallarmé, who was at the time nursing a prolonged bout of influenza, read the review of Morice's lecture in *Le Figaro*, since he wrote the lecturer a note of thanks. He must have read on the same page of *Le Figaro* a report by his friend Jules Huret, who had famously interviewed him for the same newspaper in 1891, that "between two and six o'clock, the Cinématographe-Lumière recorded more than 1200 admissions." In the first year, the short clips of the first movie shows—*Leaving the Lumière Factory at Lyons, Feeding Baby, The Blacksmith, Arrival of a Train, Boat Leaving the Port*—attracted as many as 2,500 viewers a day. Among the numerous projection houses that sprang up in Paris during the year 1896, the Pirou-Normandin, at 86, rue de Clichy, in Mallarmé's own neighborhood, would have caught his attention. Even closer, on May 1, 1897, the Lumières, who at first resisted selling the Cinématographe on the open market, opened a dealership at 35, rue de Rome.

Mallarmé was known to have commented directly on movies only once. In January 1898, in response to a poll on illustrated books, the print-bound poet told *Le Mercure de France*, "I am for—no illustrations. Everything that a book evokes should happen in the mind of the reader: but, if you replace photography, why not go all the way to the Cinématographe, whose unrolling will supplant favorably many a volume, images and text."[37]

Mallarmé's fear that Wagner had usurped the proper place of poetry and that "nothing was left to do" must have paled next to the effects of early cinema. Indeed, the close chronological relationship between the invention of cinema in late December 1895 and Mallarmé's composition of "One Toss of the Dice" six months later was not accidental, and one can imagine the following scenario. For thirty years, the poet had wrestled with the next-to-impossible project of *The Book*. During the whole long period between the crisis of his midtwenties and retirement, the only rival form was Wagnerian opera, which, alongside the spectacular but singular performances of Augusta Holmès's *Triumphal Ode* in 1889, came as close as one could imagine at the time to the total work of art. The advent of the movies in late 1895, however, represented a powerful reminder of the possibility of transformative "future spectacle." For the poet, it was now or never, and within six months, having made the necessary home improvements to the poetry-writing cottage in Valvins, he began his masterwork.

MARLLARMÉ'S ORIGINAL PREFACE

to the 1897 *Cosmopolis* Edition of
"Un Coup de Dés Jamais N'Abolira le Hasard"

I would prefer that this Note not be read or, if skimmed, that it be forgotten. It offers the clever Reader little beyond his own perceptions: but it might confuse the inexperienced one obliged to look at the first words of this Poem, so that those that follow, arranged as they are, lead to the last, the whole of it without novelty except for the spacing of the text. The "blanks," in effect, assume importance because they strike the reader first; the versification usually demanded them, as the surrounding silence, to the point that any one portion, of a lyric or even of just a few measures, occupies about a third of the page on which it is centered: I do not violate this procedure, only scatter it on the page. The paper intervenes every time an image, on its own, ceases or withdraws, accepting the succession of others; and, since it does not concern, as it usually does, regular sound patterns or verse so much as the prismatic subdivisions of the Idea, the instant they appear and for the duration of their role in some exact spiritual setting, near or far from the implicit guiding thread, for the sake of verisimilitude, the text imposes itself. The literary advantage, if I may call it that, of this copied distance which mentally separates groups of words or words from each other, is that it seems to accelerate or slow down the movement, stressing it, even intimating it by a simultaneous vision of the Page: this being the leading principle, as elsewhere the verse or the perfect line is. The fiction shows through, then quickly dissipates, following the expressiveness of the writing, around the fragmentary interruptions of a central sentence, introduced by the title and continuing on. Everything that occurs is, by foreshortening, hypothetical; narrative is avoided. Add that from this stripped-down method of thought, with its withdrawals, prolongations, flights, or from its very layout, there results, for whoever reads it aloud, a musical score. The difference in typefaces, between the dominant size, a secondary and adjacent ones, dictates their importance for oral performance, and the range, in the middle, at the top or bottom of the page, will indicate how the intonation may rise or fall. Only a certain number of daring directions, infringements, etc., forming the counterpoint to the prosody, remain in their elementary state in a work which lacks precedents: not that I respect the appropriateness of timid attempts; but it does not seem right to me, except in one's own self-publications, in a Periodical however valiant, gracious and open to experiments, to step too far beyond custom. I shall have pointed out, nevertheless, about this Poem a "state" rather than a sketch, and one that does not break with tradition at all; extended its application in many senses without having offended anyone: sufficiently to open some eyes. Today, or without presuming on the future that will follow on it—nothing or something like a new art—let us readily acknowledge that the attempt participates, in unforeseen ways, in a number of pursuits dear to our time, free verse and the prose poem. They are joined, I know, under a strange influence, that of Music as heard at a concert; one discovers here several methods which seemed to apply to Literature and which I adopt. Its genre, if it should gradually become one like the symphony, alongside the art song, leaves intact the ancient technique of verse, which I continue to worship and to which I attribute the empire of passion and of dreams; this would be the preferred place to treat (as may yet follow) subjects of pure and complex imagination or intellect: there is no reason to exclude them from Poetry—the unique source.

ONE TOSS OF THE DICE

NEVER

EVEN WHEN THROWN IN THE MEASURELESS

CIRCUMSTANCES

FROM THE DEPTHS OF A SHIPWRECK

EVEN
      if

            the Abyss

      turned white
            stalled
                  roiling
                        beneath a desperately
                              sloping incline

                              of its own

                                    wing

                                          in

advance fallen back from the difficulty of trimming its sails
and stopping the gushing
preventing the surges

deep in the very heart

the shadow buried in the deep by this alternative sail

almost the length
of the wingspan

of the great hull's gaping breadth

a vessel

listing from side to side

THE MASTER

      risen

          implying

               from this conflagration

                  that there is

                 as one threatens

             a unique Number which cannot

                        hesitates

                   by its arms a corpse

rather

        than playing sides

            like a cranky graybeard

            on behalf

            of the waves

                      one

                that shipwreck

beyond old calculations
where skills are lost with age

once he grasped the helm

at his feet
of the seamless horizon

readied
moiling and merging
with the fist that would clasp it
fate and the winds

be any other

Spirit
to heave it
into the storm
to fold up division and pass proudly

separated from the secret it guards

invades the head
flows through the undulant beard

of the man himself

without a ship
no matter
where vain

from ancient times not to open the hand
                               clenched
                   above the worthless head

        legacy amidst disappearance

                        to someone
                                   ambiguous

            the ulterior immemorial demon

having
        from dead lands
                   led
the old man toward this final meeting with probability

                             this one
                                      his boyish shade
caressed and polished and restored and washed
                          made supple by the waves and freed
                      from the hard bones lost between the planks

                          born
                             of a revel
the sea enticing the sire or the sire against the sea
                an idle chance

                                                       Betrothal

whose
        veil of illusion fluttered their obsession
        like the phantom of a gesture

                        will tremble
                        will collapse

                           madness

WILL ABOLISH

AS IF

                                          A simple

                                    in the silence

                                  in an oncoming

                                        hovers

insinuation

tangled in irony
                or
                   the mystery
                                hurled
                                      howled

eddy of hilarity and horror

round the vortex
                    without scattering
                                       or fleeing it

            and cradles its virgin symbol

                                        AS IF

a solitary wandering plume

save

a glancing encounter with a toque of midnight
that fixes it
in velvet crumpled by a dark guffaw

this rigid whiteness

ridiculous

in opposition to the sky
too much
not to mark
faintly
anyone

bitter prince of the reef

wears it like a heroic headpiece
irresistible but limited
by his trifling manly mind

in a thunderbolt

anxious

       expiatory and pubescent

                      mute

                 The lucid and lordly aigrette
                   on the invisible brow
            scintillates
                then shadows
                  a delicate dark form
              in its sea siren's sinuosity

             with impatient terminal scurf

laughter

      that

IF

of vertigo

upright

    time enough
        to slap
forked

      a rock

   false manor
       all at once
          evaporated in mists

       which imposed
         a limit on infinity

IT WAS
born of the stars

IT WOULD BE
worse

neither

more nor less

indifferent but as much

THE NUMBER

IF IT EXISTED

other than as agony's flickering hallucination

IF IT BEGAN AND ENDED

rising only to be denied and shut down when revealed
at last
by some profusion lavished in scarcity

IF IT HAD AMOUNTED

to a totality however meager

IF IT HAD ILLUMINATED

CHANCE

Falls
    the plume
        rhythmic suspense of disaster
                            to be sunk
             in the first foam
   whence once its delirium surged to a peak
             withered
       by the identical sameness of the vortex

NOTHING

of the memorable crisis
or the event
might

have been accomplished with no result in sight
                              human

WILL HAVE TAKEN PLACE
an ordinary swell pours out absence

                              BUT THE PLACE
some lapping below as if to water down the empty act
                              abruptly which else
                         by its lies
                    would have justified
                         extinction

in this region
              of waves
                    where all reality dissolves

EXCEPT

       in the heights

                PERHAPS

                           as far as a place

can fuse with the beyond

                        apart from the interest
                  assigned to it
                              in general
by such a slant and such a slope
                                  of fires

          toward
                what must be
                     the Septentrion or North

                                   A CONSTELLATION

          cold from neglect and disuse
                         not so much
                    that it does not count
              on some empty and superior surface
                the successive shock
                              from the stars
           of a final reckoning in the making

watching
           doubting
                rolling
                     blazing and brooding

                            before stopping
               at some last point that consecrates it

                All Thought casts one Toss of the Dice

UN COUP DE DÉS

JAMAIS

QUAND BIEN MÊME LANCÉ DANS DES CIRCONSTANCES

ÉTERNELLES

DU FOND D'UN NAUFRAGE

SOIT
que

l'Abíme

blanchi
étale
furieux
sous une inclinaison
plane désespérément

d'aile

.

la sienne

par

avance retombée d'un mal à dresser le vol
                    et couvrant les jaillissements
                                coupant au ras les bonds

        très à l'intérieur résume

l'ombre enfouie dans la profondeur par cette voile alternative

                    jusqu'adapter
                            à l'envergure

        sa béante profondeur en tant que la coque

                d'un bâtiment

            penché de l'un ou l'autre bord

LE MAÎTRE

surgi
    inférant

            de cette conflagration

                 que se

              comme on menace

          l'unique Nombre qui ne peut pas

                       hésite
                cadavre par le bras
plutôt
     que de jouer
        en maniaque chenu
           la partie
         au nom des flots
                    un

           naufrage cela

hors d'anciens calculs
où la manœuvre avec l'âge oubliée

jadis il empoignait la barre

à ses pieds
de l'horizon unanime

prépare
s'agite et mêle
au poing qui l'étreindrait
un destin et les vents

être un autre

Esprit
pour le jeter
dans la tempête
en reployer la division et passer fier

écarté du secret qu'il détient

envahit le chef
coule en barbe soumise

direct de l'homme

sans nef
n'importe
où vaine

ancestralement à n'ouvrir pas la main
                         crispée
              par delà l'inutile tête

       legs en la disparition

                   à quelqu'un
                             ambigu

         l'ultérieur démon immémorial

ayant
          de contrées nulles
                    induit
   le vieillard vers cette conjonction suprême avec la probabilité

                     celui
                            son ombre puérile
       caressée et polie et rendue et lavée
                    assouplie par la vague et soustraite
              aux durs os perdus entre les ais

                      né
                             d'un ébat
     la mer par l'aïeul tentant ou l'aïeul contre la mer
                une chance oiseuse

                                                              Fiançailles
   dont
          le voile d'illusion rejailli leur hantise
          ainsi que le fantôme d'un geste

                        chancellera
                        s'affalera

                              folie

N'ABOLIRA

COMME SI

Une insinuation

au silence

dans quelque proche

voltige

simple

enroulée avec ironie
                    ou
                le mystère
                            précipité
                                    hurlé

tourbillon d'hilarité et d'horreur

autour du gouffre
                    sans le joncher
                            ni fuir

                et en berce le vierge indice

                                COMME SI

plume solitaire éperdue

sauf

que la rencontre ou l'effleure une toque de minuit
et immobilise
au velours chiffonné par un esclaffement sombre

cette blancheur rigide

dérisoire
en opposition au ciel
trop
pour ne pas marquer
exigüment
quiconque

prince amer de l'écueil

s'en coiffe comme de l'héroïque
irrésistible mais contenu
par sa petite raison virile
en foudre

soucieux

        expiatoire et pubère

                                        muet

La lucide et seigneuriale aigrette
au front invisible
scintille
puis ombrage
une stature mignonne ténébreuse
en sa torsion de sirène

par d'impatientes squames ultimes

rire

que

SI

de vertige

debout

   le temps
      de souffleter
bifurquées

    un roc

   faux manoir
      tout de suite
        évaporé en brumes

       qui imposa
        une borne à l'infini

C'ÉTAIT
issu stellaire

CE SERAIT
     pire
            non
                 davantage ni moins
                             indifféremment mais autant

LE NOMBRE

EXISTÂT-IL

autrement qu'hallucination éparse d'agonie

COMMENÇÂT-IL ET CESSÂT-IL

sourdant que nié et clos quand apparu

enfin

par quelque profusion répandue en rareté

SE CHIFFRÂT-IL

évidence de la somme pour peu qu'une

ILLUMINÂT-IL

LE HASARD

Choit

la plume

rythmique suspens du sinistre

s'ensevelir

aux écumes originelles

naguères d'où sursauta son délire jusqu'à une cime

flétrie

par la neutralité identique du gouffre

RIEN

de la mémorable crise
ou se fût
l'évènement

accompli en vue de tout résultat nul

humain

N'AURA EU LIEU
une élévation ordinaire verse l'absence

QUE LE LIEU

inférieur clapotis quelconque comme pour disperser l'acte vide
abruptement qui sinon
par son mensonge
eût fondé
la perdition

dans ces parages

du vague

en quoi toute réalité se dissout

EXCEPTÉ

    à l'altitude

        PEUT-ÊTRE

            aussi loin qu'un endroit

fusionne avec au delà

        hors l'intérêt
      quant à lui signalé
             en général
selon telle obliquité par telle déclivité
              de feux

    vers
      ce doit être
        le Septentrion aussi Nord

              UNE CONSTELLATION

      froide d'oubli et de désuétude
            pas tant
           qu'elle n'énumère
      sur quelque surface vacante et supérieure
          le heurt successif
              sidéralement
      d'un compte total en formation

veillant
    doutant
      roulant
        brillant et méditant

          avant de s'arrêter
       à quelque point dernier qui le sacre

      Toute Pensée émet un Coup de Dés

Six

"THERE, I'VE ADDED A BIT OF SHADOW"

Journalists aiming to entertain the readers of fin-de-siècle France turned to Mallarmé on topics from poetry to fashion trends, bicycles to house pets. In January 1897, *Le Figaro* sought the poet's views about haberdashery to commemorate the centenary of the stovepipe hat, which had been introduced to France just after the Revolution. "You frighten me to speak about this topic," he replied, "whoever wears such a thing cannot take it off. The world may end, but not the top hat, which probably always existed in some invisible state."[1] For some time after that, grateful hat manufacturers included in their advertising, "the world may end, but not silk hats."

Two years earlier, Mallarmé had been asked by a journalist, "What do you think of punctuation?" The poet, who must have already begun thinking about "One Toss of the Dice," offered, by his own account, a long and complicated disquisition on the "use or rejection of conventional signs . . . to indicate the distinction between prose and verse." Verse might dispense with punctuation by offering a pause to constrain the forward thrust of the voice. Prose, however, required punctuation. The confused interviewer begged Mallarmé for a single sentence to sum up his point of view. "He knows what he is doing, clever chap," the poet quipped. "Could such a thing be a sentence?" "Wait," Mallarmé called out to the departing journalist, one foot out the door, "for decency's sake, let me add at least a little obscurity."[2]

Something similar occurred three months later, after the funeral of Paul Verlaine, which brought together motley bohemians and the cream of Parisian literary life, on January 10, 1896. Mallarmé—one of the pallbearers, along with the poets François Coppée, Catulle Mendès, and Robert de Montesquiou—delivered a eulogy in the church of Saint-Étienne-du-Mont, just behind the Pantheon. To the journalist Alidor Delzant's request for a copy of his oration, Mallarmé replied that he had nothing in writing. Delzant proposed that he try to reconstitute it after the burial in Batignolles, while lunch was being prepared. And in his beautiful hand, round and majestic, decorated with a few knowing flourishes, Mallarmé wrote down twenty or so lines. "Then his face, Mephisto-like, contracted, a circumflex of a wrinkle knotted his brow. Furiously, he made a few corrections and additions." Handing Delzant the sheet of paper, he said, "There, I've added a bit of shadow."[3]

Mallarmé's search for shadow has contributed to his reputation as an intentionally difficult poet—not only in his poetry, but in his prose writings, correspondence, and everyday exchanges as well. The American expatriate man of letters Robert Sherard recounted that in 1891 he invited the poet to lunch with Oscar Wilde and the Greek-born Symbolist poet Jean Moréas. Mallarmé responded via *pneumatique*, one of the little blue letters that circulated as a form of rapid communication—with delivery guaranteed in a matter of hours—throughout Belle Époque Paris. Sherard was unable to make out from its contents whether his invitation had been accepted

or refused. "It was not until Mallarmé arrived at the *café* that I gathered that his involuted phrases had implied an acceptance."[4] The
critic Jules Renard famously quipped that Mallarmé's poetry was
untranslatable, even into French.[5]

The difficulty of Mallarmé's writing, his attack upon conventional
verse, can be seen first in his rejection of the ordinary poetic lines
that allow an easy distinction between poetry and prose and make
for poetry's musical effects. The scattering of the words of his masterwork shifts the traditional appeal of poetic sound, meter, rhythm,
and rhyme from the ear to the eye. "One Toss of the Dice" was not
intended to be read aloud, much less memorized. It was meant to be
seen and to be taken in as much as a feat of graphic design as of
aural effect.

In keeping with the intensely visual character of our own era,
which began with the invention of cinema, Mallarmé's epic stands
as the world's most deeply optical poem. In a lecture he delivered on
Mallarmé and Verlaine at the Théâtre du Vieux Colombier in 1913,
André Gide expressed regret at not having the original copy of
"One Toss of the Dice" from the magazine *Cosmopolis*, the only
extant edition at that time, to show his audience. If he had brought
it along, Gide maintained, he would not have read it aloud. Instead,
he would have held it up to show to the audience, since Mallarmé's
last work was more visible than readable: "the characters are so
majestic that, even the most nearsighted person might have read it
from the back of the room."[6] The poem as an eye chart would
resurface ironically in 1969, when the artist Marcel Broodthaers
published a purely graphic edition of "One Toss of the Dice," pre-
serving the layout of the type, but with its words replaced by thick
horizontal black bars.

A key element of Mallarmé's "attack on verse" lies in his breach
of the simplest rules of syntax. The poet referred to himself as a

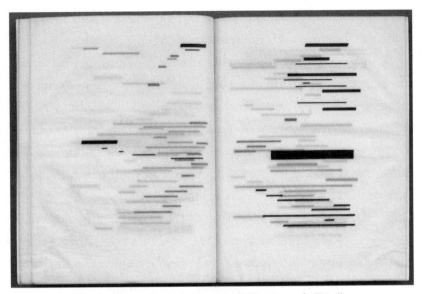

Marcel Broodthaers, folio from "Un Coup de Dés."
Broodthaers, Marcel (1924–1976) © ARS, NY. "Un coup de dés jamais n'abolira le
hasard" by Stéphane Mallarmé. 1969. 20 photolithographs. Purchased with funds
given by Howard B. Johnson in honor of Riva Castleman (178.1994.16).
The Museum of Modern Art Digital Image © The Museum of Modern Art/
Licensed by SCALA I Art Resource, NY.

"syntax man," making the connection between even the empty margins that surround every poem and the big blank spaces of "One Toss of the Dice," which interrupt the flow of language and meaning in some more shocking way. "If one accepts the invitation of the great white space left on purpose at the top of the page as if to separate from everything the already-read-elsewhere, if one comes to it with a new and virgin soul, one recognizes then that I am profoundly and scrupulously a syntax man [*syntaxier*], that my writing is devoid of obscurity, and my sentence is what it should be and be forever."[7]

What could such a wildly implausible claim mean? Surely the poet could not have expected his readers to find his writing—poetry or prose—to be easy. Nor could he have believed that his sentences, devoid of obscurity, would last forever. How is it possible to reconcile the difficult syntax of "One Toss of the Dice" with the poet's denial of obscurity—his boast of clarity?

Both English and French are "analytic languages." Unlike, say, Latin, in which the form of a word determines its role in a sentence, meaning in English and French is determined by word order. And although the arrangement of the words is generally more flexible in a poem than in prose, "One Toss of the Dice" pushes our expectations of syntactic sequence to an extreme beyond which the loose logic of the sentence threatens the logic of sense.

The basic syntax of "One Toss of the Dice" is difficult to decipher. The sudden interruption of the flow of a phrase, reversals of word order, abrupt interjections, and missing connections are a puzzle to even the most skillful grammarians. To diagram the relations between the poem's uncertain and shifting parts of speech would be impossible, even if we were, as below, to render a compressed, punctuated version in which the spatial gaps that the poet claimed to be the unique quality of his verse have been eliminated:

ONE TOSS OF THE DICE NEVER, EVEN WHEN THROWN IN THE MEASURELESS CIRCUMSTANCES FROM THE DEPTHS OF A SHIPWRECK, EVEN if the Abyss turned white, stalled, roiling beneath a desperately sloping incline of its own wing, in advance fallen back from the difficulty of trimming its sails, and stopping the gushing, preventing the surges deep in the very heart, the shadow buried in the deep by this alternative sail, almost the length of the wingspan of the great hull's gaping breadth, a vessel listing from side to side

THE MASTER, beyond old calculations, where skills are lost with age, risen, implying, once he grasped the helm, from this conflagration at his feet of the seamless horizon, that there is readied, moiling and merging, with the fist that would clasp it, as one threatens fate and the winds, a unique Number which cannot be any other Spirit, to heave it into the storm, to fold up division and pass proudly, hesitates by its arms a corpse separated from the secret it guards, rather than playing sides, like a cranky graybeard, on behalf of the waves: one invades the head, flows through the undulant beard, that shipwreck of the man himself without a ship, no matter where, vain

from ancient times not to open the hand clenched above the worthless head, legacy amidst disappearance, to someone ambiguous, the ulterior immemorial demon having, from dead lands, led the old man toward this final meeting with probability, this one, his boyish shade caressed and polished and restored and washed, made supple by the waves, and freed from the hard bones lost between the planks, born of a revel, the sea enticing the sire or the sire against the sea, an idle chance Betrothal, whose veil of illusion fluttered their obsession, like the phantom of a gesture will tremble, will collapse, madness, **WILL ABOLISH**

AS IF A simple insinuation in the silence, tangled in irony, or the mystery hurled, howled, in an oncoming eddy of hilarity and horror, hovers round the vortex without scattering or fleeing, and cradles its virgin symbol AS IF

a solitary wandering plume, save a glancing encounter with a toque of midnight that fixes it in velvet, crumpled by a dark guffaw, this rigid whiteness, ridiculous, in opposition to the sky, too much not to mark faintly anyone, bitter prince of the reef wears it like a heroic headpiece, irresistible, but limited by his trifling manly mind, in a thunderbolt

anxious expiatory and pubescent mute laughter that IF The lucid and lordly aigrette of vertigo on the invisible brow scintillates, then shadows, a delicate dark form, upright in its sea siren's sinuosity, time enough to slap with impatient terminal scurf, forked, a rock, false manor, all at once evaporated in mists, which imposed a limit on infinity

IT WAS THE NUMBER, born of the stars, IF IT EXISTED other than as agony's flickering hallucination; IF IT BEGAN AND ENDED, rising only to be denied and shut down when revealed at last by some profusion lavished in scarcity; IF IT HAD AMOUNTED to a totality, however meager; IF IT HAD ILLUMINATED, IT WOULD BE worse, neither more nor less, indifferent but as much, **CHANCE** *Falls the plume, rhythmic suspense of disaster, to be sunk in the first foam, whence once its delirium surged to a peak, withered by the identical sameness of the vortex*

NOTHING of the memorable crisis or the event might have been accomplished with no result in sight human WILL HAVE TAKEN PLACE, an ordinary swell pours out absence, BUT THE PLACE, some lapping below, as if to water down the empty act abruptly, which else by its lies would have justified extinction, in this region of waves where all reality dissolves

EXCEPT in the heights PERHAPS, as far as a place can fuse with the beyond, apart from the interest assigned to it in general, by such a slant and such a slope of fires, toward what must be the Septentrion or North A CONSTELLATION cold from neglect and disuse, not so much that it does not count, on some empty and superior surface, the successive shock from the stars of a final reckoning in the making, watching, doubting, rolling, blazing, and brooding before stopping at some last point that consecrates it

All Thought casts a Toss of the Dice

The syntax of "One Toss of the Dice" is as hard to decipher when regularly spaced and punctuated as it is as radical free verse. Even when smoothed out in the above translation of the poem into prose, the cavernous syntactic gap between "**ONE TOSS OF THE DICE NEVER**" at the beginning of the first stanza and "**WILL ABOLISH**" at the end of the third stanza needs to be closed. The verse demands that the reader make sense of numerous phrases that intervene between the main subject, the main verb, and its object. Mallarmé's epic poem requires keeping in mind the sentence, set off in capitals and 16-point type: "**ONE TOSS OF THE DICE NEVER . . . WILL ABOLISH . . . CHANCE**."

Although the title of the poem may be enigmatic, it is nonetheless a complete sentence that makes a certain amount of sense, and is easily retained in our mind. It is like a proverb, a sentence of wisdom with an epigrammatic ring. However, "NEVER" ("JAMAIS") and "WILL ABOLISH" ("N'ABOLIRA") are separated in Mallarmé's original by six pages of intervening text, and "WILL ABOLISH" and "CHANCE" ("LE HASARD") are separated by another eight pages. Though we know the shape and the meaning of the whole, we must wait, while reading, for the sequential unfolding through time of the words of the central sentence. The same is true for the sentence, all in capitals, but in 8-point type, spread over four pages: "NOTHING . . . WILL HAVE TAKEN PLACE . . . BUT THE PLACE . . . EXCEPT . . . PERHAPS . . . A CONSTELLATION" (pp. 184–87). The "NOTHING" and the "WILL HAVE TAKEN PLACE" are separated in the original French by sixteen words, the "WILL HAVE TAKEN PLACE" and the "BUT THE PLACE" by five words, the "BUT THE PLACE" and "EXCEPT" by thirty words, the "EXCEPT" and "PERHAPS" by two words, and the "PERHAPS" and "A CONSTELLATION" by thirty-two words.

Mallarmé's syntactic suspensions circle back and forth between one phrase and its interruptions, as if the reader were moving in time, while repeatedly returned to a fixed place in time—or, if it is not fixed, to a place that is moving syntactically at a different pace than the interruptions. At every moment of reading we hold in mindful suspense the main and subordinate clauses of a single sentence fractured by enclaves of intervening phrases and subphrases, exclamations and detached bits of syntactic information; the whole punctuated by the menace of dissolution in the "extinction / in this region / of waves / where all reality dissolves" (p. 185).

Like the fugue and counterfugue of certain musical compositions, the intervening subordinated phrases, subphrases, parentheses, and ellipses, which are themselves interrupted by smaller
segments and shards of meaning, are designed to interrupt the com-
prehension of the central sentence, whose words are strung like
pearls on a string. The Mallarméan sentence thus is plastic. Some
have compared its sinuosity to the organic arabesque designs of contemporary Art Nouveau, the style of "One Toss of the Dice" a poetic
style métro. It spreads out branches, disjunctive pseudopods, that take
us in one direction, then in another, before rejoining the original
line of language and thought.

Alongside wide gaps of meaning held in suspense, "One Toss of
the Dice" is packed with syntactic reversals and inversions of expected
word sequence. The normal syntax of the sentence *Un coup de dés
jamais n'abolira le hasard* is *Un coup de dés n'abolira jamais le hasard*; here, the
jamais ("never"), an adverb of time, comes before, instead of after, the
verb, as it almost never does in French, thus reversing time syntactically and chronologically. Elsewhere, possessive adjectives are placed
after the possessing noun, *aile la sienne* (p. 192); demonstratives, after
the modified noun, *naufrage cela* (p. 194); adjectives, before the noun,
which in French, with some exceptions, are normally placed after the
noun, *béante profondeur* (p. 193), *l'unique Nombre* (p. 194), *anciens calculs*
(p. 195), *l'inutile tête* (p. 196), *le vierge indice* (p. 199), *La lucide et seigneuriale
aigrette* (p. 202), *mémorable crise* (p. 206), *inférieur clapotis* (p. 207); adjectives, both before and after the noun, *durs os perdus* (p. 196), *impatientes
squames ultimes* (p. 202); adjectives, after the noun that ordinarily pre-
cede the noun, *point dernier* (p. 209); verbs are placed before the subject *Choit la plume* (p. 205); adverbs occur before, and not after, the
verb, JAMAIS . . . N'ABOLIRA in the title, but also in the phrases
très à l'intérieur résume (p. 193) and *ancestralement à n'ouvrir pas la main* (p.
196). In each case, the reversal of traditional word order, and of the
ordinary time of reading, loosens the unidirectional grip of chrono-

logical time, so that we are moving both back and forth along time's continuum.

Ellipses abound in "One Toss of the Dice": omitted negatives, *Soit que* instead of *ne Soit que* (p. 192), *sourdant que nié et clot quand apparu* (p. 205); omitted articles, *naufrage cela* (p. 194), *Fiançailles dont* (p. 196), *plume solitaire éperdue* (p. 200) *prince amer de l'écueil* (p. 201); omitted verbs, *l'homme sans nef n'importe où vaine* (p. 195) So separated are the words that modify each other—articles and nouns, adjectives and nouns, nouns and verbs, adverbs and verbs—that it is hard to tell whether something is missing, or whether the phrase should be structured in some other way. Mallarmé's poem resembles a great cosmic telegram whose terse syntactic leaps make sense along the lines of juxtaposition and not subordination. The overall impression is one of enormous compression.

Villiers de l'Isle-Adam had an uncanny perception of the condensed Mallarméan style in a dream that he recounted to the novelist and playwright Gustave Guiches. In his sleep, Villiers saw himself remove a packet of cigarette papers from his pocket. But, instead of the usual brand of Job, which recalled his biblical brother, he saw in miniature writing *The Collected Works of Stéphane Mallarmé*. Starting to read the papers, he saw that they followed one after the other, until he awoke, finally, to find *Afternoon of a Faun* lying open on his bed. "There is only one poet," concluded Villiers, "capable of capturing the infinite in such a small space!"[8]

Mallarmé's simultaneous syntax, which combines the impression of chronological linear time with that of being outside of time, does not build on acquired understandings of how literally to read the words on the page. Often, the beginning of a sentence yields little clue as to where it will end, so vivid and disorienting are the darts and dodges, the feints, flashes, and flickers of what France's "Prince of Poets" defined, in the context of Impressionist painting, as the "aspect of things, which perpetually lives but dies every moment,"[9] which flares into focus in the phrase "The lucid and lordly aigrette of vertigo on the invisible brow scintillates then shadows" (p. 180) or, in "agony's flickering hallucination . . . rising only to be denied and shut down" (p. 183).

The "syntax man" created in "One Toss of the Dice" a great simultaneous sentence that renders both the objective uniform passage of clock time and the vast stillness of eternity. He cinched such a sensation through a framing symmetry that is not unlike the first and last page of the ideal *Book*. "One Toss of the Dice" begins and ends with the phrase "*Un coup de dés*," which means that we find ourselves, having read the whole, at the place of beginning. In this, the modern poem reproduces the ring structure of ancient and medieval epics, a technique of oral poetry that allowed the singer to keep in mind the overall structure of plot while concentrating upon more local moments of narration.

Such containing symmetry is part of the modernist aesthetic. The last sentence of Joyce's *Finnegans Wake*, a sentence about circulation and recirculation, completes the first: "A way a lone a last a loved a long the / riverrun, past Eve and Adam's, from swerve of shore to bend of bay, brings us by a commodius vicus of recirculation back to Howth Castle and Environs." Likewise, Marcel Proust's three-thousand-page *Remembrance of Things Past* begins with "For a long time, I used to go to bed early" (*Longtemps, je me suis couché de bonne heure*) and ends with the word "Time" (*Temps*) and a meditation upon the relationship of chronological time to immeasurable recurrent time:

> If at least, time enough were allotted to me to accomplish my work, I would not fail to mark it with the seal of Time . . . , and I would therein describe men, if need be, as monsters occupying a place in Time infinitely more important than the restricted one reserved for them in space, a place, on the, con-

trary, prolonged immeasurably since, simultaneously touch-
ing widely separated years and the distant periods they have
lived through—between which so many days have ranged
themselves—they stand like giants immersed in Time.[10]

Like the effects of "One Toss of the Dice," the Proustian long
sentence, with its multiple subordinate clauses, both places us in
time and loses us in the reticulated twists of a thought process
according to which every moment is contained in every other
moment, and punctual linear time gives way to uninterrupted
presence.

The framing symmetry of the beginning and end of "One
Toss of the Dice," is reinforced by the central symmetry of the
poem's middle pages (pp. 176–77) with five two-page spreads on
either side, which begins and ends with the words "*AS IF.*" At its
two ends and in the middle, Mallarmé's masterpiece is built upon
a mirror image that both progresses, from beginning to middle
and from middle to end, through time, yet returns cyclically to
words that are identical, and thus gives the impression that time
has not moved at all. A similar principle operates at the level of
certain of the discernible pages, phrases, and sentences of the
poem. The words *mer* and *aïeul* are the mirror images of each
other—"the sea enticing the sire or the sire against the sea"
(p. 174). The phrase "RIEN . . . N'AURA EU LIEU . . . QUE LE
LIEU" ("NOTHING . . . WILL HAVE TAKEN PLACE . . . BUT
THE PLACE") (pp. 184–85) is a tautology that performs an unfolding of time and a resistance to time. Though the sentence progresses, with subject, verb and object or predicate nominative, it
fails to progress through time. The future perfect tense, the "WILL
HAVE TAKEN PLACE," a completed action in the future, renders perfectly time folding back upon itself.

Mallarmé's sentences recall the syntax of Latin when Latin suits

the desired effects of time simultaneity. He uses, for example, a participle, either present or past, in absolute apposition to a noun, as in
l'Abîme blanchi ("the abyss turned white") (p. 192), *la manoeuvre avec
l'âge oubliée* ("where skills are lost with age") (p. 195), *Une insinuation
simple au silence enroulée* ("A simple insinuation in the silence")
(pp. 198–99). The poet's noun and participle phrases derive from
the Latin ablative absolute, a form that designates an action having
been completed or a condition having been fulfilled as essential to
the action of the sentence's main verb. Such a structure is perfect
for the simultaneous syntax of "One Toss of the Dice," since, like
the future perfect tense, which designates in the present a completed action in the future, the ablative absolute designates a completed action in the past with consequences for the present. In both
cases, future and past bleed into the present in a great affirmation of
the fungibility of time—the timeliness of a toss of the dice and the
timelessness of chance.

Mallarmé's privileging of nouns and relative negligence of verbs
make for an environment of states of being disrupted only occasionally by punctual action. Verbs are the poor cousins of Mallarmé's
poetic universe. He often eliminated active verbs in successive revi-
sions of his poems. When the verb was retained, more often than
not it took the form of an infinitive or of a participle, either the present participle or gerund, a verb phrase that can be used as a noun
phrase, *couvrant, coupant* (both p. 193), *inférant* (p. 194) *veillant doutant
roulant brillant et méditant* (p. 209); or the past participle, *celui son ombre
puérile caressée et polie et rendue et lavée assouplie par la vague et soustraite aux
durs os perdus entre les ais né* ("this one his boyish shade caressed and
polished and restored and washed made supple by the waves and
freed from the hard bones lost between the planks") (p. 174); *le mys-
tère précipité hurlé* ("the mystery hurled howled") (p. 177). In the most
spectacular example of the dominance of nouns to be found elsewhere in the poet's *Oeuvre*, Mallarmé's preface to William Beckford's

Gothic novel *Vathek* contains a sentence of some fifty-five words with only one finite verb.

The simultaneous syntax of Mallarmé's masterwork contributed to more theoretical discussions of what time is and how it should be measured as part of the historical quest, between 1870 and 1920, to coordinate clocks in France and in the rest of the world.

The desire for universal time in France was in part a function of the railroads, and there is a case to be made that the sudden exclamations of "One Toss of the Dice," the discontinuous phrases and ellipses, reproduce the sensation of train travel, with its abrupt appearances and disappearances of close objects that pass by like little surprises in a rapidly moving visual field. Mallarmé was, as we have seen, a frequent traveler by train between Paris and Valvins.

Before 1888 there were at least three temporal systems in use in France. Every town had its own local or solar time tied to the moment when the sun passed through the meridian at that longitudinal location. Local inhabitants were also aware of Paris Time, or mean solar time along the meridian of the Paris Observatory. Finally, clocks in French railway stations displayed an offset time—in advance by five minutes—in the track area in order to discourage missed trains. The establishment of a single temporal measure by which cities and towns linked by trains might schedule arrivals and departures was essential to smooth operation along the rails. In January 1888, M. F. S. Carnot, the president of the Republic, announced the formation of a commission to study the question of a single civil time for the entire country, and on March 15, 1891, a law was passed making Parisian Time "the legal hour of France, Algeria, and Tunisia."

The great impetus to French unification of time came from Germany. In an address on the very day after the French passed their law, and just a month before his death, the formidable Prussian general Helmuth von Moltke, who had defeated Napoleon III at Sedan in 1870, reminded the members of the Reischtag of the importance of railroads for military maneuver and of the significance of a single time zone for the coordination of trains. On April 1, 1892, Germany adopted for all railway, postal, and telegraphic services Greenwich Time plus one hour, or Central European Time.

The question of time simultaneity was, of course, inseparable from that of universally recognized spatial meridians. No one disputed the meridian as a unit of global measure: the earth is divided longitudinally into 360 degrees, the sun rotates every 24 hours or 1440 minutes, and each degree represents 4 minutes of longitude. Nationalism erupted, however, in the matter of fixing a prime meridian to be used worldwide for navigational maps and charts, or for astronomical and scientific purposes. In the area of spatial measurement, the French assumed they would play a dominant role as they did in the treaty—written in French and signed by seventeen nations in Paris on May 20, 1875—establishing the meter as the international standard of length. A prototype, made of 90 percent platinum and 10 percent iridium alloy, was stored at the International Bureau of Weights and Measures at Sèvres, with thirty exact copies distributed worldwide.

In 1870, up to fourteen different prime meridians were still being used on European topographical maps, with three main contenders: that passing through Ferro, the most westerly of the Canary Islands, 20 degrees west of Paris; the Paris meridian, passing through the Paris Observatory; and the meridian passing through the Royal Observatory at Greenwich. At the International Geographic Congress held in Antwerp in 1871, Greenwich was adopted for sea charts, but land maps were still predicated upon local meridians.

The International Meridian Conference held in Washington, D.C., in the fall of 1884 established a universal day. Of the twenty-five nations in attendance, only France abstained from recognizing the English prime meridian. Unable to hold out any longer, however, a bill was introduced in the Chamber of Deputies in October 1896—that is, at the very time that Mallarmé wrestled with time simultaneity in "One Toss of the Dice"—to change France's prime meridian from the Paris Observatory to Greenwich. The bill was immediately amended to read, "The legal time in France and Algeria is the mean time of Paris, retarded by 9 minutes, 21 seconds," which corresponded exactly to the longitudinal difference between Paris and Greenwich. It was only on March 9, 1911, fourteen and a half years later, that the bill became law, and France reluctantly joined the world community in acknowledging both universal time and the prime meridian of the English national observatory.

Time signals were first transmitted from the Eiffel Tower on May 23, 1910, but on July 1, 1911, the signals shifted to reflect Greenwich Time. From Paris, the almost instantaneous transmission of wireless signals to eight relay stations worldwide solved the problem of time simultaneity and aided in the plotting of location as well. The Mallarmé of "One Toss of the Dice" would have been moved, though perhaps not surprised, believing as he did in the interconnection of all earthly things, to know that some of the earliest uses of telegraph signals dispatched worldwide involved shipwrecks: the rescue in 1909 of 1,600 passengers from the White Star Liner *Republic*, which collided with the S.S. *Florida* off the coast of Nantucket, and, on the night of April 14, 1912, the distress call and calculation of the exact location of the *Titanic*: "MGY (*Titanic*) CQD in 41.46 N. 40.14 W. Wants immediate assistance."

"One Toss of the Dice" participated, alongside cinema, in the worldwide quest for time simultaneity. Yet Mallarmé's epic poem also summoned ideas that were much older than the technological advances and poetic breaks of the last decade of the nineteenth century. The dream of animating individual things, still and detached, by making them part of a greater whole, reached all the way back to the thinking of such questions in the West. Mallarmé can be situated within the great Platonic articulation of the relation of the realm of matter and the senses, both of which are limited by time, to that of ideas, which are conceived to exist outside of time. His last poem sits alongside Neoplatonic, and even theological, understandings of the troubling link between language, which is time-bound, and the divine, which is imagined to be beyond earthly time.

"One Toss of the Dice" responds more powerfully than any poem I know to the age-old question that still presses powerfully upon modern philosophy: How is it that we can conceive of whole, universal, abstract things, yet we cannot capture their wholeness in language? Why is it that we cannot render—speak or write, or even think—their unified ideal nature through words?

The answer has to do in part with the relation of the visual to the verbal. "One Toss of the Dice" is a poem that is structured at the level not of the line of verse, nor even of the strophe, but of the page, extended in Mallarmé's ambitious final version to two pages. As a visual unit, we take in the page all at once, though we must read it through time. We can see many things, including many words, all at once, logically and simultaneously. We cannot, however, understand them without the successive orderings of one word placed after another in sequence. Given that we see and can conceive of many things at once, holding them in our mind, Mallarmé was obsessed by the question of how the simultaneity of what the eye sees or the mind imagines might be translated into patterns of thought, might manifest in figures of speech, might be communicated from speaker to listener, or, most important, might be captured in writing and communicated from the written or printed page to the reader—all of which requires that words be spoken, written, or read in time.

No one has gone further in thinking about the relation of the wholeness of what we can conceive to the fragmentary nature of what we can think, say, write, or read than Augustine of Hippo, who lived fifteen centuries before Mallarmé. The most profound of all the early Church Fathers, the main conduit of Plato, Christianized, to the West, and a man for whom words and the Word stood at the center of all understandings of personal, social, and religious experience, Augustine articulated the relation of the wholeness of ideas to the fragmentary nature of language in terms of God's Creation of the world on the model of human speech. "Just as when we speak of matter and form," Augustine wrote in *De Genesi ad litteram* (*The Literal Meaning of Genesis*), "we understand that they are simultaneously implicated in each other, but we cannot pronounce one and the other simultaneously. So it is that we need a brief space of time when we pronounce these two words, to pronounce one before the other, so it is too in the unfolding of a narrative, it is necessary to recount the creation of one before that of the other, even though God, as we have said, created both simultaneously."[11] Augustine was fascinated by the question of how God could have held the words of Creation in His mind long enough to arrive at the end of the sentence, which made sense of the whole, just as he wondered how this is possible in the sentences spoken by one human being to another. Every sentence, spoken, written, or read, each creation of meaning in words, participates—for both Augustine and Mallarmé—in the drama of the original creation of the world.

It is unlikely that the poet, living under the desperately secular regime of Third Republic France, as amid positivist faith in empirical science and emerging social sciences, ever read the writings of the fifth-century bishop of Hippo. Yet the two men engaged in a common thinking of the relation of words to the world that makes it seem that some questions are so deep and enduring that they appear naturally in the most disparate of places.

Mallarmé, like Augustine, equated human language with creation, or at least the ability to summon things with words. "I say: 'a flower!' then from that forgetfulness to which my voice consigns all floral form, something different from the usual calyces arises, something all music, essence, and softness: the flower which is absent from all bouquets."[12] Reading the poet's sentences, whether in verse or in prose, is a creative process, which mimes Augustine's account of God's Creation of the world. In "One Toss of the Dice" in particular, we are obliged to keep in mind words pronounced in time, substantial swaths of syntax, while other words interrupt to break the chain of meaning, or start other chains, all before returning to the originally interrupted phrase, which may seem never to end. All the while, we maintain some idea of the meaning of the whole.

Mallarmé sought in his epic poem to produce the sensation of an aboriginal speech act, the sentence that God spoke in creating the world. No less than Augustine, he attempted, in his reversals of word order, ellipses and omissions, interruptions of meaning, and wild syntactic jumps, to create a kind of artificial simultaneity resembling what Augustine attributed to "God's coeternally present Word." Mallarmé and Augustine aspired to an understanding that contains the whole of Creation, that exists before the material words that make vibrations in the air, that, when pronounced in time, created the physical world, the world of time, in time. "Nothing," wrote the bishop of Hippo, in a phrase whose syntactical complication prefigured that of Mallarmé, "could be created which, if before time, is not coeternal with the Creator, or if at the beginning of time or at some time, does not base the reason for its creation—if the term 'reason' is not used improperly—in the partaking of a life coeternal in the Word of God coeternal with the Father."[13]

If all this thinking about how language structures the poetic effects of "One Toss of the Dice" seems a little removed from the everyday and a little abstract, bear in mind that poetry in this regard is no different from any other language act, no different from the combinations of words we use all the time. Nothing, in fact, could be closer to our experience of how it feels to think, to speak, or to write about even the smallest things.

When we think, our thought gives the impression of a great full simultaneity in which all parts of the equation are present—what Augustine calls an "intuition" or "intellection."[14] However, as soon as we begin to put such thoughts into words, something is lost. The same is true when we read one word after the other in a sentence, and even more so when we write, writing being synonymous with the shadowy ink that obscures the blank neatness of white paper. The poet Georges Rodenbach reported having asked Mallarmé, at a café and in the presence of the art critic and novelist Edmond de Goncourt and the novelist Alphonse Daudet, if he did not "willingly withdraw into the shadows, in order to be alone with an elite, with himself, or his dream?" There was a long silence: Daudet tipped his monocle, Goncourt smirked, and "then, Mallarmé, with his smiling serenity, made one of those gestures (a little priest, a little dancer) with which he seemed each time to *enter* the conversation as one enters on the stage, and said: 'But doesn't the act of writing itself require putting black on white?' "[15]

Mallarmé aimed in "One Toss of the Dice" to recover in time the sensation of fullness that is outside of time, and which makes us feel spiritually alive, in essence, by putting black on white. "Let us have no more of those successive, incessant, back-and-forth motions of our eyes, traveling from one line to the next and beginning all over again," he wrote in his famous essay "The Book, a Spiritual Instrument." "Otherwise we will miss that ecstacy in which we become immortal for a brief hour, free of all reality, and raise our obsessions to the level of creation."[16]

"One Toss of the Dice" chronicles the shipwreck of speech and of writing: that in laying out our thoughts through time, they lose their wholeness, become fragmented, seem arbitrary, wrecked, partial. This is something that each of us experiences when we begin to write, or even to organize our thoughts before writing. The fullness of our imagining of things never enters language, to the extent that if we use a word, the thing itself is absent. The golden glow of our unarticulated ideas, a state of pure potential and boundless hope, in which the whole of things is vaguely perceptible along with the relation of parts, is punctured by the necessity of choosing one word instead of another, of eliminating some meanings in favor of others. Such wholeness is further shattered by the putting of one thought, one word, before another in the making of phrases, sentences, and paragraphs—what Mallarmé in the poem's preface termed the "prismatic subdivisions of the Idea." The making of small, sequential, meanings, compared to the seamless integrity of the imagination, feels like disaster.

"One Toss of the Dice" engages the thought process at large, the writing process at large, the relation of writing to thought and to intuition, and the relation of small, physical, particular events and things (the material world and the world of history) to universals and abstractions—to ideas that, if they are true or even axiomatic, are not conceived to exist in time or to be bound by time. The relation of individual happenings and things to universal ones is, to take up the terms of our poem, that of any single toss of the dice to the concept of chance itself, or, to adopt the first proposition of the poem, a single toss of the dice "THROWN IN THE MEASURE-LESS CIRCUMSTANCES" (p. 169). Our prediction about how any particular roll might come out, in light of the infinity of all possible rolls, is a flawed calculation, but something nonetheless accessible to the imagination or the mind. Chance may set the background of each toss of the dice, but it has no purchase upon its result; nor does any particular roll change the nature of chance, our ideas about chance, or our chances in relation to the next roll. Each new toss of the dice is a wholly new beginning, in which the odds of any specific outcome are identical to every other toss—past, present, or future.

The incommensurability of individual material things to abstract ideas has haunted the West in one form or another, from Plato's distinction between the soul and the material world accessible to the senses, to the early Church Fathers' distinction between God and the earthly realm, to Descartes's mind-body split, to Hegel's universal and particular, the infinitude that moves finite things, Spirit and Nature. There is some indication that Mallarmé, at the behest of Villiers de l'Isle-Adam, read Hegel, whose thought via translation entered France, alongside of the music of Wagner, beginning in the 1860s.

The dice image itself is one of metaphysical gambling with a theological ring. Against the abstract background of chance, any individual toss of the dice poses the question, at the core of philosophy since the sixth-century B.C.E. philosopher Heraclitus, of the relationship of what is timeless to that which is in time, of being to becoming, and of ideal abstraction to historical event. For the ancients, the question of how an individual moment in time relates to the series of all such moments was subsumed in the paradoxes of another pre-Socratic philosopher, Zeno of Elea, who in the fifth century B.C.E. articulated the conundrum of the race between Achilles and the tortoise, which we know from Aristotle: "In a race, the quickest runner can never overtake the slowest, since the pursuer must first reach the point whence the pursued started, so that the slower must always hold a lead." Or, in the paradox of an arrow moving along a trajectory in space: "If everything when it occupies an equal space is at rest, and if that which is in locomotion is always occupying such a space at any moment, the flying arrow is therefore motionless."[17] Aristotle took up the paradoxes in his assertion of the reality of individual things in distinction to Plato's insistence upon the illusory nature of all sublunar reality, the knowledge of which enters the mind through the senses. For Plato, individual things were merely the degraded images of Ideas, which alone are real and true.

The question of the reality of individual things versus universals ran like a rich vein through the Middle Ages, tipping from Platonic belief in the reality of Ideas to a recognition of particular things as part of a new interest in empirical observation and science at the time of the Renaissance of the twelfth and thirteenth centuries. As part of the Renaissance of the sixteenth and seventeenth centuries, the English philosopher Francis Bacon would reject the "intellectual sciences" and philosophy, which, he maintained, lead to disputations rather than knowledge. He favored an inductive scientific method based upon the close scrutiny of particular natural events. For Bacon, the senses may deceive, but "they also supply the means of discovering their own errors."

Leo Tolstoy recovered Zeno's paradox in his discussion of the causality of historical events in *War and Peace*. Is it great men and the spirit of the times or the swarm of unknown individuals whose wills coalesce into the collective feelings that make for social movement? Given the infinite divisibility of the instants that make up the continuum of time, how is it possible, Tolstoy asked, to know when any particular event begins or ends?

Interest in Zeno's paradox, which lies at the philosophical core of "One Toss of the Dice," quickened among mathematicians around the time of the poem's composition. The German mathematician Richard Dedekind, looking at rational and irrational numbers, concluded that there are no discontinuities along the number/line continuum. The mathematician Georg Cantor, considered to be the father of set theory, distinguished between real numbers, which are not countable, and natural numbers, which are countable, leading to what were known at the end of the century as set-theory paradoxes.

In 1897, the very year "One Toss of the Dice" appeared, the Italian mathematician Cesare Burali-Forti articulated one such conundrum that resembles the core phrase of Mallarmé's poem: "the ordinal number of the sets of all ordinal numbers must be an ordinal." Bertrand Russell would pick up the contradiction from Burali-Forti in his 1903 *The Principles of Mathematics*. Contemporaneous mathematicians and philosophers who looked at the irrational numbers between whole numbers asked into how many parts a line might be divided, how many numbers lie between zero and one.

The most important philosopher of fin-de-siècle France, Henri Bergson, the son of a Jewish pianist from a prominent Polish family, married a cousin of Marcel Proust, who served as best man at his wedding. Both the philosopher and the novelist placed the role of human memory at the core of their thinking of the world, and both were obsessed by the relationship of individual moments in time to time as a continuum. Bergson took up the relation of individual things—points in space and instants in time—to the collective experiences that subsume them, encompass them, make them disappear, and transform them into the sensation of something more whole and higher than the sum of individual parts. In *Matter and Memory*, published in 1896, the philosopher posited consciousness itself as "a threading on the continuous string of memory of an uninterrupted series of instantaneous visions." He was fascinated by the ways we transform individual experiences, which are at first conscious and particular, into the unconscious habits of living, the flow of life itself, what he termed "duration" (*la durée*).

Mallarmé aimed in "One Toss of the Dice" to resolve the contradiction between temporal atomism and temporal continuity by writing a sentence that reproduced the sensation of being both in and outside of time. In Bergson's terms, the poet collapsed discrete temporal moments into seamless duration. What may appear as the poet's obscurity is, in reality, an attempt to reproduce the world as an idea, whole and abstract, alongside the things, partial and concrete, that might fill that world—a creation that would be both outside of language and time and yet still part of the time-bound fragmentary orderings that language brings. The reader is obliged to make sense of the disorderings, which is divinely challenging, but which simulates the power of all creations—God's Creation of the world via the Word alongside the poet's summoning of a flower with words. It is not that Mallarmé introduced shadow for shadow's sake or was difficult for the sake of difficulty. It is that he, like Augustine, and like all of us, wanted it all—to be and to know, to feel and to be conscious of feeling, to be ourselves and to see ourselves as others see us, to be outside of time and in it, to be both dead and alive.

Seven

THE DICE ARE TOSSED

In the autumn of 1896, Stéphane Mallarmé received an invitation from *Cosmopolis*, a cultural magazine with headquarters in London and local offices in Berlin, Paris, and Saint Petersburg to publish the poem or article of his choice. Whether "One Toss of the Dice" was the first draft, or a first chapter, or even a finished version of *The Book*, it had found a worthy venue, which was important, given the poem's unusual format and syntactic provocation. The poet would not face a repeat of the humiliating rejection that had accompanied his submission of *Afternoon of a Faun* to the timidity or resentment of editors and other writers.

The good fortune of such an open-ended invitation deepened when Mallarmé was honored by one of the most lavish, indeed, still remembered, banquets of those "banquet years," as Roger Shattuck came to call the period between 1885 and World War I. Younger poets, who acknowledged Mallarmé as their leader, organized not a twelve-, but a fifteen-course dinner in his honor on February 2, 1897. The poet, a gourmand who appreciated exquisite food and wine as well as fine furniture and *bibelots*, consumed with pleasure the potage valois, fillets of sole à la vénitienne, roasted chickens, pheasants surrounded by partridges, steak tenderloin in Madeira sauce, cheeses and fruits, pralines and ice cream, washed down by Mâcon, Chablis, Côte Saint Jacques, Champagne, coffee, and liqueurs. The venue was the elegant Au Père Lathuille restaurant on Paris's avenue de Clichy, situated just beyond the city line, in what is now Paris's seventeenth arrondissement, in order to escape the city tax on wine. Nearly a century before, the owner of Au Père Lathuille had distributed the contents of his cellar to the troops of the First Empire. He urged them to drink his wine so that it would not fall into the hands of invading Russian, Austrian, and Prussian troops, whose capture of Paris in March 1814 led to Napoleon I's downfall and exile. In 1879, Édouard Manet rendered the famous restaurant's luxurious soft light and pastel colors, delights of table and talk, lush plants and flowers in his painting *Au Père Lathuille*. Mallarmé, famous for delivering eloquent toasts to others at some of the greatest banquets of France's Belle Époque, had been feted at a good address. As exacting as he was in all things sensual and esthetic, he pronounced the evening "unique and perfect."

In an exchange of letters that preceded the appearance of "One Toss of the Dice" in the spring of 1897, André Lichtenberger, the Paris editor of *Cosmopolis*, informed Mallarmé that "the originality of the form of your poem provoked some objections from our English publisher," who is afraid of offending "our readership, which is a little conservative when it comes to artistic matters." In his response of March 4, 1897, the poet reminded Lichtenberger that he had broken no rules; and, besides, "a journal neither informs nor approves the work which it publishes."[1] In the end, the editors persuaded Mallarmé to compose a statement that would address the unconventional appearance of "One Toss of the Dice." The poet's initial reluctance to frame his masterwork with explanation can still be seen in the preface to the *Cosmopolis* edition, which begins, "I would prefer that this Note not be read or, if skimmed, that it be forgotten" (p. 163).

The editors of *Cosmopolis*, hoping not to compromise the circulation of their magazine, restrained Mallarmé's typographic ambitions to only ten pages, while his own design had called for twenty, plus a title page. "*Cosmopolis* was brave and delightful," he wrote to André Gide, "but I could only offer them half of what I had intended, it was already such a risk for them!"[2] The initial page was significant. There, we learn that Mallarmé baptized his work a "poem"; and there, the spinal sentence, the poem's title, "Un Coup de dés jamais n'abolira le hasard," would be assembled in full. The poet thought of his poem as a complete book that should stand alone between two covers, which drew the accusation, as Mallarmé reported to Gide, that he was trying to make money by selling blank space.

By the time "One Toss of the Dice" appeared in *Cosmopolis*, Mallarmé had already planned in detail the layout of a more elaborate version, the undertaking of the art dealer Ambroise Vollard, with illustrations by Odilon Redon. Two hundred copies of the luxury edition were to be sold for the considerable sum of fifty francs. The poet was anxious that Redon's drawings not be integrated into the visual layout of his words. They were to appear on separate pages, set against a shaded background in order not to rival "One Toss of the Dice" as a work of graphic design in its own right.[3] Mallarmé was meticulous in his correction of the proofs for the expanded edition. Using graph paper to plot the layout across the two-page spreads, he issued written orders about the spacing of lines, the alignment of words, measurement of left, right, and center margins, type size and weight, and even warnings that "bad" letters—that is, those made from worn type, which might not make a full impression—be checked. The poet envisaged a full-folio presentation of this volume, 27 × 36 centimeters, but, in its final corrected version, it never saw the light of day.

For Stéphane Mallarmé, the dice were tossed on May 4, 1897, when "One Toss of the Dice Never Will Abolish Chance" became available to the conservative readers of *Cosmopolis*. As chance would have it, however, the literary event was eclipsed by news of a catastrophic fire that broke out the very same day at a gala to aid the indigent children of Paris. At three o'clock in the afternoon, just after the papal nuncio had bestowed his benediction upon the orphans and their clerical chaperones at the Bazar de la Charité, a movie projector, run not by electricity but by a mixture of ether and oxygen, burst into flame. A makeshift tent, the kind still used for charity benefits, on the rue Jean-Goujon in Paris's chic eighth arrondissement, was quickly consumed. In the panic to escape through a single exit, 126 members of France's social elite, mostly women, lost their lives. Some of the dead were burned so badly that they could be identified only by their teeth, in what was one of the earliest instances of forensic dentistry.

The disaster at the Bazar de la Charité, so prominent because the very rich were involved, was seen by some as divine punishment. The movie projector, invented by the Lumière brothers only two years before, and the elegant but highly flammable clothes of the victims figured as instruments of Satan. The charitable ladies, the poet François Coppée said, had come together to do good. "Everyone, of course, accuses God."[4] Everyone, that is, except God's representatives on earth. A solemn mass was held the following Saturday in the Cathedral of Notre-Dame. At ten o'clock in the morning, the Republican Guard cleared the parvis in front of the west façade, with its elaborate sculptural program of birth and resurrection. Onlookers could be seen sitting on the branches of nearby trees and leaning out of the windows of the Hôtel-Dieu on the northern side of the square. The procession of mourners, government officials, and journalists filed past a mound of wreaths laid at the foot of the equestrian statue of Charlemagne and into the central door of the church. There, in the presence of President Félix Faure, the Père Ollivier blamed the infernal human invention of moving pictures for the tragedy of the Bazar de la Charité: "Without doubt, O sovereign Master of men and societies . . . , You have turned against him the conquests of science . . . ; and, the fire that he pretends to have wrested from Your hands like Prometheus of old, you have made the instrument of your vengeance. That which gave the illusion of life produced the horrible reality of death."[5]

Certain of the women who perished in the Bazar de la Charité fire showed remarkable bravery. The Duchesse d'Alençon, sister of Empress Elisabeth of Austria, refused the aid of a worker who had offered to help her escape. "Because of my title I had to be the first to enter here. I shall be the last to go out," she is reported to have said.[6] She was later identified only by her dental records and the ring on her finger: "28 septembre 1888, Ferdinand d'Orléans à Sophie de Bavière." Many of the aristocratic men, as in the shipwreck of the *Titanic* some fifteen years later, acted very badly, clawing their way to safety. The Catholic decadent writer Léon Bloy reported that one man cried, "It's everyone for himself," and it was widely rumored that men had used their canes, an aristocratic accessory, to fight their way out of the panicked crowd. *Le Journal* reported that "among the men, two were admirable, as many as ten did their duty. But the rest bolted, and not only saved no one, but cleared a path through feminine flesh with kicks of the feet and fist, and thrusts of the cane."[7]

Mallarmé's friend and sometime *Mardist* Count Robert de Montesquiou, known visually by the painting by Giovanni Boldini, which depicts him gazing lovingly at his cane, may have been there. He apparently showed up the next day and, pretending to look for friends, used his cane to lift the sheets covering the bodies laid out on the floor of the temporary morgue set up in the Palace of Industry. One of the policemen on duty is reported to have scolded, "One does not touch the dead with the end of a cane, Mr. Clubman! If it disgusts you, I can do the unveiling!" News of Montesquiou's extreme bad taste reached the poet and novelist Jean Lorrain. From there it spread to fellow *Mardist* Henri de Régnier, whose sister-in-law, the daughter of poet José-Maria de Heredia, and mother-in-law, were injured trying to escape. Régnier suggested that at the upcoming party of the Baronne Alphonse de Rothschild, Montesquiou might do well to leave his cane at home and carry a muff. The day after the reception, the count "left his cards" at Régnier's home, challenging him to a duel.[8] Régnier, who confessed to an "almost complete ignorance" of swordsmanship, took several lessons. The duel took place in a remote area of the Park of Neuilly, and ended when Régnier managed to inflict a slight thumb wound upon Montesquiou, who went on to become one of the models for the dissolute Baron de Charlus in Marcel Proust's *Remembrance of Things Past*.

Despite his closeness to the Mallarmé family during the illness of eight-year-old Anatole in the summer of 1879, Montesquiou had broken temporarily with his master because of what he felt to be an indiscretion on Mallarmé's part. In 1882, the consummate dandy introduced Mallarmé to his fantastic apartment on the quai d'Orsay late one evening. Two years later, the portrait of the overripe aesthete Des Esseintes surfaced in Joris-Karl Huysmans's novel *Against the Grain*. Montesquiou became convinced that the poet had shared with Huysmans such details of his nightcap in the "Cave of Ali-Baba" as the sanctus bell used as a doorbell, the gold painted tortoise, and the rooms decorated as a monastery cell or as the cabin of a yacht. This did not prevent Montesquiou, however, from declaring "One Toss of the Dice" to be "the last word of all human thought."

On the day of the fire at the gala of the Bazar de la Charité, Mallarmé was in Paris, having returned from a brief stay in Valvins. He was aware of the event, since he wrote to José-Maria de Heredia to wish his wife and daughter a speedy recovery, as well as to the society painter Jean-François Raffaëlli, whose own wife and daughter were injured in the crush. By May 8, the poet was back in Valvins to prepare the summer house for the arrival of Marie and Geneviève, as he did each summer.

For weeks after the fire, French newspapers spoke of little else. Their failure to take notice of Mallarmé's "attack on verse" seemed an unfortunate, but relatively minor consequence of a major national tragedy. Yet, how could the poet, having published on the very same day an epic poem about disaster and chance, not have wondered if its appearance and the explosion of a movie projector in Paris's eighth arrondissement were mere coincidence or part of a larger and more meaningful pattern of events? The question lies at the heart of "One Toss of the Dice."

Fellow poets with whom Mallarmé had shared his epic poem were his best audience. André Gide, who was vacationing in Florence at the time, wrote to his mentor to praise the poem's "literary boldness . . . like a strangely jutting high promontory, beyond which there is nothing but night—or the sea and the sky full of dawn."[9] Yet, for Mallarmé, the version Gide had read was not bold enough. He expressed appreciation that the editors of *Cosmopolis* had taken the risk of publishing such an unusual work. The poet was dissatisfied, however, with the layout, and promised to send Gide the first suitable proof of his revision, which was already in the process of being published in the Vollard edition by the well-established printer Firmin Didot.

This second edition of "One Toss of the Dice," Mallarmé assured Gide, would feature a proper layout. Lines of text crowded together on a single page of *Cosmopolis* would be spread across two pages, the separation rendering visually, and not just semantically,

the meaning of the words. The phrase "by its arm a corpse . . . separated from the secret it guards" (*cadavre par le bras . . . écarté du secret
qu'il détient*) (pp. 194–95), which occupied a single folio of the poem's
first printing, would, in the full edition, be physically laid across
two folio pages, the word *écarté* ("spread") designating the very process of thrusting apart. The same would be true of the phrase "with
impatient terminal scurf . . . forked" (*par d'impatientes squames ultimes
. . . bifurquées*) (pp. 202–3), the "forked" pointing to the words, on
one page in *Cosmopolis*, situated along the fold of the book upon two
separate pages in Mallarmé's design for the full edition. Something
similar occurs on pages 198 and 199 where the phrase *voltige . . .
autour du gouffre* ("hovers . . . round the vortex") literally crosses the
gutter or depressed fold—a vortex or abyss (*gouffre*)—that lies
between the open pages of the printed book.

More startling, Gide would see in the full twenty-page version of
"One Toss of the Dice," when Mallarmé describes a boat about to
sink amid the scattered debris of a shipwreck, that the typographical
layout, the actual words, displayed across two pages, would dip
across their full breadth and depth from left to right. The words will
go down with the boat. "The vessel lists," he promises, "from the
top of one page to the bottom of the other."[10]

In his response to Gide, Mallarmé referred to pages 192 and
193, one of those sheets in which the visual layout of the words
on the page coincides with their syntactic outlay and their meaning. The essential images, which move in a descending arc, gain-
ing typographic mass across the double-page spread, involve a
feathered wing descending through the whitened, spread-out,
roiling abyss toward the sail of a rocking and listing boat, which
eventually rights itself. The first word on this folio page is only
the eighteenth word of the French poem, and plunges us full gale
force into the attempt to make the appearance of the poem coincide with its meaning.

EVEN

    if

            the Abyss

      turned white

        stalled

          roiling

                beneath a desperately

                  sloping incline

                      of its own

                          wing

                              in

The top half of the folio page in the original French displays just fifteen words disposed in eleven lines, eight of which hold only a single word, and four of which contain only a single syllable. While the layout of the page does not wholly stop the process of reading, it certainly slows it down in the very place that the words themselves—"stalled roiling"—designate a halt to the forward motion of the boat. The layout of English page 170 is sparse, the syntax halting, and the image evoked, along with the meaning of the words themselves, summon a pale, roiling, halted abyss.

The descending type that speaks of sinking in the sea on pages 170 and 171 leaves us gasping for air, as if we were really going under. And though we lurch and almost sink on the top left portion of the double page, on the lower right third we settle, as the sinking ship has righted itself, and we are saved from drowning. The form of the sentence made from "the Abyss . . . beneath a desperately sloping incline of its own wing" appears to descend, while "in advance fallen back from the difficulty" mirrors the sudden updraft of wind in a sail, or the swoop of a winged bird. The listing ship rights itself in a series of lines that become increasingly symmetrically poised on top of one another, as the disposal of words on the page coincides with their meaning—a hull which has regained its balance in a series of centrally justified lines on page 171.

advance fallen back from the difficulty of trimming its sails

and stopping the gushing

preventing the surges

deep in the very heart

the shadow buried in the deep by this alternative sail

almost the length

of the wingspan

of the great hull's gaping breadth

a vessel

listing from side to side

Mallarmé's use of space and design to render meaning was an early version of Marshall McLuhan's famous dictum "the medium is the message." It anticipated a world in which software programs for lay-out and display on screens and in print have endowed us all with the potential, if not to write visual poetry, at least to organize our thoughts along the lines of a PowerPoint presentation, with different sizes and forms of type, bullet points and subpoints, decorative and plain backgrounds, image and text boxes, SmartArt, headers and footers, inserts and fades, all of which are designed to project the shape of our thoughts upon a screen. Such "talking points" are merely technical versions of the kind of graphic art that began with "One Toss of the Dice."

In an even more stunning coincidence of typographical layout with meaning, Mallarmé promised that on the final page of the authorized version of "One Toss of the Dice," Gide would "see that the constellation will take the shape, according to precise laws and as much as it is possible in a printed text, fatally, of a constellation."[11]

The layout of the type on pages 186–87 resembles a toss of the dice, a descending arc of a line, at the end of which the scatter of words reproduces the dispersion of dice, the whole held up by the concluding phrase "All Thought casts a Toss of the Dice." More important, the shape of the tossed dice duplicates the figure of the Big Dipper, part of the constellation Ursa Major, by which the northern pole star, Polaris, might be located. The poem thus appears literally as a constellation, the projection of points in space—in the instance, words scattered on the page—upon an imagined plane.

Mallarmé knew the Ursa Major, a pattern of stars in the northern celestial hemisphere, originally recognized by Ptolemy in the second century C.E., and one of eighty-eight constellations still acknowledged today. His readers, much closer to the world of celestial navigation than we are in a world of global positioning systems, would have recognized in the Big Dipper or the Plough an asterism of seven bright stars within the Ursa Major. The constellation's brightest star, Polaris, was a way of determining true north for the purpose of earthly navigation.

Mallarmé and his contemporaries were also more familiar with the mythological significance of the Ursa Major. At the age of twenty-one, in the first version of what would become his prose poem "Autumn Complaint" ("Plainte d'automne"), a lament for his dead sister, the poet singled out the constellation as the place of dead souls and the source of his own solitude: "Since Maria left me on her journey to another star—oh, which one? Orion, Sirius, the Great Bear?—I have always cherished solitude."[12] In *The Ancient Gods*, his translation and adaptation of William Cox's *Manual of*

Mythology, written some seventeen years after "Autumn Complaint," Mallarmé discussed the seven great sages of Hindu astronomy, the Rishis, in terms of the blended roots in Sanskrit of the words for "wise ones" and "shining ones," which were converted in Greek to "'*arctoi*' or 'bear,' belonging also to this root."[13]

Mallarmé's shaping of his verse to resemble the Big Dipper, his final orientation in the direction of the northern pole star at the end of "One Toss of the Dice," goes further than mere consolation to set the world aright, to heal the threat of shipwreck in a world that many modern writers and thinkers declared to be without meaning. Like the Ursa Major, which points reliably north, the end of "One Toss of the Dice" situates the reader, fixes us in the universe, and makes the connection between poetic and geographic orientation. Mallarmé thus affirmed poetry's power to identify familiar patterns amid the seeming chaos of looking into unordered space.

"One Toss of the Dice" is filled with nodal points of threat and rescue. The words in places disorient and tug us under. We lose our bearing—only to be delivered at other points by the coincidence of the material layout of words on the page with their meaning. Words may seem unlimited, arbitrary, chaotic. Properly disposed, they make for the discernment of constellations of meaning just as the stars, scattered throughout the sky, coalesce in discernible patterns oriented around the Septentrion or North Star.

The ending of "One Toss of the Dice" is determining and significant for our understanding of Mallarmé's poetry and of modernity writ large. It answers the question of whether life, in the absence of some guiding presence outside of man—the role that God used to play—might have meaning. The righting of the listing boat along with the whirling universe pointed, finally, north puts Mallarmé on the side not of waffling, degenerate, impotent indeterminacy, but of the great Platonic connection of all things, man the microcosm of

the wider world. "Yes!" Mallarmé exclaimed, in his essay "Literature. Doctrine," "With its twenty-four signs, this Literature exactly
called Letters, along with multiple couplings in the form of phrases,
then verse, a system disposed as a spiritual zodiac, implies its own
doctrine, abstract, esoteric like some theology."[14]

Paul Valéry visited Mallarmé at his summer home just two weeks
after the appearance of "One Toss of the Dice." He reported in a
letter to André Gide that their mentor called him over to his desk,
opened a drawer, pulled out a copy of "One Toss of the Dice," then
recited it to him privately "in a low voice, unmodulated, without the
least 'affect,' as if he were reading it to himself."[15] Valéry also
described the walk from the house to the train station. The two
poets experienced what was apparently an incredibly starry night in
Valvins: "The sky moreover was full of extraordinary tosses of the
dice." Mallarmé reported to his wife and daughter on the very same
evening that it was "a night of stars without equal."[16] If chance had
spoiled the publication of "One Toss of the Dice," the poet must
have wondered if the dice in the stars had not arrayed themselves in
constellations in imitation of his masterwork. Valéry later remarked
that Mallarmé "tried to raise a page to the power of the starry sky!"[17]

One could find no better example of signs reproducing the thing
signified than Mallarmé's writing a poem whose imagery summons
writing itself. The sail of "One Toss of the Dice" combines with falling feathers—quills—to reproduce the very motion of putting pen
to paper. The poet described writing as an "oar stroke," and the sail
as a "white page."[18] Henri de Régnier recalled that Mallarmé the
sailor took pleasure in cruises on the league of the Seine between
Samois and Valvins, at the mercy of the moving sail, rectangular and
white, which, he said, with a smile and a finger pointing in that
direction, reminded him of "the white page on which one writes."[19]

Mallarmé sailing on the Seine.
Bibliothèque littéraire Jacques Doucet, Paris, ms MNR 1864.

De Régnier also reported that at the Tuesday meeting of March 27, 1894, Mallarmé announced that he was going to publish something on sails. "When I am dreaming on the river, stretched out on my boat, it is really the white page on which one writes," the poet said, according to Régnier. It contains all of philosophy. It implies the identity of opposites, because one tips it to the left to go right, and also the other way around."[20]

Two feathers and one feathered wing that appear out of nowhere in "One Toss of the Dice" fall through the air, as Mallarmé duplicates the sensation of thought coming into being from nowhere, and of the feather-pen descending to transcribe thought to paper. In correcting the proofs of "One Toss of the Dice" as part of the preparation of the enhanced version in the months after the *Cosmopolis* edition had appeared, the poet picked up his own pen and crossed out the ordinary printed "f," substituting a handwritten flowing "f," more like the florin "*f,*" used as a symbol for the coin, in order to give it the appearance of a feather.

A wing appears in "One Toss of the Dice" as a hesitating feather, tossed in the wind. It descends from the white abyss in the direction of the sail of a rocking and listing boat. At the bottom of page 170, the feathers take shape "beneath a desperately / sloping incline / of its own / wing." On page 171, "this alternative sail" comes to rest, "almost the length / of the wingspan / of the great hull's gaping breadth." The disposition of type on the two folios reproduces the visual effects of a falling feather, which sways gracefully in the air from side to side, from "EVEN" to "Abyss," left to right; then, in starts and stops, from "turned white" to "of its own," right to left; then, from "of its own" to "in," right to left, again. The shape of the whole can be taken for a large open wing encompassing all the words—feathers on the wing—between "EVEN" and "in."

The second dropping of the feather/plume/pen in "One Toss of the Dice" renders the sensation of what it feels like when the ideal wholeness of an idea is broken into bits of language—words—arrayed on the page, one after the other.

Falls

     the plume

          rhythmic suspense of disaster

                    to be sunk

               in the first foam

     whence once its delirium surged to a peak

            withered

        by the identical sameness of the vortex (p. 183)

Whereas the first feather is lost in "*rigid whiteness / ridiculous / in opposition to the sky,*" the second sinks into an eddy of the sea. It is as if, in not making a mark, it avoids disaster, remains pure potential, coalesces into *"the identical sameness of the vortex"* without ever assuming a particular material shape. The pen's written depiction of the failure of the plume to make its mark is, of course, a contradiction, but "One Toss of the Dice" is built upon a world of alternative logics, which seek both to respect and infringe logical laws as we read.

The impossible thing that Mallarmé wishes to come momentarily true is just the opposite of the obscurity of which he is sometimes accused. He brought about a literal coincidence of signs with the thing signified, of the words of his poem with the images that the words evoke. The impulse was pervasive. Édouard Dujardin, editor of the *Revue indépendente*, reported that in editing one of Mallarmé's articles, he reminded the poet of the grammatical impossibility of placing an exclamation point in the middle of a sentence. To which Mallarmé replied with a couplet, now famous among his occasional pieces: *"Ce point, Dujardin, on le met / Afin d'imiter un plumet"* ("This point, Dujardin, you will resume it / In order to imitate a plumet").[21] We have seen that the falling plumes of "One Toss of the Dice" represent the process of writing, the pen lowered to paper. The warning to Dujardin goes even further in aligning the cast of the grammatical sign with its meaning, the shape of the exclamation point with that of a feather.

In the copy of "One Toss of the Dice" sent to his friend the *Mardist* Camille Mauclair, Mallarmé expressed the possibility of an unmediated relation between language and the world at the level of the sentence or larger linguistic unit. "I believe that every phrase or thought, if it has a rhythm, should model it on the object that it depicts and reproduce, cast all naked, immediately, as sprung in the mind, a little of the disposition of this object in every way. Literature shows this; no other reason to write on paper."[22]

The goal of uniting the appearance of words and their meaning has a long history in the West, beginning with Plato's dialogue *Crat-*

ylus, which turns around the question of whether words are divinely imposed and maintain some necessary relationship with their referent or are merely the result of social convention, and are therefore unreliable as vehicles of proof or truth. Saint Augustine picked up the Platonic thread in late antiquity. "Everyone seeks," he affirmed, "a certain resemblance in his ways of signifying such that signs themselves reproduce to the extent possible, the thing signified."[23] The harmony of words and things was, for the early Church Father, the equivalent of a sacrament, the melding of symbols—wine and wafer—with the blood and body of Christ, the eucharistic presence of Christ's body in the words of the mass. In the seventh century, the Spanish bishop Isidore of Seville transformed the search for etymologies, the "causes of the original imposition" of names upon things based upon the resemblance of letters and the objects to which they refer, into the basis of all natural and moral philosophy.

Ancient and medieval ideas about the etymological relationship of language and meaning resurfaced in the nineteenth century with the birth of the science of comparative philology in Germany among the Romantics and its implantation in France after the Franco-Prussian War. At the end of the eighteenth century, the naturalist Georges Cuvier had advanced the theory that one could recognize the whole of an organism by only a part of the skeleton. Linguists of the period focused upon the bits of surviving linguistic material that allow us, according to phonetic laws originally formulated by the fairy-tale writer Jacob Grimm in the 1820s, to trace the history of words back to that primitive place where words, meaning, and the world converge, which is Mallarmé's driving ambition for "One Toss of the Dice."

The man usually considered the first philologist, the German Franz Bopp, published a *Comparative Grammar* between 1833 and 1852. Bopp's work, building on the discovery of Sanskrit texts in the eighteenth century, traced the etymology of words beyond Hebrew and the Semitic languages to their Indo-European roots, which were thought to contain the basic elements of all human speech. Interest in Bopp's work was sparked in France by the translation in 1866 of his *Comparative Grammar* by the linguist Michel Bréal. The son of a rabbi, the original force behind the marathon at the first modern Olympic Games in 1896, and an early defender of Dreyfus in the affair that would quicken in the interval between the composition and the appearance of "One Toss of the Dice," Bréal was one of the pioneers of modern semantics. Mallarmé had met Bréal at the home of none other than Napoleon III's American dentist, the Parisian social gadfly Dr. Thomas Evans. Both men were present at a gathering of the Comité des Universités de Paris et d'Amérique that Evans hosted on October 12, 1895, for the purpose of countering the excessive influence of German universities in the United States.

Before that, Mallarmé had come across the early ideas of comparative anthropology, the combined origins of languages and of peoples, through Max Müller's *Science of Language*, translated into French in 1864. "It is said that blood is thicker than water, but it may be said with even greater truth," Müller asserted, "that language is thicker than blood." The assimilation of pure language and pure blood culminated for Müller in the Aryan languages of northern India: "the blood which circulates in their grammar is Aryan blood."[24] Müller's racialist ideas were vulgarized in English by William Cox and, as previously mentioned, Mallarmé translated into French Cox's *Manual of Mythology* and *Mythology of the Aryan Nations* under the title of *Les Dieux antiques*.

Mallarmé was interested in the origins of languages. Throughout his life, he nurtured the vague project of completing the equivalent of a Ph.D. in comparative linguistics. As early as 1865, he compiled notes that, according to Edmond Bonniot, included a Latin thesis on "The Divinity of Intelligence (the spirituality of the soul)."

"Finally, what remains for me to do," Mallarmé wrote to Eugène Lefébure, on March 20, 1870, "is a little German, with which, around Easter, I should begin the study of a comparative Grammar (not in translation) of the indo-germanic languages, I mean Sanskrit, Greek and Latin, this for two years later to do a 'licence'; then, I will start a more external study of Semitic languages which I will arrive at via Zend (middle Persian)."[25]

In the thinking of the Romance philologists of the nineteenth century, all modern languages derived from "the Aryan family." Mallarmé, however, did not study Sanskrit, Zend, or the Semitic languages. He studied English, and he crafted "One Toss of the Dice" by drawing on English roots and forms that he concluded came closer than those of his native tongue or the verbal patterns of Latin to "the miraculous stamp of Truth Herself Incarnate."[26] French, even more than English, had become distanced from the primordial attachment of the sound of words to things. Mallarmé chose for an example of the obscurity of French the very words that designate "shadows" along with the words that point to "day" and "night." The poet claimed to be disappointed that in French the word *ténèbres* ("shadows") does not seem very dark when compared with the opacity of the word *ombre* ("shade"). Likewise, he was frustrated at the perverseness and contradiction that lends dark tones to *jour* ("day") and bright tones to *nuit* ("night").

Like the Septentrion or North Star, which orients us at the end of "One Toss of the Dice," English is superior because of its northern roots. English escaped the influence of classical languages, which it would not encounter until the Norman Conquest of 1066, in the form of Norman French. It thus preserved in sounds and spellings some of the original spirit of the primordial Sanskrit roots. "He who wants to speak wisely can only say one thing about English, that this idiom, thanks to its monosyllabic character and the neutrality of certain forms apt to mark several grammatical functions at once, lays bare its Radicals: if by this designation one means certain words (even though all can equally aspire to such), simple in their notion and aspect."[27] Oddly, too, since Mallarmé envisaged a return via poetry to the truth that lies in the origin of words, English also points to the direction in which language will evolve. The poet was convinced that English grammar, though rooted in very ancient and sacred beginnings of language, was headed toward some great future linguistic point. "English: Contemporary Language par excellence, the one that marks the double character of the era, retrospective and advanced."[28]

Mallarmé developed his anthropological ideas about language in *English Words*, completed in 1878, just before his son Anatole's illness and death. There, he maintained that "certain keys" exist "between languages, or sometimes even in one language," and that English is especially vital in the keys that survive from its ancient Indo-European rudiments. The words "house" and "husband," for example, have always been linked, since the husband is the head of household. The poet rejoiced in the English affiliation between the word "loaf" and "lord," since the role of a lord is to distribute bread; between "spur" and "spurn"; between "well" and "wealth"; and between "thrash," the floor for beating grain, and "threshold."[29] He insisted that the letter "k" was a key to the verbal kinship between English words: revealing "the sense of knottedness, of joining, etc. Take note of the group '*kin, kind, king*,' from which comes the notion of family goodness."[30]

The survival of families of sound reveal clusters of meaning, which were especially visible in the first consonant, or combination of consonants, of English words. The initial letters of words were, for the poet, the equivalent of Cuvier's skeletal parts by which one might recognize the whole animal as well as its relation to other species. The poet thus organized the words discussed in his *English Words* alphabetically, because the first letter of a word, unlike the first name of a person, was the equivalent of a family name. The truth contained in the beginning of words was fixed in the body and indicative of family relations.

Alliteration, rhyme based on the first stressed syllable of a series of words within a single line of verse, was, for Mallarmé, "one of the sacred or perilous mysteries of Language";[31] and it was much more of an English than a French metric principle. English alliteration reached all the way back to Anglo-Saxon poetry, and it culminated in the works of Edgar Allan Poe. As a teenager, Mallarmé had copied and translated Poe's verse, and the translation he published in 1875 of "The Raven," with illustrations by Édouard Manet, preserved Poe's repeated occlusive "g" sounds: the original "What this grim, ungainly, ghastly, gaunt, and ominous bird of yore / Meant in croaking 'Nevermore'" was rendered by *"à ce que ce sombre, disgracieux, sinistre, maigre et augural oiseau de jadis signifiait en croissant: 'Jamais plus!'"*[32] Alliteration affirmed the original connection of words via the vestigial sounds of their Aryan roots still affixed to the first syllable, and was thus the guarantee of an original connection of words to things as well as of things among themselves.

For Mallarmé, the role of poetry was to reunite families of words separated through time, and whose relationship, attested only by similarities of sound, was no longer apparent. The genius of the poet—Mallarmé's "purifying the words of the tribe"—was to sense such relations, which he might not necessarily fully understand, but which he, or his genius, or some invisible spiritual source beyond the consciousness of any individual, would transcribe from thought, or intuition, or inspiration, to paper. "I have found the genuine poetry that men have lost since Orpheus!" the poet exclaimed in a phrase harking back to the origins of verse.[33]

"One Toss of the Dice" is filled with repeated consonant sounds that not only imitate the alliterative potential of English but fix the French sounds of Mallarmé's poem in the original organic elements

of human speech—a "similitude between verses and the old pro-
portions."[34] The falling feather of pages 200–201, the "solitary
wandering plume," starts atop a page dominated by the florin "*f*,"
"f": *sauf / que la rencontre ou l'effleure une toque de minuit / et immobilise /
au velours chiffonné par un esclaffement sombre . . . prince amer de l'écueil /
s'en coiffe comme de l'héroïque"* (pp. 200–201) ("*save / a glancing encounter
with a toque of midnight / that fixes it / in velvet crumpled by a dark guffaw
. . . bitter prince of the reef / wears it like a heroic headpiece*"; pp. 178–79).
In Mallarmé's discussion of English consonants, "f," especially in
combination with "l," denotes the act of flying or beating space,
examples to be found in "to fall," "to flow," "to float," "to fly," "to
flap," "to flutter," "to flit."[35] Though the "f's" of page 201 are not
initials, and only in the word "*l'effleure*" is an "f" bound to an "l," it
is hard not to see in their repetition along the trajectory of the falling feather, whose shape is bound to the "*f*," an attempt to elide
organically letter, sound, and sense.

   True alliteration is to be found in the falling feather of page 205,
especially if we count the "ch" and the soft "c" of "*cime*" and the
ligature "s" sound of "*aux écumes*" among the sibilant "s's": "***Choit /
la plume / rythmique suspens du sinistre / s'ensevelir / aux écumes originelles
/ naguères d'où sursauta son délire jusqu'à une cime / flétrie***" ("Falls / the
plume / rhythmic suspense of disaster / to be sunk / in the first
foam / whence once its delirium surged to a peak"; p. 183). The "s's"
of "One Toss of the Dice," like the florin "*f*" for feather, are ideo-
graphs, letters that take the visual shape of the thing they represent.
Mallarmé's notes, written just before "One Toss of the Dice," and
published after his death, indicate as much: "'S,' I say, is an analytic
letter: dissolving and disseminating, par excellence. . . . I find in it
the occasion to affirm the existence, outside of verbal value as much
of a purely hieroglyphic one . . . , of a secret direction, confusedly
indicated by orthography, and which converges mysteriously upon
the pure general sign made to indicate verse."[36] The letter "S" points

and curls back and forth, like a hieroglyph of the wavering arc of the wafting feather as it falls.

"S" bound to another consonant is, Mallarmé averred, a sinister sound. "SNEER is a *'bad smile'* and SNAKE, a perverse animal, *le serpent*, SN impresses an English reader as a sinister digraph. . . ."[37] "*S*, alone, however, has no other sense than that very clearly of to place, to seat, or, on the contrary, to seek."[38] How perfect, then, to trace the path of the falling feather, whose meaning is allied with the lowering of the plume/pen seeking paper, in "s" sounds, beginning with the "ch" of *choit*, third-person singular of the archaic verb *choir*, "to fall," which shares a root with "chance," from the popular Latin *cadentia*, plural neutral of the present participle *cadere*, "to fall." And how perfect that the "s," which connotes placement or seating, should come to rest (p. 209) on the sibilant surface of the North Star: "*sur quelque surface vacante et supérieure / le heurt successif / sidéralement*" ("on some empty and superior surface / the successive shock / from the stars"; p. 187).

"One Toss of the Dice," a shipwreck poem littered with debris on the surface of water, features prominently the liquid sounds "m," "n," "r," and "l." In Mallarmé's Anglo-cratylism, the letter "L" "seems sometimes incapable of expressing anything other than a natural desire [*appétition*] followed by no outcome, slowness, stagnation of things which drag or lag or continue even; it recovers spontaneity in meanings like to leap and all its powers of yearning in meanings of listening and loving, satisfied by the group of *loaf* to *lord*."[39] Pages 194–95 hold a series of "l's" in stressed position, which depict the ship's captain, slowed by the stalled sea and full of desire to regain his former mastery of the boat, yet unable to do so: "LE MAÎTRE / hors d'anciens calculs / où la manoeuvre avec l'âge oubliée." ("THE MASTER / beyond old calculations / where skills are lost with age"; pp. 172–73). Nor is he able, when the time comes, to cast the dice clasped in his raised fist.

The symmetrical alliterative "la mer par l'aïeul tentant ou l'aïeul contre la mer" ("the sea enticing the sire or the sire against the sea") turns around the liquids "l" and "m" in what might be seen as one of those tautologies of "One Toss of the Dice" which expresses desire with no outcome, the ultimate form of which is to be found on pages 206–7: "RIEN / de la mémorable crise / ou se fût l'évènement / accompli en vue de tout résultat nul / humain / N'AURA EU LIEU / une élévation ordinaire verse l'absence / QUE LE LIEU / inférieur clapotis quelconque comme pour dis- perser l'acte vide" ("NOTHING / of the memorable crisis / or the event / might have been accomplished with no result in sight / human / WILL HAVE TAKEN PLACE / an ordinary swell pours out absence / BUT THE PLACE / some lapping below as if to water down the empty act"; pp. 184–85).

"The stagnation of things" rendered by "L's" is fully expressed in the dorsal dominant phrase "RIEN . . . N'AURA EU LIEU . . . QUE LE LIEU" ("NOTHING . . . WILL HAVE TAKEN PLACE . . . BUT THE PLACE"), as "desire followed by no outcome" is conveyed in "l'évènement accompli en vue de tout résultat nul humain." Against the passivity conveyed by the "L," one finds the alliterative "inférieur **cl**apotis **qu**el**c**onque **co**mme pour disperser l'**ac**te vide," dominated by the velar hard "c," including the *que-* of *quelconque.* "Words in 'C,' a consonant with a ready and decisive attack," Mallarmé contended, "are seen in great number, receiving from this initial letter meaning connected to lively acts like to embrace, to split, to climb, thanks to the addition of an '*l*'; and with '*r*', splinter and break: 'ch' implies a violent effort and with that pre- serves an impression of roughness."[40] On the penultimate folio of "One Toss of the Dice," the active "C's" and "Ch's" do battle with "passive" "L's," mirroring the more general theme of states of being or background interrupted by an event, smooth sailing, in the instance, punctured by a shipwreck.

In Mallarmé's linking of the sounds of English to their primordial meaning, "'M' translates the power to do or to make, thus the joy, male and maternal; then, according to a meaning coming from very far in the past, measure and duty, the number, meeting, fusion and the middle term: by a reversal, not as sudden as it appears, inferiority, weakness or rage."[41] "N" connotes purity, because it "cannot support the presence of another consonant at the beginning of a word . . . 'N,' less frequent than 'M' marked with the seal of plenitude: judge it rather incisive and clean, as in the act of cutting or in the senses expressed by the Families of NAIL and NOSE, *'ongle'* and *'nez,'* from which *'bec'* [NOZZLE]." Pages 191–93, full of "m's" and "n's," are covered by the "weakness and rage" of the "stalled roiling abyss."

JAMAIS / QUAND BIEN MÊME LANCÉ DANS DES CIRCONSTANCES / ÉTERNELLES / DU FOND D'UN NAUFRAGE / SOIT / que / l'Abîme / blanchi / étale / furieux / sous une inclinaison / plane désespérément / d'aile / la sienne / par / avance retombée d'un mal à dresser le vol / et couvrant les jaillissements / coupant au ras les bonds / très à l'intérieur résume / l'ombre enfouie dans la profondeur par cette voile alternative
NEVER / EVEN WHEN THROWN IN THE MEASURE- LESS / CIRCUMSTANCES / FROM THE DEPTHS OF A SHIPWRECK / EVEN / if / the Abyss / turned white / stalled / roiling / beneath a desperately / sloping incline / of its own / wing / in / advance fallen back from the difficulty of trimming its sails / and stopping the gushing / preventing the surges / deep in the very heart / the shadow buried in the deep by this alternative sail

The "veill**ant** / dout**ant /** roul**ant** / brill**ant** et médit**ant** / av**ant** de s'arrêter / à quelque point dernier qui le sacre" ("watching / doubting rolling / blazing and brooding / before stopping / at some last point that consecrates it") of the final page of "One Toss of the

Dice" offers a series of nasal present participle suffixes that renders states of being and plenitude, ended incisively by a "stopping," a cutting short. *Couper* in French means "to cut," and a *coup de dés*, a "cut of the dice," seals and consecrates the entire poem, just as writing fixes or "cuts short" the fullness of an idea.

Mallarmé took the sounds of English to be close to the truth of things, and he used English phonology in "One Toss of the Dice" to make visible the hidden relationships between them. So, too, the poet uses many French words with their English connotation: *dénier* as "to deny," in the sense of "to refuse," which was an archaism in French; *vacante*, meaning "open" as in English, and not "vacant" or "unoccupied," as in French; *vain* and *veuf* as synonyms of "empty," as in English, and not "vain, ineffectual, useless" or "bereft," as in French. Mallarmé uses *Sûr*, at the beginning of a sentence, like the English "Sure," which ordinarily in French would be *Certes*, and *coin* to refer to money, a pure anglicism that does not exist in French.[42] Certain phrases of "One Toss of the Dice" seem to have been borrowed from English, "*prince amer de l'écueil*" (p. 201) "bitter prince of the reef," "*la mémorable crise*" (p. 206), *mémorable* being a French word, more usual in English as "memorable" than in the rare French from "*mémorable.*" The word "*résume*" appears on page 193 of "One Toss of the Dice," "*très à l'intérieur résume*," in its etymological sense of "to take back," closer to the English "to resume" than to its French sense of "to summarize" or "to sum up." "*Alternative*" is also found on page 193 as an "alternating" and not as in the French, more literally "alternative," except in the restricted realm of "alternating current," *courant alternatif.*

The word order of "One Toss of the Dice" derives in part from modern English, especially the placement of adjectives before nouns, as in "*la mémorable crise.*" On some deep level, however, under the assumption that the oldest forms of English were the most authentic, Mallarmé turned to archaic examples of recognizable

English, found in Low German, which he reproduced in *English Words*. There, the poet, in a completely improbable effort to recover the lost truth of words as a key to the truth of things, offered a translation of the Bible of the fourth-century bishop Ulfilas, from what he calls Mœso-Gothic, into both English and French:

1) Vairthai vilja theins, svê in himina yah ana airthai
   BE-DONE WILL THINE AS IN HEAVEN YEA ON
   EARTH
   (*Être faite veut ta . . . comme au ciel oui sur la terre*)
2) Hlaif unsarana thana sinteinan gif uns himma daga
   LOAF OUR THE CONTINUOUS GIVE US THIS DAY
   (*Pain notre le perpétual donne-nous ce jour*)
3) Svasve yah veis afletam thaim skulam unsaraim
   SO-AS YEA WE OFF-LET THOSE DEBTORS OF
   OURS
   (*Comme oui nous laissons de côté ces débiteurs des nôtres*)[43]

In a world where the origin of words was the guarantee of their authenticity, the closer one gets to Aryan roots, the closer one is to the "Immortal Truth Herself." For Mallarmé, this meant the astonishing prospect of sentences written at the end of the nineteenth century that imitated the jumbled word order of the fourth-century Gothic Bible, or at least the poet's word-by-word translation of the Bible of Ulfilas. The contours of the sentences of "One Toss of the Dice" had been in place since the fourth century, and participated in the spiritual aura of the Word of God. "All the great masters, ancient and modern, plagiarized Homer," Mallarmé observed, "and Homer plagiarized God."[44]

Eight

"IT'S THE SAME FOR THE MAN OF SCIENCE"

Two years after beginning "One Toss of the Dice," and a little over a year after its publication, Mallarmé was plagued by bouts of what was thought to be tonsillitis. He had been coughing all spring. The return to Valvins in late April 1898 to prepare the house for the arrival of Marie and Geneviève brought intermittent relief. The discomfort seemed at some times to subside and, at others, to be chronic, often within the space of a single day. On May 1, he wrote to his wife and daughter that he "was practically no longer coughing, and felt, even, the good encroachment of repose." Later that evening, after a dinner with the poet Édouard Dujardin at which he remained "completely sober," he wondered if he had not caught whooping cough from one of the local girls who brought it home from school that winter.

The poet made the usual calls at neighboring houses, and some of the local residents dropped by to indulge in the yearly round of gossip and news with the humble man who sometimes appeared lost in his thoughts, and who was now world famous. A purveyor of construction materials, Monsieur Maire, predicted that there would be no unemployment in the coming year. The postman was bitten in the leg by a dog, and had to be taken home in a horse-drawn cart. He would be incapacitated for a few days. The liberal candidate from Fontainebleau, Gustave Hubbard, was not reelected to the Chamber of Deputies. Queen Victoria, then in the fifty-first year of her reign, passed through on the rail line just behind Valvins on her way back to London from Nice. The weather had been so intemperate that Méry Laurent, who was to spend time with Mallarmé and other friends near Valvins, postponed her holiday. Once he had settled in, the poet visited the cemetery where Anatole lay, writing plaintively back to wife and daughter, "for we had been four, my poor friends. . . . I carried your thoughts with me there. . . . I have almost stopped coughing."[1]

In the France all around him, tension between the accusers and the defenders of Captain Alfred Dreyfus came to occupy more and more space in newspapers and in popular debate. The arc of what would become the Dreyfus affair and that of "One Toss of the Dice" were, in some uncanny sense, entwined. In the summer of 1896, as Mallarmé began to write his masterwork, Lieutenant-Colonel Georges Picquart, head of the Bureau of Statistics, the French intelligence services, received a packet of thirty or forty shredded pieces of paper collected by a cleaning lady from the wastebasket of the German military attaché in Paris, Maximilien von Schwartzkoppen. Once he had reassembled the fragments of the "little blue" *pneumatique*, Picquart recognized that the evidence used to convict Captain Dreyfus had been falsified. It would be another three years before Dreyfus was, if not exonerated, at least pardoned. The case against him began to unravel in the spring and summer of 1898.

That January, Mallarmé's friend Émile Zola had published an article in Georges Clemenceau's newspaper *L'Aurore* under the banner headline "J'accuse." In what was perhaps the most powerful speech act of the nineteenth century, Zola accused President Félix Faure and the general staff of the French army of judicial misconduct and anti-Semitism in the prosecution of the case against Captain Dreyfus. Condemned to life imprisonment, Dreyfus languished in a military prison on Devil's Island. Within a month, the author of "J'accuse" found himself as well on trial, and he was convicted of criminal libel on February 23, 1898. To avoid prison, Zola fled to London, where he registered under the name of M. Pascal, one of the characters in *The Rougon-Macquart*, his epic series of novels about a family under the Second Empire.

Mallarmé and Zola admired each other from a distance, but their views of literature could not have been further apart. Zola criticized Mallarmé for being "so constantly preoccupied with the rhythm and arrangement of words that he ends up losing awareness of their meaning."[2] Mallarmé had written to Zola on February 3, 1877, to congratulate him on the success of his novel about alcoholic decline, *L'Assommoir*, with the provocative claim that the apathy of modern life may be more destructive than alcohol.[3] Despite their differences in matters of art, the poet wrote to the novelist on the very day of his conviction in Paris's supreme court to praise the courage of his intervention in the Dreyfus affair, which would divide the French into factions whose enmity has endured in one form or another to the present day. Mallarmé confided to Marie at the end of April that he felt as if he were in prison "in Zola's place."[4] He noted that Fernand Labori, Dreyfus's and Zola's lawyer, summered in nearby Samois. Labori, who would be shot by an anti-Dreyfusard in August 1899 in the course of Dreyfus's retrial in Rennes, had converted a former convent into a summer home that, in its sumptuous heyday, accommodated up to a thousand guests for lunch.[5]

That spring and summer, artistic circles in and around Mallarmé were in an uproar about the rejection of Auguste Rodin's sculpture of Honoré de Balzac. The sculptor had been commissioned in 1891 by the Société des Gens de Lettres to create the official monument to France's greatest epic novelist before Zola. Balzac had been one of the Society's original founders and its former president. Zola was instrumental in persuading this guild of writers to grant the commission to Rodin, who was at the time less well-known than the other contenders, Henri Chapu and Marquet de Vasselot. Yet, Rodin took an unheard-of seven years, during which time he read Balzac's prodigious novelistic corpus and, despite his goal of creating a psychological rather than merely a physical portrait of the writer, depicted Balzac nude and clothed. He even went so far as to order a reproduction of the novelist's writing cloak to be made by Balzac's former tailor. When the final result in plaster was unveiled at the yearly salon of the Société Nationale des Beaux-Arts in 1898, those who had originally bestowed the commission upon Rodin refused to accept the finished work, or to pay him. Rodin wrote a personal note to Mallarmé as the "*Aeropagite*," or arbiter of taste in France, to inform him of the unhappy outcome of his dealings with the Société des Gens de Lettres. The poet, who in the "Rodin affair" was resolutely on the side of the sculptor, wrote to console his fellow artist: "nothing, caddishness above all, can touch the profound serenity of your work."[6]

The poet sailed very little, if at all, between June and August 1898. Paul Valéry visited his mentor for the July 14 holiday and reported that "on the sill of a window, which opened onto the calm landscape, Mallarmé had spread out the magnificent proof-sheets of the great edition composed at Lahure's. He did me the honor of asking me for my opinion about certain details."[7] The Lahure edition of which Valéry spoke would have been the authoritative copy of "One Toss of the Dice" meant to appear with illustrations by Odilon Redon; it had occupied the poet's attention ever since the original publication two years before in *Cosmopolis*. Valéry wrote to André Gide that in the course of this visit, Mallarmé "changed his shirt in front of me, gave me some water for my hands and poured a bit of his cologne over me himself."[8] Whistler, too, came to Valvins. The poet, the painter, and Geneviève took long walks along the Seine. Mallarmé, who was once categorized in an interview about cats as a "catophile," suggested that Whistler paint the Mallarmé family's old black cat, Lilith. The artist managed to place only a couple of strokes of ink on paper when Lilith scampered under the table.[9] It was a perfect lesson, in the mode of "One Toss of the Dice," about the difficulty of capturing the essence of things on canvas or in print.

Having published two years before "One Toss of the Dice," which was as close as he ever came to a version of *The Book*, Mallarmé returned to the unfinished epic poem *Hérodiade* and, apparently, to *The Book*, to which he referred in a letter as "jottings for the dream," both conceived in the psychic crisis of his midtwenties. Sometime, too, in August, Mallarmé responded to an interview conducted by *Le Figaro*: "Your ideal at age twenty?" "I chose to write," the poet wrote, "to which I was faithful, in order that my life might have a meaning. This implies . . . removing daily from my native illumination the perilous [*hasardeux*] layer of dust that gathers under the name of experience. Fortunate or vain, my choice at age twenty survives intact."[10]

Mallarmé's faith in the redeeming power of poetry sustained him throughout a lifetime of economic difficulty, professional frustration, and personal loss. "One Toss of the Dice," in turn, nourished from the outset the literary works, painting, and music that would, over the course of the century following its publication, come to define modernism in the arts. The poet's urge to reconcile the shape of his verse with its meaning, along with his modeling of the effects of time simultaneity in his difficult body of works, struck to the core of twentieth-century art, and would surface in twentieth-century scientific thought as well.

Of all the poets of that first generation not to have known Mallarmé personally, Apollinaire put forth in his *Calligrammes* a striking example of graphic poetry in the wake and mode of "Un Coup de dés." Guillaume Albert Wladimir Alexandre Apollinaire de Kostrowitzky could not have been more unlike Mallarmé when it came to lifestyle or the contents of his works. By the age of twenty-one, he was earning a living as an author of such pornographic novels as *Mirely, or the Little Hole That Doesn't Cost Much; Memories of a Young Don Juan;* and *The 11,000 Penises.* The last was a play on the Catholic veneration of the Eleven Thousand Virgins, in which the French word for "virgin" (*vierge*) mixes with the word for "stick" (*verge*), which is slang for the male member. At one point, Apollinaire founded a literary review, *Aesop's Feast;* when it failed, he changed the name to *The Immoralist's Review,* and continued to edit it out of a building owned by the Catholic Church. The poet and pornographer nourished the legend that began to grow around him of an obscure foreign birth, of market expertise coupled with financial fraud, of formidable appetites, and a capacity for conversation. Apollinaire loomed as a poet, editor, journalist, bohemian, and overall exotic personality, yet one who still visited his mother every Sunday for a meal and to pick up his clean laundry. He was known for his art criticism, having invented the term *"les peintres cubistes,"* and for a futurist manifesto proclaiming "suppression of poetic grief . . . syntax, punctuation, lines and verses, houses, boredom."

In 1914, Apollinaire fought two duels and began *Les Calligrammes,* which continued Mallarmé's project of concrete visual poetry. That same year, he volunteered for military service, and, in March 1916, was wounded by a shell while reading in a trench. The poet survived the operation to remove the shrapnel that had lodged in his brain but died on November 9, 1918, two days before the armistice ending World War I, a victim of the pandemic Spanish flu.

In *Les Calligrammes,* Apollinaire stripped poetry of all rhetorical ornament. The rhythm base of poetry—its relation to music, measure, beat, and time—disappeared. Like the disposition of type that took the shape of a listing boat or a constellation in "One Toss of the Dice," the layout of the calligrammes reproduced the actual subject of verse. Their original title, "lyric Ideograms" (*Idéogrammes lyriques*), captured the poet's desire, a Mallarméan ambition if ever there was one, that alphabetic writing take on the visual power of the hieroglyph.

In May 1897, just a week after the appearance of "One Toss of the Dice," Guglielmo Marconi demonstrated that wireless signals were capable of crossing open water. Apollinaire, who was fascinated by the telegraph, composed his calligramme "Wireless" ("TSF") to mimic the shape of radio waves dispersed in all directions. The words on the page are like snippets of telegraphic speech and sound, including political slogans ("Vive le Roy," "Vive la République," "Down with priests"), slang expressions and sexual innuendos, street utterances ("Stop driver," "Move on please ladies"), and newspaper advertisements ("Proprietor of 5 or 6 apartments").

The verses of the calligramme "It's Raining" are aligned diagonally with a vertical pitch, as if the lines of poetry were sheets of rain falling from the sky to the ground. The elegiac tone and the evocation of lost loves contained in the words themselves render, like tears, a liquidation of sentiment and a freeing from the past: "listen to it rain while regret and disdain cry an old music / listen to the falling of the cords [*liens*] which hold you back from top to bottom." The play on the French expression "raining cords," equivalent to the English "raining cats and dogs," is reproduced in the typographic bands that stretch from top to bottom of the page, and are doubled by reference to the cords or sentimental ties which bind.

In his masterwork, "Zone," Apollinaire picked up the Mallarméan ambition of being at once in and outside of chronological time. The title "Zone" referred to the border between France and

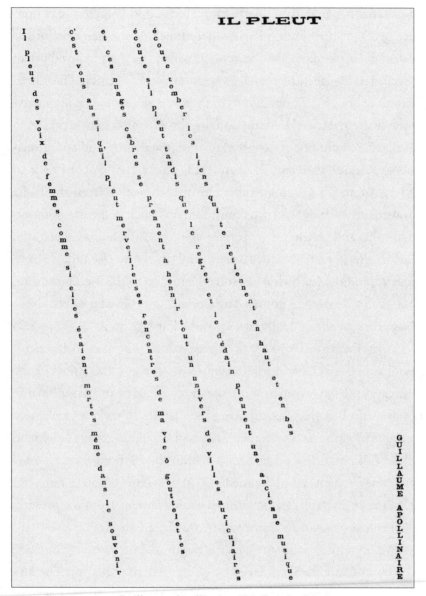

Guillaume Apollinaire, "It's Raining"

Switzerland, where Apollinaire found himself in 1912; to the periphery or zone surrounding Paris, where much of the narrative of the poem takes place; and to the zone to which the marginalized urban dweller is displaced by the city's seeming lack of center. The varied length of lines in "Zone" and its uneven stanzas, from one to twenty-nine lines, its lack of punctuation, its abrupt transitions, work, as in Mallarmé's epic poem, to obscure traditional time and space relations. "Zone" is a pan-Parisian, trans-European, global poem in which we move instantaneously through the city—from the Eiffel Tower, across bridges, down familiar streets, such as the rue Aumont-Thiéville and avenue des Ternes; to the Gare Saint-Lazare, the Jewish ghetto on the rue des Rosiers and the rue des Écouffes, Montmartre, and the Cathedral of Notre-Dame; on to the Mediterranean, Marseilles, Coblenz, Rome, Amsterdam, and Gouda; to the Near East; then, at the end, all the way to the Far East.

As in Picasso's *Demoiselles d'Avignon*, which joins two distinct cultural zones—a classical triad of muses on the left two-thirds of the canvas, and two women with the faces of African masks on the right—Apollinaire superimposes a shared "Greek and Roman antiquity" upon a communal Christian religious past: "God who dies Friday and rises on Sunday." Within the Catholic past, "Zone" contains elements from the medieval past, such as "Notre Dame has seen me at Chartres," which mingle with elements from the present: "The most up-to-date European is you Pope Pius X."

Along with Apollinaire's cubist poem, cubist painting followed the trail of simultaneity blazed by Mallarmé's masterwork. The loss of Renaissance perspective and the flattening of pictorial space, as well as the dissolving of the substance of objects—whose outlines are broken, whose parts are fragmented into smaller areas within larger masses, whose seemingly distinct planes dovetail and overlap with one another—go hand in hand with the global syncretism of "Zone" and the splicing of enclaves of meaning in "One Toss of the

Dice." The presentation of a single object from multiple points of view collapses time into space in a way that, like Mallarmé's virtual simultaneous syntax, makes it seem as if one is at once part of punctual chronological time and the flow of endless duration.

In autumn 1913, the futurist journal *New Men* (*Les Hommes nouveaux*) published a visual and verbal poem by Blaise Cendrars, a Swiss novelist, and Sonia Delaunay, a Russian painter, both living in Paris: "The Prose of the Trans-Siberian and of Little Jehanne of France." This design poem, like a multicolored version of "One Toss of the Dice," was printed on a single sheet of paper, seven feet long, in an edition of 150 copies, which, unfolded and placed end to end, attain the height of the Eiffel Tower. An accompanying advertisement described "The Prose of the Trans-Siberian" as a "simultaneous book," in which text and image were meant to be read at the same time. Apollinaire's commentary on Cendrars and Delaunay's syncretic color poem emphasized the identity of their ambition with that of "One Toss of the Dice": "Blaise Cendrars and Mme Delaunay-Terk have carried out a unique experiment in simultaneity, written in contrasting colors in order to train the eye to read with one glance the notes placed up and down on the bar, even as one reads with a single glance the plastic elements printed on a poster."[11]

Simultaneity was part of the Italian painter and sculptor Umberto Boccioni's *Futurist Manifesto* of 1912, which stressed the "synthesis of what one remembers and what one sees."[12] Fellow futurist Giacomo Balla's *Dynamism of a Dog in Motion* of that same year showed the blurred feet and tail of a dog, the sweep of a leash, and the steps of the dog's master, all presented as a series of motions, which the viewer sees simultaneously, but which he knows unfold sequentially through time. So, too, Marcel Duchamp's *Nude Descending a Staircase*, which combines the cubist overlapping of fragmented semisolid planes with the futurist commitment to motion, captured on a single flattened plane the dynamic steps of a figure through the successive stages of a single continuous action. Duchamp's 1913 painting was the heir not only to the intermittent stop-motion of cinema but also to "One Toss of the Dice."

The legacy of Mallarmé's masterwork extended to modern music, and was especially felt in the works of Erik Satie. Like Apollinaire, the composer could not have been further from Mallarmé in temperament or life course. Satie was born in 1866 in the coastal town of Honfleur of a French father and an English mother, who died when the child was two. Raised by grandparents, Satie joined his father at the age of twelve in Paris, where he entered the music conservatory. When the time came for the obligatory year of military service, Satie joined the army and contracted bronchitis on purpose in order to be discharged. Around that time, be began work on his first musical composition, "Les Gymnopédies," and to play piano at the café Le Chat Noir. Upon his father's death in 1892, Satie moved to Montmartre to an apartment rigged up as a musical studio and religious shrine, which he called "the closet," and, after a brief infatuation with the Rosicrucians, founded his own religion, the "Metropolitan Church of the Order of Jesus the Conductor." With the small inheritance his father had left him, the increasingly quirky composer bought a dozen identical corduroy suits and presented himself, well dressed, for election to the Académie Française.

In 1898, the composer moved across Paris to Arcueil, carrying a chest, a bed, and his suits in a wheelbarrow. He continued to play in the music and dance halls of Montmartre, often walking the six miles from home with a hammer in his pocket for protection. Satie made an infinitesimal income from the publication rights to his compositions, noting that he earned seventy-three *centimes* in the first quarter of 1903. Some large proportion of the money he made from his piano playing was spent on drink, as he grew increasingly eccentric. He was seen wearing a clay pipe in his suit pocket with the stem in his ear. In cafés, he demanded the bottom portion of cognac out of a graduated carafe. He applied for a scholarship to the Schola Cantorum, France's institute of sacred music, which he attended, graduating first in his class in 1908. While continuing to compose fanciful piano pieces—"Irksome Example," "Agreeable Despair"— the composer turned to politics, joining the radical-socialist party of Arcueil, where he organized a series of musical events for children, wrote a social column in the local newspaper, "A Fortnight in Society," and offered free music lessons every Sunday at ten a.m. Satie's only other musical work of this period is *Three Pieces in the Shape of a Pear*, written in response to Claude Debussy's criticism that his music lacked form. Then, after seven years of complete silence, Satie began in 1910 a series of humorous pieces, including "Sketches and Annoyances of a Fat Good Fellow in Wood," "Chapters Turned in All Directions," "Unappetizing Chorale," "Dried Embryos," "Next to Last Thoughts," and "Bureaucratic Sonata," often with such facetious notations on scores as "Like a nightingale with a toothache" and "Turn page with an amiable and smiling finger."

In the mode of Mallarmé's alliance of the shape of words with their meaning and of Apollinaire's calligrammes, Satie wrote concrete visual music in which the arrangement of notes on a musical score corresponds not so much to the sound, but to the visual appearance of the page of sheet music. In the collection *Sports et Divertissements*, written in 1914, the composer reproduced, in the graphic layout of "La Balançoire," the leisurely back-and-forth motion of a seesaw or swing. In the thirty-six sixteenth notes that descend from treble clef high F sharp to low D in line three of "Le Water-chute," Satie imitated the cascade of a waterfall. The humorous piece was composed without a key signature or bass notations, techniques akin to Mallarmé's and Apollinaire's lack of punctuation in poetry. Satie warned the listener: "If you have solid nerves, you will not be too sick. It will be like falling off a scaffolding. You will see how curious it is. Watch out! Don't change color. I feel uncomfortable. That

Erik Satie, "Le Water-chute"
Harvard University, Houghton Library, Typ 915.14.7700.

proves that you needed to be amused." A similar series of rising six-teenth notes in line four of "Le Golfe" is the unmistakable visual sign of the swing of a golf club. A certain buoyant constancy in the treble clef on top of the regular rise and fall of eighth notes in the bass clef of the first line of "Le Bain de Mer" reproduces visually the lapping of waves and the sensation of swimming in the sea, which was reinforced by a doodle in Satie's own hand of wavy water at the very beginning of this short composition.

As in the time simultaneity of Apollinaire's "Zone," cubism and futurism in painting, and Cendrar and Delaunay's "Prose of the Trans-Siberian," Satie's musical rhythms were part of the legacy of "One Toss of the Dice." The syncopated cadences, beat and offbeat, of his ragtime music-hall numbers resonate with the Mallarméan syntax insofar as they produced the sensation of being both in the moment and slightly beyond the moment. The iconic work of ragtime, Scott Joplin's "Maple Leaf Rag," was published in 1899. Satie encountered the rhythms of ragtime sometime after John Philip Sousa's visit to the International Exposition of 1900, and especially after he listened to recordings of Jelly Roll Morton brought back to France by the Swiss conductor Ernest Ansermet in 1916. The cakewalk figured prominently in Satie's ballet *Parade*, performed at the Théâtre de Châtelet a year later.

Parade featured the insertion, amid musical strains, of the actual sounds of revolver shots, a siren, a Morse code ticker, a typewriter, an airplane propeller, a lottery wheel, and what Satie called "squish puddles" (*flaques sonores*), made by striking a cymbal with sponge-tipped sticks. As zany as they may seem, such antics were the logical end points of Mallarmé's conscious alignment in "One Toss of the Dice" of the shape of things and their artistic representation, which, in Satie's ballet, have become one and the same.

The poet, playwright, and filmmaker Jean Cocteau recognized that Satie's "acoustical illusions" were introduced "in the same spirit as the cubist painters used optical illusion."[13] The cubist integration of everyday objects to their works—newspaper, sheet music, matchbook covers, chair caning, and stamps, textures of marble, or cloth—reached an extreme in the readymades of the Dadaists in Zurich and Paris, beginning in 1914. Without even the frame of music or painting, Marcel Duchamp, who withdrew from traditional painting after 1913, transformed everyday objects—a bicycle wheel, a urinal, a bottle rack, a check to his dentist, a Monte Carlo bank bond—into freestanding works of art. Duchamp's insight—that art can be made by changing the context of ordinary things—would culminate in the pop art of the middle of the twentieth century, in Andy Warhol's reproductions of common commodities like Campbell's tomato juice or Brillo boxes, or his carrying of a portable recorder with him wherever he went (his "wife,"as he delicately referred to it), in order to tape everything he or anyone around him said. All are part of the evolution that began with "One Toss of the Dice" to align the shape of artistic expression with its meaning.

"One Toss of the Dice" inspired Satie's minimalist musical compositions, where traditional theme and variation were replaced by "circular melodic motion" that obscures progression. And Satie's "furniture" or white music, in turn, anticipated the trance music of the 1980s. In his late twenties, Satie had become involved briefly with Susanne Valadon, a former tightrope walker, painter, and model for Renoir and Toulouse-Lautrec, as well as the mother of Maurice Utrillo. Bitter over their breakup, he composed "Vexation," thirteen bars of music to be repeated 840 times, with the warning: "It would be advisable to prepare oneself in advance, in the most profound silence, by a period of serious immobility." John Cage's Pocket Theatre Relay Team performed "Vexation" in New York in September 1963. The eleven participating pianists remained seriously immobile at the piano for eighteen hours and forty minutes, after which one of the six remaining members of the audience shouted, "Encore!"[14]

The most compelling English successor to "One Toss of the Dice" was T. S. Eliot's *The Waste Land.* Eliot initially had been wary of what he referred to as Mallarmé's "mossiness." Yet by the early 1920s, he recognized that "every battle" the French poet "fought with syntax represents the effort to transmute lead into gold, ordinary language into poetry." In 1926, Eliot wrote an essay in French on Poe and Mallarmé in which he praised the latter's "discovery of new objects for new emotions," expressed in a syntax so complex that "it prevents the reader from swallowing the phrase or verse in a single blow [*d'un seul coup*]," which may, in fact, be a direct reference to *Un Coup de dés.* The American-born poet admired Mallarmé's ability to transform the "accidental into the real" via an "*incantation* . . . which relies on the primitive power of the Word."[15]

In *The Waste Land*, Eliot transforms the "accidental into the real" by inserting quotidian sounds and conversations that are part of daily life in London. Some are imitated from nature: the nightingale's "'Jug Jug' to dirty ears," "Twit twit twit / Jug jug jug jug jug jug / So rudely forc'd / Tereu" or the cock's crow, "Co co rico co co rico." Others are banal dialogues, overheard or imagined: "My nerves are bad to-night. Yes, bad / Stay with me. Speak to me / Why do you never speak? Speak / What are you thinking of? What thinking? What? / I never know what you are thinking. Think." Still others belong to cries heard on the street or tavern talk, as in the famous monologue interspersed with notice of the closing pub that reproduces the diverse typography of Mallarmé's masterwork: "When Lil's husband got demobbed, I said / I didn't mince my words, I said to her myself / HURRY UP PLEASE ITS TIME / Now Albert's coming back, make yourself a bit smart."[16]

Eliot produced in *The Waste Land* effects of time simultaneity analogous to those of Mallarmé in "One Toss of the Dice." Current perceptions of the city are mixed with personal memories of a recent and more distant past, both blended with the collective history of an entire civilization. Yet, unlike "One Toss of the Dice," in which a rudderless boat, after rocking wildly, managed to right itself, and a disorienting universe was finally tethered to the North Star, *The Waste Land* manifests a world so thoroughly unmoored as to offer only a minimal sign of life and no hope of catching one's bearing:

> What are the roots that clutch, what branches grow
>
> Out of this stony rubbish? Son of man,
>
> You cannot say, or guess, for you know only
>
> A heap of broken images, where the sun beats,
>
> And the dead tree gives no shelter, the cricket no relief,
>
> And the dry stone no sound of water.[17]

Where the collapse of time for Mallarmé—the creation of the sensation of an eternal present—was a means to secular salvation, time for Eliot was not redemptive, but a sign of disenchantment with the world. He no longer identified with the great Platonic tradition that nourished Mallarmé's belief in the insuperable but divine relation between words and ideas. In the two epigraphs that preceded the "Burnt Norton" section of the *Four Quartets*, Eliot reached beyond Plato to Heraclitus, whose cryptic affirmations of the hidden harmonies of nature only confirmed for him a sense of his own alienation (*"Although logos is common to all, most people live as if they had a wisdom of their own"*) and paralysis (*"The way upward and the way downward are the same"*). "One Toss of the Dice" may be challenging to understand, but, as Mallarmé repeatedly affirmed, the things we do not understand, the "mystery in letters," is the guarantee of poetry's power to heal the broken relation between consciousness and the world.

In his articulation of time simultaneity in "One Toss of the Dice," Mallarmé participated in the evolution of elemental ideas about time and space since Descartes and Newton. The poet's great intuition about the relation of a unique event to the infinite possibility of all such events anticipated in its own artistic way the coming into being of quantum physics in the first half of the twentieth century.

In the very year following the publication of "One Toss of the Dice," the mathematician Henri Poincaré, cousin of Raymond Poincaré, the minister of public education who had signed the paper authorizing Mallarmé's retirement, psychologized Newton's absolute, theological time by making all time into a construct, a social convention. For H. Poincaré, there was no direct intuition of simultaneity, nor was it possible to assess the relative length of two durations. "If we think we have this intuition," the great mathematician wrote, "this is an illusion." The rules for measuring time were not necessary, and could be discarded without compromising the laws of physics, mechanics, or astronomy. We choose these rules, Poincaré concluded, not because they are true, but because they are convenient.[18]

Poincaré's dematerializing of space and time was only a prelude to that of Albert Einstein, who, having completed his studies at the Zurich Polytechnic Institute, took a job in 1902 as technical expert class three in the Bern Patent Office.[19] There, he examined applications for patents on a variety of inventions, among which were numerous devices for coordinating clocks in local schools, railway stations, and businesses. Einstein's life in Bern resembled that of Mallarmé in superficial ways. Both were domestically situated with wife and children, both worked for the state in essentially bureaucratic jobs, and both maintained informal evening gatherings for the purpose of enriching intellectual life. Tuesdays *chez* Mallarmé found a Swiss, scientific, Jewish equivalent in the Olympia Academy, created by Einstein, the mathematician Conrad Habicht, and the philosopher Maurice Solovine. Along with the mechanical engineer Michele Besso, the mathematician Marcel Grossman, and Einstein's wife, Mileva Marić, they met regularly in the Einstein apartment on the second floor of Kramgasse No. 49 to discuss philosophy and physics. But the author of what may be the world's most difficult poem and the author of the world's most famous equation resembled each other in some ways that are not so superficial. They expressed similar fundamental ideas about the source of poetic and scientific genius, about time and space, about simultaneity, about the intersection of particular things and abstract concepts, and, finally, about the mystery underlying all such relations.

It is unlikely that Einstein, however well versed he was in literature and philosophy, read Mallarmé's epic work. How is it, then, that what is arguably the scientist's most famous sentence about nonscientific matters takes up the terms of "One Toss Of the Dice Never Will Abolish Chance"? Einstein wrote to his friend Max Born in

December 1926, "The quantum mechanics is very imposing. But an inner voice tells me that it is not yet the real thing. The theory says a lot, but does not really bring us any closer to the secret of the 'old one.' I, at any case, am convinced that *He* is not playing at dice."[20]

Mallarmé and Einstein were each concerned with the thought process writ large, and with the nature of poetic and scientific inspiration. The French poet was obsessed with how images formed in the mind are translated into words, how an idea such as chance (which remained pristine and unified as long as it was only an idea) might be expressed in words, which, by their particular material quality, make the concept seem less whole, satisfying, or necessary. Einstein, too, attributed an independence of "the miracle of thinking" from language. In his account, shared with psychologist Max Wertheimer, of how he came to the theory of relativity, the scientist distinguished between concepts and words. "These thoughts did not come in any verbal formulation. I very rarely think in words at all. A thought comes, and I may try to express it in words afterward."[21]

Einstein was acutely aware of the identity of poetic and scientific inspiration. In the 1930s, after Einstein had resettled in the United States, he invited the French poet and diplomat Saint-John Perse to Princeton University, where he asked him, "How does the idea of a poem come?" The poet spoke of the role played by intuition and imagination. "It's the same for the man of science," Einstein responded with delight. "It is a sudden illumination, almost a rapture. Later, to be sure, intelligence analyzes and experiments confirm or invalidate the intuition. But initially there is a great forward leap of the imagination."[22]

Both Mallarmé and Einstein were convinced of the primordial role of intuition in artistic and scientific creation. The poet relied upon flickers and sparks in "One Toss of the Dice" to reproduce the effects of what he defined as "the aspect of things, which perpetu-

ONE TOSS OF THE DICE 281

ally lives but dies every moment." The scientist claimed that his greatest insights came as a result of sudden intuitive flashes. The first occurred just before the astonishing months in the spring and summer of 1905 during which he wrote the five papers in and around "The Special Theory of Relativity." "I'm going to give it up," Einstein is reported to have lamented to his friend and coworker Michele Besso, whom he had run into on the street. As they discussed it, however, "I suddenly understood the key to the problem." When Einstein saw Besso the next day, he declared without greeting him, "Thank you. I've completely solved the problem."[23] What he had understood was that "an analysis of the concept of time was my solution. Time cannot be absolutely defined, and there is an inseparable relation between time and signal velocity." Five weeks after this "eureka" moment, Einstein completed his paper "On the Electrodynamics of Moving Bodies," which formed the basis of the special theory of relativity.

The scientist, whose extraordinarily abstract and mathematical thought often emerged from concrete examples, began his founding article with a visual problem with significance for understanding "One Toss of the Dice": "It is known that Maxwell's electrodynamics—as usually understood at the present time—when applied to moving bodies, leads to asymmetries which do not appear to be inherent in the phenomena. Take, for example, the reciprocal electrodynamic action of a magnet and a conductor."[24] Einstein noted that it was generally assumed that, in a field where each moves relative to the other, the effect is different when the conductor moves relative to the magnet from when the magnet moves relative to the conductor. Yet, he had come to understand, the effects in both cases were the same. It not only made no difference which moves relative to the other, but there was no such thing as a body in motion or a body at rest. Extended to the cosmos, a conceptual state of absolute rest implicit in the Newtonian world-view, Einstein's insight meant that there was no way of determining whether an object orbiting around the earth moves or the earth moves, as long as each was in motion relative to the other.

The disparate syntactic zones of "One Toss of the Dice" unfold independently of each other in a way thoroughly analogous to Einstein's discovery. It is impossible to tell whether the spinal core sentence "ONE TOSS OF THE DICE NEVER . . . WILL ABOLISH . . . CHANCE" or the intervening words that make up the rest of the poem takes priority, one over the other. They move, in other words, relative to each other, as in the case of Einstein's magnet and conductor, or earth and orbiting object. There is a great logical leap, of course, and more than eight chronological years, between the poem of 1897 and the first relativity of 1905. Yet Mallarmé's poem brings to the imagination of the reader discrete verbal clusters, and subclusters, circling one another in such a way as to open new possibilities of meaning, new mental structures that—on a different level and in a different cultural medium—open vistas to Einstein's thinking about the relativity of moving bodies.

The one physical law that remained invariable for Einstein, like Mallarmé's North Star at the end of "One Toss of the Dice," was the speed of light, which was central to the theory of relativity. He attempted to reconcile theories of light as a series of discrete quanta or particles with theories of light as a continuous electromagnetic wave.[25] The ultimate effect of Einstein's synthesis of the particle and wave theory of light, along with his banishment of fixed coordinates of time and space, was the elimination of the ether, a nebulous undetectable substance that was supposed to reside between the solid masses which make up our world, as well as to be the fluid through which electromagnetic effects and light were transmitted. "According to this theory," Einstein wrote in an explanation of relativity for the general public, "there is no such thing as a 'specially favored' (unique) coordinate system to occasion the introduction of the 'aether-idea,' and hence there can be no aether-drift, nor any experiment with which to demonstrate it."[26] Einstein's elimination of the ether—reckoned by Newton, in the eighteenth century, and by James Clerk Maxwell and Hendrik Lorentz, in the nineteenth, to reside in the interstices of matter—coincided with Mallarmé's own definition of the novelty of "One Toss of the Dice": the introduction of space between the words on the page. "The whole of" the poem "without novelty except for the spacing of the text. The 'blanks,' in effect, assume importance because they strike the reader first" (see p. 163).

Einstein influenced, among other things, cubist painting, whose overlapping visual planes necessitate the simultaneous perception of a single object from multiple points of view; the poetry of Guillaume Apollinaire and T. S. Eliot, with its fractious spatial displacements; and the novels of Marcel Proust and Franz Kafka, for whom time became elastic, detached from any notion of regular chronological sequence. James Joyce, William Faulkner, and Virginia Woolf also practiced powerfully the technique of time compression. Woolf condensed several lifetimes into a single day in *Mrs Dalloway* (1925), and Faulkner did the same in *The Sound and the Fury* (1929). Joyce played all kinds of tricks with time in *Ulysses* (1922), squeezing as he did Odysseus's twenty years of travel into sixteen hours in the life of Leopold Bloom. In an epic smearing of time calculations, Joyce's unheroic hero tries to determine when he last weighed himself, scrambling methods for the calculation of time: "the twelfth day of May of the bissextile year one thousand nine hundred and four of the Christian era (jewish era five thousand six hundred and sixty-four, mohammedan era one thousand three hundred and twenty-two), golden number 5, epact 13, solar cycle 9, dominical letters C B, Roman indication 2, Julian period 6617, MXMIV."[27]

Mallarmé's epic poem suggests that the loosening of time and space relations began earlier, and began not only among scientists and mathematicians but among the makers of modern poetry. "One Toss of the Dice" was the first poem of literary relativity. The equation would not have surprised Einstein, who regarded scientific principle as a kind of fiction, arrived at not through observation and deduction, but by a purely conceptual act of mind that Mallarmé called the "ideal." "The rational and empirical components of human knowledge stand in eternal antithesis," the father of scientific relativity wrote in 1933, "for propositions arrived at by pure logical means are completely empty as regards reality. In this sense, the fundamentals of scientific theory, being initially free inventions of the human mind, are of purely fictional character."[28] Like the poet, the scientist sought a single key, a central idea, a general field theory that would explain all observable phenomena of the natural world. "Will we ever in our lifetime," he asked his friend Michele Besso, "get hold of the redeeming idea?"

Einstein's "redeeming idea" might look something like Mallarmé's project of *The Book*. The poet, haunted by "the mystery of letters," the Book of Nature before which we stand in reverent awe, anticipated the scientist, who described the world in his *Autobiographical Notes* as "a great, eternal riddle, at least partially accessible to our inspection and thinking."[29] Mallarmé may have aimed in his masterwork to write the sentence that God pronounced when He created the world, but Einstein wanted "to know how God created this world. I am not interested in this or that phenomenon, in the spectrum of this or that element. I want to know His thoughts, the rest are details."[30] In rehearsing his theory, as it developed between special and general relativity, the scientist compared what he had done to the very kind of mystery that Mallarmé identified with letters. "Hardly anyone who has truly understood this theory," Einstein noted in a paper presented in 1915, "will be able to resist being captivated by its magic."[31]

Some of the irresistible magic of Einstein's theory began with the vision of a poet like Mallarmé, who, in "One Toss of the Dice," stretched the perceptual world out of which so many new cultural forms, including scientific theories, emerged. Mallarmé and Einstein worked in the same mental universe, which, for several decades and on multiple fronts, had been immersed in the question of time simultaneity. The poet expressed the blurred boundary between continuous space and linear time via the medium of verse whose scattered words were meant to be read one after the other, yet taken in all at once—an approximation of the simultaneity that Einstein articulated via imaginary thought problems and mathematical equations. Mallarmé's prescient poem defined the spirit of the age, what the historian of science Peter Galison called a "critical opalescence," and the popular psychologist Malcolm Gladwell termed a "tipping point" toward the digital revolution.

At its furthest reach, Mallarmé's practice of interactive reading, as expressed in "One Toss of the Dice," and his vision of an infinitely connected universe, as expressed in the idea of *The Book*, have materialized in the hypertext of contemporary media, and in the global, public computer network system, the World Wide Web.

"One Toss of the Dice" is a seafaring poem, and "cybernetics" is a nautically derived term: its roots, in the Greek word "*kubernetes*," hark back to the third-century philosopher Plotinus, who used it to refer to the "steersman" of a boat. Almost all the characteristics of our cybernetic world are as if preordained in the terms that Mallarmé used to describe this "total word" and "Poem of Humanity"; this "terrifying and harmonious plenitude"; this "immaculate grouping of universal relationships come together for some miraculous and glittering occasion"; this "latent conducting wire" that "would explain all earthly existence"; this Universal Library whose fluid pages exceed the bindings of any traditional book; and this alchemical source of limitless wealth that would transform the nature of the human community. In turn, the ambitions of those who made computers, their software, and the Internet elide surprisingly with those of France's "Prince of Poets."

Early contributors to the development of the Internet emphasize the associational logic that we have seen to be an integral part of "One Toss of the Dice." In a landmark article published in *The Atlantic Monthly* of July 1945, Vannaver Bush, an engineer and inventor in charge of the U.S. Office of Scientific Research and Development during World War II, spoke of "wholly new forms of encyclopedias . . . , ready made with a mesh of associative trails running through them." Information technology pioneer Ted Nelson, the son of Hollywood director Ralph Nelson and actress Celeste Holm, wrote in 1965 of "literary machines," computers that would enable people to write and publish in a new, nonlinear format, hypertext, which, when combined with graphics, video, and audio, constituted a new way of imagining knowledge: hypermedia. For Nelson, "hypermedia" meant "nonsequential" text, "in which a reader was not constrained to read in any particular order, but could follow links and delve into the original document from a short quotation." The English computer scientist Tim Berners-Lee, working at the European Organization for Nuclear Research in the late 1980s, developed HTML, a universal language by which various computer software programs might communicate with one another. He emphasized the decentered nature of hypertext in the earliest version of the Web, Enquire, which allows us to break out of ordinary linear modes of thought and to "make intuitive leaps across the boundaries—those coveted random associations."[32]

Mallarmé's integral vision of *The Book* is echoed in the totalizing push of the World Wide Web. Vannaver Bush asked us to imagine a "future device for individual use, which is a sort of mechanized private file and library." He suggested we call this device a "Memex," "in which an individual stores all his books, records, and communications." Tim Berners-Lee imagined that the universal HTML language might connect "all the bits of information . . . on the planet" into "a single, global information space."[33]

Cybernetic information sharing and storage, in the wake of Mallarmé's original poetic articulation, have revived the ancient dream of assembling boundless, unified fields of knowledge in a single volume. The poet's *Grand Oeuvre* may, in fact, be most fully realized in the electronic encyclopedia, available worldwide in a plethora of languages, Wikipedia, and in Google's attempt, announced around the beginning of the twenty-first century, to organize the world's books by scanning the holdings of five American research libraries. A Chinese company, Superstar, reported that, as of 2006, it had digitized 1 million books in Chinese, or half the titles published since 1949. With whole libraries accessible online, we imagine that whatever we wish to know or to have or to do is somehow to be found or obtained or done via the World Wide Web, a virtual mirror of the universe that carries to completion Mallarmé's vast project of writing on everything by assembling writing about everything.

The Internet has brought to fruition the poet's ambition to compose a work that would "change the nature of the human community," whose isolated parts are now connected worldwide. Mallarmé, writing in the 1880s and 1890s, imagined his project of *The Book* along the lines of a peculiar theatrical performance, one in which those in attendance would read a series of folios alongside the "operator," the "simple reader," or the "first reader." The poet provided for a participatory community of readers that anticipated the new communities of readers on the Web. Whether in a bar in Brazil, an office in Bangalore, a basement in Beijing, an attic in Brooklyn, a beach on the Riviera, or a bistro in Beirut, internauts are potentially in contact with one another. As long as someone has an online device, he or she can read, author, correct, comment, and contest information on the World Wide Web. Today's global websites are forums in which participants exhibit still photographs and video; make restaurant and travel reservations; read dining, hotel, theater, and shopping reviews; play interactive games; meet online, and mingle via social media; rent apartments and houses; and buy and sell real estate as well as all manner of consumer goods and services.

Mallarmé, who suffered from a lack of money his whole life, may have seen *The Book*, alongside *The Latest Fashion*, as a get-rich scheme. Ready to burn "the furniture and the rafters of the roof, to feed the furnace of the *Grand Oeuvre*," he described its potential for generating wealth in alchemical terms. When it came to an actual business plan, however, his ideas focused on the conventional means of selling a large quantity of books, whose blank spaces, like those in "One Toss of the Dice," would be loaded with advertising inserts. The poet, who wrote an advice column for women and endorsed some of the most exclusive luxury merchandise of fin-de-siècle France, could not have imagined the potential of the Internet for generating exponential sums via the sale of advertising, commissions on transactions over commercial websites, or the explosive increase in the market value of stocks in companies that in some cases have yet to turn a profit. Both the Web and the poet's unrealized project of *The Book* hold the potential for mysterious, wanton wealth, whose source and limits are unclear.

Mallarmé's master poem indisputably and unapologetically set the agenda for artistic modernity, for the associative logic of the modern novel and poetry, the flattened perspective of modern painting, the atonal harmonies and syncopated rhythms of modern music. The poet's masterwork was the first of a series of great break with traditional notions of time and space, which, along with an emphasis upon the quanta of matter, are the stuff of modern physics The enchantment of the world that Mallarmé envisaged via poetry prefigured astonishingly the World Wide Web, whose speed, vastness, and endless possibilities of connection bring the times in which we live closer than any in the past to that great Platonic harmony, of which "One Toss of the Dice" is an early beacon and a guiding light.

Throughout the summer of 1898, Mallarmé continued to experience a general fatigue. The "Pen Man" complained in a letter to old friend and musician Léopold Dauphin that a "laziness of the pen had set in."[34] A cough persisted despite the prognosis of the country doctor in Valvins that the discomfort in his throat would pass in a few days. Congestion on the night of September 8 was cause to summon the doctor back. By morning the gagging had subsided, and the poet managed to dictate a letter to his daughter. When the doctor arrived around eleven a.m., Mallarmé, who loved turning the smallest everyday things and events into imaginative fancy, joked that the redness in his face made him look like a puffing "snake charmer" or a "ruddy cock." The doctor again pronounced the patient fit, but, as he began to leave, Mallarmé, seized by a sudden loss of breath, fell to his knees. Grasping the doctor, and looking in horror toward Marie and Geneviève, France's most celebrated poet choked to death within a matter of minutes. Together, wife and daughter lifted him onto the bed. Geneviève picked up her father's pen and began to write to friends, "Oh! Dear Sir, father died this morning. The burial is Sunday afternoon."

On the hot Sunday of September 11, 1898, the train that the poet had taken so often between Paris's Gare de Lyon and Valvins brought the poets José-Maria de Heredia, Henri de Régnier, and Paul Valéry to Fontainebleau. They were joined by Julie Manet, painters Edouard Vuillard and Auguste Renoir, sculptor Auguste Rodin, *Mardists* Edouard Dujardin, Edmond Bonniot, and Henry Roujon, poets Catulle Mendès and Léon Dierx, intimate friend Méry Laurent, Thadée and Misia Natanson, Georges Clemenceau, and a crowd of local farmers and boatmen in their Sunday best.

Many of the Parisians, taken by surprise at the suddenness of the event, rushed to Valvins still wearing their everyday clothes. Unlike the large crowd that had attended the public funeral of Paul Verlaine, including the bohemians and prostitutes whom he had frequented in the course of decades of carousing in Paris's Left Bank, this was an intimate gathering of neighbors and the best-known artists and writers of the Belle Époque. The crowd of mourners assembled on the lawn between the boatman's house and the Seine. They walked with the coffin on a horse-drawn cart to the cemetery of Samoreau, where Mallarmé, who had visited his son earlier that summer, was buried next to Anatole.

In the course of the customary words of adieu, some of the most articulate writers in France were now mute with grief. Henri Roujon, who was designated to pay homage on behalf of the poets of an older generation, broke down in tears before he could finish. Valéry, who was to represent younger poets, was also unable to speak. He would not write another poem for twenty years after his mentor's death. At the gathering at the Mallarmé house after the burial, Rodin, a towering figure with the sadness on his face of one of his Burghers of Calais, was reported to have said, "How long will it take for nature to make another such a mind?" Renoir remarked enigmatically, "It's not every day that one buries Mallarmé." Vuillard, Bonnard, and Renoir spent the night with the Natansons at their nearby summer house, La Grangette. The crowd of mourners, artists inside and local residents outside the cottage, lingered late into the night, the poet's boat bobbing without a captain on its mooring along the Seine.

In the days following the funeral, Geneviève—no longer wearing her habitual white long dress with balloon sleeves but cloaked in black, like her mother had been ever since the death of Anatole—began to delve through the papers on her father's desk. Next to a book on Beethoven and Wagner, she found a note scribbled in pen-

Mallarmé's boat without its captain.
Bibliothèque littéraire Jacques Doucet, Paris, ms MNR 1876.

cil and tucked inside a pad of blotting paper. It seemed that only he
had suspected the worst. "The terrible fit of coughing which I have
just suffered may return in the night and see me off . . . ," he had
written the night before his death. "My thoughts turn to this semi-
secular mountain of notes, which will only cause you difficulties. . . .
I alone could make sense out of what remains. . . . Burn everything.
. . . There is no literary heritage, my poor children. . . . I leave no
unedited papers, except a few printed bits and pieces that you will
find, then the 'Coup de Dés' and *Hérodiade*, finished if fate so
wills."[35] He referred, of course, to the definitive edition, still in
progress, of his master poem, a work about chance that he had left
to chance.

Geneviève would not burn her father's papers. Rather, she shared
them with the man she would marry in 1901, Dr. Edmond Bonniot,
a *Mardist* who began as a law student and subsequently completed
medical school. After Geneviève died of cancer in 1919, Bonniot

published a number of unedited pieces by his late father-in-law before his own premature death in 1930. His literary executor, the poet Henri Charpentier, would become the secretary of the Académie Mallarmé, founded in 1937. The direct chain continued when Charpentier left his share of the Mallarmé's papers to his daughter Françoise Morel, who, finally, after over a century, published in 2007 an edition of "One Toss of the Dice" to the poet's specifications. After Mme Morel's death, the handwritten copy of "One Toss of the Dice" that was to be published by the art dealer Ambroise Vollard came up for auction at Sotheby's Paris. A few days before the sale, lot 163, which Vollard originally had described as "the mythic manuscript of the most beautiful edition in the world," was declared by the French Ministry of Culture to be a national treasure, and thus not eligible for export. As representatives of foreign libraries and dealers stepped aside, bidding on the night of October 15, 2015, became fierce. When the hammer finally fell, the house burst into resounding applause. The autograph copy of Mallarmé's masterwork had been sold for 963,000 euros to art collector Marcel Brient.

Dr. Henri Mondor, whose biography of Mallarmé is the primary source of information about his last days, had amassed some 8,000 to 10,000 letters and documents connected to the poet. Mondor was a professor of surgery and, more than anyone else, was responsible for the revival of interest in the poet after almost half a century of neglect. He began his *Life of Mallarmé* with an evocation of the terrible events of June 1940: "June 14, when one saw the German regiments occupy Paris . . . , we chose to study an existence that no one had yet tried to capture, and in which one finds, in order to reconcile the present with certain French glories of the past, extraordinary virtues."[36] As crowds were fleeing the capital in automobiles, on bicycles, and on foot, Mondor stayed behind, with the image of Mallarmé as an example of courage in adversity fixed in his mind.

A week after the German bombardment of Paris in June 1940,

Mondor confided his collection of Mallarmé papers, along with a brand-new Chrysler sedan to the poet Raymond Cortat, with instructions to drive both to his native Auvergne, in central France, but to deposit the papers in the National Library should he not survive the war. Cortat recounted that he got as far as the suburbs of Moulins, some 200 miles from Paris, when he encountered the invading German army. He decided to abandon the "flaming new" Chrysler and to continue on foot and whatever public transportation was available.[37]

At the end of the war, the Chrysler was miraculously retrieved in perfect condition, having spent four years under a canvas awning. Mondor recovered his collection of letters and other documents, all completely unscathed. He eventually donated them to the Bibliothèque Jacques Doucet, where they occupy fifty-nine linear feet of shelf space. The poet's notes for *A Tomb for Anatole* can be accessed online at http://bljd.sorbonne.fr/resource/a011429863484jFv9sT/. Mallarmé's notes for *The Book* now reside in Harvard University's Houghton Library and are available online at http://pds.lib.harvard .edu/pds/view/46152340. A copy of the corrected proofs of "One Toss of the Dice Never Will Abolish Chance," mentioned in a holographic will composed the night before the poet's death, turned up for sale in 1960 at the Parisian rare book dealer Pierre Bérès; it was purchased by an American, who either sold or donated it to the Houghton Library, where, like Stéphane Mallarmé next to Anatole in the cemetery of Samoreau, it lies entombed next to *The Book*.

NOTES

Throughout the notes, I have used abbreviations to refer to three frequently cited works, two different editions of Mallarmé's complete works and the eleven-volume set of his letters:

Correspondance   Stéphane Mallarmé, *Correspondance de Stéphane Mallarmé*, 11 vol., ed. Henri Mondor and Jean-Pierre Richard (vol. 1) and Henri Mondor and Lloyd James Austin (vol. 2–11) (Paris: Gallimard, 1959–1985).

OC-Marchal (1 or 2)   Stéphane Mallarmé, *Oeuvres complètes*, 2 vol., ed. Bertrand Marchal (Paris: Gallimard, 1998–2003).

OC-Mondor   Stéphane Mallarmé, *Oeuvres complètes*, ed. Henri Mondor and G. Jean-Aubry (Paris: Gallimard, 1945).

Introduction

1. *Correspondance*, 8:146.
2. Ibid., 140, 144, 132.
3. Ibid., 151.
4. Henri Mondor, *Vie de Mallarmé* (Paris: Gallimard, 1941), 731.
5. *Correspondance*, 1:191.
6. *OC-Mondor*, 664.
7. *Correspondance*, 11:34.

8. These details are contained in Jean-Luc Steinmetz, *Stéphane Mallarmé: L'absolu au jour le jour* (Paris: Fayard, 1998), 424ff.

9. *OC-Mondor*, 662.

10. Suzanne Bernard, "Le 'Coup de Dés' de Mallarmé replacé dans la perspective historique," *Revue d'histoire littéraire de la France* 51, no. 2 (1951): 181–95; Virginia A. La Charité, *The Dynamics of Space: Mallarmé's UN COUP DE DÉS* (Lexington, Ky.: French Forum, 1987); Michel Murat, *Le "Coup de Dés" de Mallarmé: Un recommencement de la poésie* (Paris: Belin, 2005).

11. Mondor, *Vie*, 746.

12. For an excellent discussion of nineteenth-century artist's books, see Anna Sigrídur Arnar, *The Book as Instrument: Stéphane Mallarmé, The Artist's Book, and the Transformation of Print Culture* (Chicago: University of Chicago Press, 2011).

13. The phrases "desperately modest man" and "sweeping cosmic manner" belong to Robert G. Cohn, a teacher with whom I first encountered Mallarmé. Cohn, who was partly responsible for the revival of critical interest in the poet after World War II, died on December 16, 2015, coincidentally, the very day I sent the final manuscript of this book off to my publisher.

Chapter I: A Poet Is Born

1. Carl Paul Barbier, ed., *Documents Stéphane Mallarmé* (Paris: Nizet, 1976), 5:53.

2. Carl Paul Barbier, ed., *Documents Stéphane Mallarmé* (Paris: Nizet, 1977), 6:40.

3. Henri de Régnier, *Nos Rencontres* (Paris: Mercure de France, 1931), 192.

4. *OC-Mondor*, 1559.

5. Ibid., 662.

6. Ibid., 1383.

7. Henri Mondor, *Mallarmé lycéen* (Paris: Gallimard, 1974), 173–74.

8. *OC-Mondor*, 10.

9. Mondor, *Mallarmé lycéen*, 176.

10. Claude Pichois, *Baudelaire*, trans. Graham Robb (London: Hamish Hamilton, 1989), 324.

11. Barbier, *Documents Stéphane Mallarmé*, 5:322.

12. Ibid., 6:35.

13. Henri Mondor, *Mallarmé plus intime* (Paris: Gallimard, 1944), 102–3.

14. Barbier, *Documents Stéphane Mallarmé*, 5:239.

15. Ibid., 346–47.

16. Laurence Joseph, "Mallarmé et son amie anglaise," *Revue d'histoire littéraire de la France*, no. 3 (July–September 1965): 457–78.

17. Gordon Millan, *Les "Mardis" de Stéphane Mallarmé: Mythes et réalité* (Paris: Nizet, 2008), 100.

18. Barbier, *Documents Stéphane Mallarmé*, 6:374.

19. Ibid., 33.

20. Mondor, *Vie de Mallarmé*, 58.

21. Barbier, *Documents Stéphane Mallarmé*, 6:51.

22. *OC-Mondor*, 662.
23. Ibid., 22.

Chapter II: The Foundation of a Magnificent Work

1. Carl Paul Barbier, ed., *Documents Stéphane Mallarmé* (Paris: Nizet, 1977), 6:51.
2. Ibid., 65.
3. Ibid., 67.
4. Ibid., 79.
5. Ibid., 67.
6. Ibid., 83.
7. Ibid., 104.
8. Ibid., 114.
9. Ibid., 117.
10. Ibid., 118.
11. Ibid., 131, 135.
12. Ibid., 155.
13. *Correspondance*, 3:232.
14. Ibid., 1:198.
15. Ibid., 114, n2.
16. Ibid., 115.
17. Ibid., 132.
18. Ibid., 139.
19. *OC-Mondor*, 489.
20. Bettina Knapp, *Judith Gautier: Writer, Orientalist, Musicologist, Feminist* (New York: Hamilton Books, 2004), 76.
21. Suzanne Meyer-Zundel, *Quinze Ans auprès de Judith Gautier* (Paris: Dinard, 1969), 65.
22. Théophile Gautier, "Le Club des Hachichins," *Revue des deux mondes* 13 (1846): 522, 530.
23. Austin Gill, "Mallarmé fonctionnaire," *Revue d'histoire littéraire de la France*, no. 1 (January–February 1968): 6–37.
24. *Correspondance*, 1:240.
25. Ibid., 242.
26. Friedrich Nietzsche, *The Gay Science*, trans. Walter Kaufmann (New York: Vintage Books, 1974), 181.
27. Martin Heidegger, *Nietzsche*, trans. David Farrell Kress (San Francisco: Harper & Row, 1987), 4:22.
28. Max Weber, "Wissenschaft als Beruf" ("Science as a Vocation"), in *Gesammlte Aufsaetze zur Wissenschaftslehre* (Tubingen, 1922), 524–55. (This speech was originally delivered at Munich University in 1918 and published the next year by Duncker & Humboldt, Munich.)
29. *Correspondance*. 1:242.
30. Ibid., 222.

31. Stéphane Mallarmé, "Le Livre, instrument spirituel," in *Mallarmé: Selected Prose Poems, Essays and Letters*, trans. Bradford Cook (Baltimore: Johns Hopkins University Press, 1956), 25; for French original, see *OC-Mondor*, 378.
32. Mallarmé, *Selected Prose*, 25; French, *OC-Mondor*, 378–79.
33. *OC-Mondor*, 663.
34. Guizot quoted in Laurent Theis, "Guizot et les institutions de mémoire" in Pierre Nora, *Les Lieux de mémoire* (Paris: Gallimard, 1984–1992), 2:583.
35. Quoted in Rosemary Lloyd, *Mallarmé: The Poet and His Circle* (Ithaca, N.Y.: Cornell University Press, 1999), 15.
36. Jean de Meun, *Le Roman de la rose*, ed. Daniel Poirion (Paris: Flammarion, 1974), verse 16,278.
37. Dante, *Purgatorio*, trans. Robert and Jean Hollander (New York: Doubleday, 2000), canto 33, 11. 85–90.
38. Stillman Drake, ed. and trans., *Discoveries and Opinions of Galileo* (New York: Doubleday, 1957), 237.
39. *OC-Mondor*, 399.
40. *Correspondance*, 4, part 1:88.
41. Ibid., 1:205.
42. Ibid., 131.
43. Mary Ann Caws, trans. www.studiocleo.com/librarie/mallarme/prose. html; French original, *OC-Mondor*, 435–54.
44. Catulle Mendès, *Rapport à M. le ministre de l'instruction publique et des beaux-arts sur le mouvement poétique français de 1867 à 1900* (Paris: Imprimerie Nationale, 1902), 137.

Chapter III: Enchanting a Devastated World

1. *Correspondance*, 1:333.
2. Guy de Maupassant, *The Necklace and Other Stories*, trans. Sandra Smith (New York: Liveright: 2015), 180.
3. Frédéric Mistral, *Memoirs of Mistral*, trans. Constance Elizabeth Maud (New York: Baker & Taylor, 1907), 304.
4. De Maupassant, *The Necklace*, 180.
5. Ibid., 181.
6. Maxime du Camp, *Les Convulsions de Paris* (Paris: Hachette, 1879), 1:22.
7. Ibid., 2:351.
8. Ibid., 1:10.
9. *Correspondance*, 1:338.
10. Ibid., 339.
11. Ibid., 356.
12. Henri Mondor, *Histoire d'un faune* (Paris: Gallimard, 1948), 223.
13. François Ruchon, *L'Amitié de Stéphane Mallarmé et de Georges Rodenbach* (Geneva: P. Cailler, 1949), 133.
14. *Correspondance*, 1:342.

15. *OC-Mondor*, 679.
16. Ibid., 872.
17. Ibid., 668.
18. Ibid., 669.
19. Ibid., 672.
20. Ibid., 674.
21. Arthur Rimbaud, *Complete Works, Selected Letters*, trans. Wallace Fowlie (Chicago: University of Chicago Press, 1966), 307.
22. *OC-Mondor*, 513.
23. Ibid., 515.
24. Ibid., 514.
25. *Correspondance*, 3:246.
26. Ibid., 2:26.
27. Stéphane Mallarmé, *Mallarmé on Fashion: A Translation of the Fashion Magazine "La Dernière mode*," trans. P. N. Furbank and Alex Cain (Oxford: Berg, 2004), 156.
28. Ibid., 153, 198.
29. Ibid., 61, 31.
30. Ibid., 107.
31. *OC-Mondor*, 743.
32. *Mallarmé on Fashion*, 68, 206.
33. Charles Baudelaire, *Curiosités esthétiques* (Paris: Garnier, 1962), 488.
34. *Mallarmé on Fashion*, 124.
35. *OC-Mondor*, 663.
36. *Mallarmé on Fashion*, 167.
37. Stéphane Mallarmé, *Collected Poems: A Bilingual Edition*, trans. Henry Weinfield (Berkeley: University of California Press, 1996), 50.
38. *OC-Mondor*, 88, 91.
39. Ibid., 125.
40. *OC-Marchal*, 1:1278.
41. *OC-Mondor*, 162.
42. Ibid., 174.
43. Ibid., 175.
44. Ibid., 163.
45. *OC-Marchal*, 1:1299.

Chapter IV: Tuesdays in the "Little House of Socrates"

1. Stéphane Mallarmé, "Crisis in Poetry," in *Selected Prose Poems, Essays and Letters*, trans. Bradford Cook (Baltimore: Johns Hopkins University Press, 1956), 42; for French original, see *OC-Mondor*, 367. See also Mallarmé's essay "Mystery in Letters," where he writes, "Yes, I know; Mystery is said to be Music's domain. But the written word also lays claim to it": Mallarmé, *Selected Prose*, 32; French, *OC-Mondor*, 385.

2. Quoted in Anne Martin-Fugier, *Les Salons de la IIIe République: Art, littérature, politique* (Paris: Perrin, 2009), 140.

3. *Correspondance*, 2:159.

4. *OC-Mondor*, 340, 299.

5. "Mallarmé par sa fille," *Nouvelle Revue française*, November 1926, 521.

6. Henri de Régnier, *Figures et caractères* (Paris: Mercure de France, 1901), 117.

7. Paul Valéry, "Au concert Lamoureux en 1893," in *Oeuvres*, ed. Jean Hytier (Paris: Pléiade-Gallimard, 1957), 1:1276.

8. *OC-Mondor*, 388.

9. Henri Mondor, *Vie de Mallarmé* (Paris: Gallimard, 1941), 330.

10. André Gide, *Si le Grain ne meurt* (Paris: Gallimard, 1928), 263.

11. Henry Roujon, *La Galerie des bustes* (Paris: J. Rueff, 1908), 39.

12. Edmond Bonniot, "Notes sur les Mardis," *Les Marges* 57, no. 224 (January 10, 1936).

13. Édouard Dujardin, *Mallarmé par un des siens* (Paris: Messein, 1936), 25.

14. *Correspondance*, 4, part 1:24–25. Buffalo Bill had visited Paris as part of the Universal Exposition of 1889.

15. Carl Paul Barbier, ed., *Correspondance Mallarmé–Whistler* (Paris: Nizet, 1964), 104.

16. *Correspondance*, 4, part 1:329.

17. *Correspondance Mallarmé–Whistler*, 129.

18. Henri de Paysac, *Francis Vielé-Griffin: Poète symboliste et citoyen américain* (Paris: Nizet, 1976), 147.

19. Jean Ajalbert, *Mémoires en vrac: Au temps du symbolisme, 1880–1890* (Charente: Du Lérot, 2005), 64.

20. *Correspondance*, 4, part 1:314.

21. De Paysac, *Francis Vielé-Griffin*, 147.

22. *Correspondance*, 6:218.

23. Bernard Lazare, *Figures contemporaines* (Paris: Didier, 1895), 243–44.

24. "Mallarmé par sa fille," 522.

25. *Correspondance*, 3:84; Dujardin, *Mallarmé par un des siens*, 29.

26. André Fontainas, *De Stéphane Mallarmé à Paul Valéry: Notes d'un témoin, 1894–1922* (Paris: Edmond Bernard, 1928).

27. Quoted in Catulle Mendès, *Rapport à M. le ministre de l'instruction publique et des beaux-arts sur le mouvement poétique français de 1867 à 1900* (Paris: Imprimerie Nationale, 1902), 182.

28. Quoted in Roujon, *Galerie des bustes*, 58.

29. Camille Mauclair, *Mallarmé chez lui* (Paris: Grasset, 1935), 89.

30. René Ghil, *Les Dates et les oeuvres* (Paris: G. Crès, 1923), 209.

31. Ibid., 114.

32. Ibid., 209.

33. "Every week he gathers round him embryonic poets and authors. . . . He strings together obscure and wondrous words, at which his disciples become stupid . . . , so that they leave him as if intoxicated, and with the impression

that incomprehensible, superhuman disclosures have been made to them": Max Nordau, *Degeneration* (New York: D. Appleton, 1895), 103.

34. Mary Ann Caws, trans. *Mallarmé in Prose* (New York: New Directions, 2001), 122; French, *OC-Mondor*, 394. The authoritative book on Mallarmé and religion is Bertrand Marchal's *La Religion de Mallarmé* (Paris: José Corti, 1988). Marchal treats the poet's transformation of art into a religion in distinction to the ways in which Mallarmé's verse and thinking about verse are in consonance with traditional Catholic theology.

35. Julie Manet, *Journal (1893–1899)* (Paris: Klincksieck, 1979), 148.

36. Cited in *Correspondance*, 5:371.

37. Ibid., 4, part 2:366.

38. Ibid., 2:202.

39. Ibid., 203.

40. Ibid., 201.

41. Ibid., 301.

42. Stéphane Mallarmé, *A Tomb for Anatole*, trans. Paul Auster (New York: New Directions, 2005), 1.

43. Ibid., 19.

44. *OC-Marchal*, 1:208.

45. Mallarmé, *Tomb for Anatole*, 46.

Chapter V: "There Has Been an Attack on Verse!"

1. *OC-Mondor*, 663.

2. Ibid., 875.

3. *OC-Marchal*, 1:1049.

4. Ibid.

5. Ibid., 1029.

6. Ibid., 1037.

7. *Correspondance*, 3:343.

8. Stéphane Mallarmé, *Lettres à Méry Laurent*, ed. Bertrand Marchal (Paris: Gallimard, 1996), 52.

9. *Correspondance*, 4, part 2:542.

10. Cited in Annegret Fauser, *Musical Encounters at the 1889 Paris World's Fair* (Rochester, N.Y.: University of Rochester Press, 2005), 120.

11. *OC-Mondor*, 481.

12. Cited in Robert Guiette, "Max Elskamp et Stéphane Mallarmé," *Le Mercure de France*, no. 1161 (May 1960): 254.

13. Quoted in Paul Valéry, *Oeuvres*, ed. Jean Hytier (Paris: Pléiade-Gallimard, 1960), 2:1208.

14. *The Times* (London), February 23, 1894, p. 7.

15. *Correspondance*, 6:227.

16. Ibid., 230.

17. Henri de Régnier, *Les Cahiers inédits, 1887–1936*, ed. David J. Niederauer and

François Broche (Paris: Pygmalion, 2002), 377. See *Correspondence*, 6:227ff. for Mallarmé's account of his trip to Oxford and Cambridge and his essay "Cloîtres," published in *OC-Marchal*, 2:247.

18. Carl Paul Barbier, ed., *Documents Stéphane Mallarmé* (Paris: Nizet, 1971), 3:260.

19. *Correspondance*, 6:232.

20. *OC-Mondor*, 643.

21. *Correspondance*, 7:144.

22. G. H. Fleming, *James Abbott McNeill Whistler* (New York: St. Martin's Press, 1991), 290.

23. Carl Paul Barbier, ed., *Correspondance Mallarmé–Whistler* (Paris: Nizet, 1964), 232.

24. This testimony is taken from the documentary history of the affair by Whistler, *Eden Versus Whistler: The Baronet and the Butterfly; A Valentine with a Verdict* (Paris: Louis-Henry May, 1899), 22.

25. *Le Soir*, May 27, 1894, cited in *Correspondance*, 6:287.

26. *Correspondance*, 9:106.

27. Henry Roujon, *La Galerie des bustes* (Paris: J. Rueff, 1908), 52–53.

28. *Lettres à Méry Laurent*, 81.

29. Ibid., 72.

30. *Correspondance*, 6:138.

31. *Lettres à Méry Laurent*, 151.

32. *Correspondance*, 6:267, n1.

33. A.-M. Bloch, "Psychologie: La Vitesse comparative des sensations," *Revue scientifique* 13 (1887), 586.

34. See Christophe Wall-Romana, "Mallarmé's Cinepoetics: The Poem Uncoiled by the Cinématographe, 1893–98," *Publications of the Modern Language Association* 120 (January 2005): 128–47.

35. Jacques Rittaud-Hutinet and Chantal Rittaud-Hutinet, *Dictionnaires des cinématographes en France (1896–1897)* (Paris: Honoré Champion, 1999), 349–50.

36. Jean-Jacques Meusy, *Paris-Palaces ou le temps des cinémas (1894–1918)* (Paris: CNRS Editions, 2002), 20.

37. *OC-Mondor*, 878.

Chapter VI: "There, I've Added a Bit of Shadow"

1. *OC-Mondor*, 882.

2. Ibid., 407.

3. Gabrielle Delzant, *Lettres—Souvenirs* (Paris: Lahure, 1904), 286.

4. Robert Harborough Sherard, *Twenty Years in Paris: Being Some Recollections of a Literary Life* (Philadelphia: George W. Jacobs, 1905), 390.

5. Hervé Joubeaux, *My Mallarmé is rich: Mallarmé et le monde anglo-saxon* (Paris: Editions d'Art Somogy, 2006), 10.

6. André Gide, "Verlaine et Mallarmé," *La Vie des Lettres* 5 (April 1914): 12.

7. "Entretien recueilli par Maurice Guillemot" in *OC-Marchal*, 2:715.

8. Gustave Guiches, *Au Banquet de la vie* (Paris: Spes, 1925), 201.

9. *OC-Marchal*, 2:455.

10. Marcel Proust, *Remembrance of Things Past,* trans. Stephen Hudson (London: Chatto & Windus, 1931).

11. Augustine, *De Genesi ad Litteram*, ed. P. Agaësse and A. Solignac (Paris: Desclée de Brower, 1972), 123.

12. Stéphane Mallarmé, "Crisis in Poetry," in *Mallarmé: Selected Prose Poems, Essays and Letters*, trans. Bradford Cook (Baltimore: Johns Hopkins University Press, 1956), 42; for French original, see *OC-Mondor*, 368.

13. Augustine, *De Genesi*, 164.

14. Mallarmé, in sync with both Plato and the Fathers of the Church, speaks of an Idea or the Word. "The Word [*Le Verbe*] is a principle which is developed through the negation of all principle, chance [*le hasard*], as the Idea, and is found forming . . . , itself, the (spoken) Word [*la Parole*], with the help of time, which permits its scattered elements to be gathered and to be joined according to rules governing such diversions": *OC-Mondor*, 854.

15. *Le Figaro*, September 13, 1898.

16. Mallarmé, *Selected Prose*, 27; French, *OC-Mondor*, 380.

17. Aristotle, *Physics* 6:9, 239b15, and 6:9, 239b5.

Chapter VII: The Dice Are Tossed

1. This letter, in a private collection, is cited by Gordon Millan, *A Throw of the Dice: The Life of Stéphane Mallarmé* (New York: Farrar, Straus & Giroux, 1994), 311.

2. *Correspondance*, 9:172.

3. Ibid., 241.

4. Quoted in Léon Bloy, *Mon Journal* (Paris: Mercure de France, 1904), 51.

5. Jules Huret, *La Catastrophe du Bazar de la Charité* (Paris: F. Juven, 1897), 148.

6. Cornelia Otis Skinner, *Elegant Wits and Grand Horizontals* (Boston: Houghton Mifflin, 1962), 40.

7. Dominique Paoli, *Il y a cent ans: L'Incendie du Bazar de la Charité* (Paris: Desgrandschamps, 1997), 32.

8. Henri de Régnier, *Nos Rencontres* (Paris: Mercure de France, 1931), 155–65.

9. *Correspondance*, 9:171, n2.

10. Ibid., 172. Gide read from Mallarmé's letter in the lecture delivered at the Théâtre du Vieux Columbier on November 2, 1913 (André Gide, "Verlaine et Mallarmé," *La Vie des letters* 5 [April 1914]: 13).

11. *Correspondance*, 9:172.

12. *OC-Marchal*, 1:433.

13. Ibid., 2:1465.

14. *OC-Mondor*, 850.

15. Paul Valéry, *Oeuvres*, ed. Jean Hytier (Paris: Pléiade-Gallimard, 1957), 1:623.

16. *Correspondance*, 9:196.

17. *Écrits divers sur Stéphane Mallarmé* (Paris: Gallimard, 1950), 18.

18. *Correspondance*, 9:34.

19. Henri de Régnier, *Figures et caractères* (Paris: Mercure de France, 1901), 122.

20. Henri de Régnier, *Les Cahiers inédits, 1887–1936*, ed. David J. Niederauer and François Broche (Paris: Pygmalion, 2002), 379.

21. *OC-Mondor*, 168.

22. Camille Mauclair, *Mallarmé chez lui* (Paris: Grasset, 1935), 116.

23. G. Combès and J. Farges, eds., *De Doctrina Christiana* (Paris: Desclée de Brouwer, 1949), 300.

24. Max Müller, *The Science of Language* (Chicago: Open Court Publishing, 1899), 35; Max Müller, "The Last Results of the Researches Respecting the Non-Iranian and Non-Semitic Languages of Asia or Europe," in C. C. J. Bunsen, *Outline of the Philosophy of Universal History* (London: Longman, Brown, Green, and Longmans, 1854), 1:268.

25. *Correspondance*, 1:318. Mallarmé, like many nineteenth-century philologists, including Bopp, thought that Zend was a language; however, it is a contraction of the Avestan word *zainti*, meaning "interpretation."

26. *OC-Mondor*, 363.

27. Ibid., 963.

28. Ibid., 1053.

29. Ibid., 919.

30. Ibid., 941.

31. Ibid., 921.

32. Ibid., 192.

33. Maurice de Fleury, "M. Stéphane Mallarmé," *Le Figaro*, February 11, 1891, p. 3.

34. *OC-Mondor*, 364–65.

35. Ibid., 921, 933.

36. Ibid., 855.

37. Ibid., 921.

38. Ibid., 947.

39. Ibid., 958.

40. Ibid., 940.

41. Ibid., 960.

42. Jacques Scherer, *Grammaire de Mallarmé* (Paris: Nizet, 1977), 50.

43. *OC-Mondor*, 905.

44. Ibid., 255.

Chapter VIII: "It's the Same for the Man of Science"

1. *Correspondance*, 10:177.

2. *Le Voltaire*, April 18, 1879.

3. *Correspondance*, 2:146.

4. *Correspondance*, 10:154.

5. Aristide Marie, *La Fôret symboliste* (Paris: Firmin-Didot, 1936), 178.

6. *Correspondance*, 10:189.

7. *Écrits divers sur Stéphane Mallarmé* (Paris: Gallimard, 1950), 16.

8. Robert Mallet, ed., *Correspondance André Gide-Paul Valéry, 1890–1942* (Paris: Gallimard, 1955), 331.

9. *Correspondance*, 10:250.

10. *OC-Mondor*, 883.

11. Guillaume Apollinaire, "Simultanisme-librettisme," *Les Soirées de Paris* 25 (June 15, 1914): 323–24.

12. Cited in Marjorie Perloff, *The Futurist Movement: Avant-Garde, Avant-Guerre, and the Language of Rupture* (Chicago: University of Chicago Press, 1986), 8.

13. Jean Cocteau, "La Collaboration de 'Parade,'" in *Oeuvres complètes* (Lausanne: Marguerat, 1946–1951), 9:53.

14. Alan M. Gillmor, *Erik Satie* (Boston: Twayne Publishers, 1988), 102.

15. T. S. Eliot, "Prose and Verse," *Chapbook* 22 (April 1921): 3–10; T.S. Eliot, "Notes sur Mallarmé et Poe," *La Nouvelle Revue française* 14 (November 1926): 524–26.

16. T. S. Eliot, *The Waste Land and Other Poems*, ed. Frank Kermode (New York: Penguin Books, 2003), 58, 68, 58, 59.

17. Ibid., 66.

18. Henri Poincaré, "La Mesure du temps," *Revue de métaphysique et de morale* 6 (1898): 12.

19. On Poincaré and Einstein, see Peter Galison, *Einstein's Clocks, Poincaré's Maps* (New York: W. W. Norton, 2003).

20. William Hermanns reports in his book *Einstein and the Poet: In Search of the Cosmic Man* (Brookline, Mass.: Branden Press, 1983) that the scientist repeated the phrase in 1943: "As I have said so many times, God doesn't play dice with the world" (p. 58).

21. In a way analogous to Mallarmé's making the visual verbal, Einstein emphasized the importance of feelings and the visual nature of such feelings before they take verbal shape. "During all those years there was a feeling of direction, of going straight toward something concrete. It is very hard to express that feeling in words. . . . Of course, behind such a direction there is always something logical; but I have it in a kind of survey, in a way visually" (Max Wertheimer, *Productive Thinking* [New York: Harper & Row, 1959], 227–28).

22. Quoted in André Maurois, *Illusions* (New York: Columbia University Press, 1968), 35.

23. Walter Isaacson, *Einstein: His Life and Universe* (New York: Simon & Schuster, 2007), 122.

24. Albert Einstein, "On the Electrodynamics of Moving Bodies," available at http://einsteinpapers.press.princeton.edu/vol2-doc/311.

25. In "On a Heuristic Point of View Concerning the Production and Transformation of Light," one of the papers published in 1905, his "annus mirabilis," Einstein staked a synthetic claim: "According to the assumption to

be considered here, when a light ray is propagated from a point, the energy is not continuously distributed over an increasing space but consists of a finite number of energy quanta which are localized at points in space and which can be produced and absorbed only as complete units": see Isaacson, *Einstein*, 98.

26. Albert Einstein, *Relativity: The Special and General Theory*, trans. Robert W. Lawson (London: Methuen, 1920), 50.

27. James Joyce, *Ulysses* (New York: Random House, 2000), 668–69.

28. Albert Einstein, "On the Method of Theoretical Physics," in *Ideas and Opinions*, ed. Carl Seelig (New York: Three Rivers Press, 1982), 271.

29. Albert Einstein, *Autobiographical Notes*, trans. Paul Arthur Schilpp (Carbondale, Ill.: Open Court Press, 1979), 5.

30. Cited in Gerald Holton and Yehuda Elkana, eds., Albert Einstein. *Historical and Cultural Perspectives* (Princeton, N.J.: Princeton University Press, 1982), 240.

31. Ibid., 104.

32. "I liked Enquire and made good use of it because it stored information without using structures like matrices or trees. The human mind uses these organizing structures all the time, but can also break out of them and make intuitive leaps across the boundaries—those coveted random associations. Once I discovered such connections, Enquire could at least store them": Tim Berners-Lee, *Weaving the Web: The Original Design and Ultimate Destiny of the World Wide Web* (Harper: New York, 2000), 10.

33. Ibid., 9.

34. *Correspondance* 10:245.

35. The account of the poet's final hours is contained in a letter from Paul Valéry to Francis Vielé-Griffin, which is itself based upon a letter from Geneviève in *Correspondance*, 10:260.

36. Henri Mondor, *Vie de Mallarmé* (Paris: Gallimard, 1941), 7.

37. Jean Binet, *Les Vies multiples de Henri Mondor* (Paris: Masson, 1993), 63.

ACKNOWLEDGMENTS

I have benefited from a number of blessings—large and small, personal and institutional, current and long past—that have made the writing of this book both easier and more pleasant. First, the generosity of Yale University, which offered a year free of teaching and administrative duties to pursue the meaning of a poem that has haunted me since I first encountered it as a graduate student at Stanford. I have profited immensely from conversations with colleagues in the Yale French Department and the Humanities Program, and from teaching Yale's Directed Studies "great ideas and works" syllabus, which is designed to encourage first-year students to think big and aim high. I am indebted to Bertrand Marchal, France's premier Mallarmé scholar, for sharing with me a tiny bit of his vast knowledge of nineteenth-century French poetry; to my wife Caroline Merrill, whose keen reading of the manuscript along the way has sharpened the conjugal grammar; and to Robert Weil, an incomparable editor, whose eagle eye upon the big picture has made the tedious bits downright jolly.

INDEX

Page numbers in *italics* refer to illustrations.